IT SHOULDN'T HAPPEN TO A LAWYER

RECOLLECTIONS BY

ALLAN AINSWORTH

IT SHOULDN'T HAPPEN TO A LAWYER

Published by Magic Flute Publications 2014
ISBN 978-1-909054-25-7

Magic Flute Publications is an imprint of
Magic Flute Artworks Limited
231 Swanwick Lane
Southampton SO31 7GT

www.magicfluteartworks.com

Cover illustration and photographs © Allan Ainsworth

A description of this book is available from the British Library

Contents

The Old Offices at Bletchley

The Eagle at Amersham

Introduction

I suppose we all end up here, looking back over our working lives and wondering how to explain to those that were not there the joys, the sorrows, the recollections and the colourful tales that now only live in memory. We think back on those years, which at the time were the ordinary progress of life: earning a living, buying the first car or the first house, raising the family, juggling the demands of work with the needs of growing children, developing a career. Along the way we share many moments with our loved ones, our friends and the colleagues we encounter during our working days.

The past 45 years working in what I proudly call "the art of the law" has fortunately given me a unique and varied working life and in consequence have stories to tell, memories to share and wonderful characters to describe. I hope that others may now want to sit down for a few hours and having read through my account will share and enjoy many of my varied experiences, together with the characters that I have met along my journey - many of whom are sadly no longer with us. Some of these people have helped to forge important parts of my career and now I feel that by telling my story and writing this book I have not only preserved their memories but also have brought them all back to life in the pages that follow. For the many hours I have taken putting all this down in this book I have felt that those that I refer to have, for all intents and purposes been standing over me while I write about them and share once again what they have contributed not only to me but what they themselves have stood for and left the indelible memories with me.

When I first started work back in August of 1970 the working environment was so completely different from that of today. It really did belong to a different generation, and as I look back now I can see that we approached life with a wholly different way of thinking, of adapting to life that may seem rather quaint to us now living in the twenty-first century.

My career started amongst old ways and customs, governed very much by a long-established social order and yet there was a craving for change. Agents for change were sometime powerful and established unions who went head-to-head with the old social order, and my working life began in this era of confrontation: strikes and short weeks, the lingering dominance of old-style customs, disciplines, politics and establishments. This first decade of my career was still dominated and run by many of the old regimented types who themselves had come through the two world war years of hard times and discipline. The established ways that had been tried and tested from the late 1800's in dress manner and style unlike today's modern ways of skills and techniques. It was always accepted without question that the "old ways were the best" and nobody questioned, tested or bucked such a system. Nowadays success is measured by imagination, motivation and success. However, in my mind one thing has never changed and that has been the fascination for the personal characters that have passed through my life and those memories that they have left now tattooed on my mind.

I hope that in the ensuing chapters I can rekindle or create the images of those past times, past characters and past circumstances to bring some explanation as to why I now feel the necessity of putting pen to paper. A period when time itself seemed to stand still embroiled in the dusty archaic ways of the established order or things and yet embroiled us with the feeling of warmth safety and protection. This was a period when Land Registries and registered land hardly existed, manual typewriters were the norm, and offices were filled with ladies in the typing pool. I can still hear today those noisy echoes of old clanking typewriters and gossip, and I can still picture the old deeds tied up with pink ribbon. Men wore dark suits and sober ties to work and ladies dressed in their very smart skirts, frocks and blouses with pearl necklaces and jewellery. Clerks and juniors were taught to accept their place in the pecking order and had to earn through age and experience their way to improvement and promotion. The senior members of staff were acknowledged and respected for being so well dressed well knowledgeable and always addressed by their minors with either "Mr" or "Sir". First name familiarities were not even considered and if and whenever junior staff were called by their surnames.

"Get me the Smith file, Ainsworth!"

If on the other hand my name was prefixed by "Mr." this was usually an indication that trouble was afoot.

"Come into my office Mr. Ainsworth." was a sure indication that I was going to face reprimand or worse.

In this my first world, offices smelt of old wood, old wax, musty paper and old deeds. The nineteenth century was not far behind and documents were still sewn by hand, and the old waxing seal was still common. Ball-point pens (we were still calling them *Biros*) were very new and even the colours had a significance of priority; black was standard, red would denote a correction, and green was reserved solely for accountants. The telephone was rarely used to conduct any part of a transaction as everything had to be covered in writing and there was always the senior member of staff that could coherently write in the old style copperplate handwriting. This skill remained essential for drafting old style deeds or perhaps formal invitations as the need arose. This time as I recall was when everything was very orderly with everyone knowing what was expected of them. Routine was well-rehearsed and everyone felt safe in such an environment.

For this reason I dedicate these memories and this book to those that have influenced me, have shaped my character and have brought me over the years to the person I now am by either direct or indirect example. These characters will walk through these pages as I journey down the years, along with the places that I have visited worked or simply passed through. I also dedicate this book to those that have stood by me with the encouragement and confidence that one day all the studying all the hard work and all the changes trials and tribulations would pay off. I would in particular highlight my eternal gratitude to my Mother who in the early days must have recognised a spark and through her confidence steered me away from a more mundane career mapped out by my less confident Father. With her blessing and backing I have been able to enter into this wonderful and varied world.

1 The Early Years

I was fast approaching the age of 18 years during the middle part of 1970. I was still at school and still so very unsure what I wanted for my future career and prospects. Most if all of my friends and school mates had long left to follow their careers in all walks of life. As for me, I had volunteered myself through the school's commercial course and felt reasonably efficient in my typing skills, having achieved some 58 words a minute on the old style manual typewriter and together with this most useful skill, I had GCE passes in English Language, Literature, Mathematics, Geography. At that time I was very interested in current affairs and politics and had fast come to the conclusion that, having spent several years dissecting Shakespeare, 20th Century short stories, *Lord of the Flies,* George Orwell and other mind-shattering novels, that continued academic education would really be a waste of time. Being a bit of a rebel I now really felt that if someone was to tell me what to do then they really should be paying me for the privilege. My problem was I had no idea really which route my career would take.

My qualifications and interests started to point towards Journalism. I could see myself with a tatty sports jacket, pen and notebook chasing the daily snippets of gossip and fact, and then writing up my findings. Local newspapers at that time had a large circulation and offered career options for the aspiring cub reporter, albeit the main life for future journalistic ambitions fell to the larger cities such as London. In those days that represented two to three hours of daily travel by steam locomotive, and, surprising as it may seem to us nowadays, such travel times were beyond contemplation for the average young person in 1970. You could se the beginnings of change in those days. Cars were becoming more affordable and those steam-powered relics were slowly being replaced by unpopular and unreliable diesel trains. Even so, I felt I was chained to work near to home. Enquiries with our own local newspaper revealed that they had just employed a local lad. I knew him and found him rather smug and personally, I did not take to him. The prospect of working with him as a colleague rather put me off. Such are the random opinions that precipitate career choices!

I was now under some pressure. Teachers were hinting rather strongly that by the summer my presence was no longer required, and this probably forced this issue.

Fortune came to my rescue when the careers officer from the school called me to his office one late spring day and suggested that there was a career opportunity available with the County Council as a trainee legal executive. At that time I can honestly say that I did not have a clue what this entailed but, to pacify the mood of both headmaster and staff, I drove myself over to Aylesbury in my newly acquired car, a Vauxhall Victor 1600, that I had bought from my part-time shelf-filling job in the local supermarket. It was my first car and my pride and joy at that time.

I attended the interview and faced a gentleman who appeared to me to be very old and a bit crusty. He made me feel very nervous and the interview from my point of view didn't go at all well, or so I thought. Something must have worked in my favour as I was indeed accepted into the status of Trainee legal executive with such duties to commence on 1st August 1970.

I started work for the grand sum of £15 per week. £2 of that provided me with a full tank of petrol, enough to manage the daily drive to Aylesbury and back and I still had plenty to spoil myself at weekends with my mates and girlfriend.

I was not the only one to be accepted as a trainee and was to start my career with two other trainees one being Gill who would keep popping up throughout my career and who has indeed recently retired herself from the local council, and also Margaret who we will discuss later but was to have an even more profound impact into my life. Our duties were primarily overseen by our immediate superior, Mr. Earl, who maintained a very rigid code of discipline. Our Office Manager, Mr. Howes, who was a lovely old gentleman from an earlier generation of courtesy and manners. In the 3 years I worked with him never lost his temper, never raised his voice nor indeed had a bad word to say about anyone. I also encountered old Fred, a legal assistant of many years standing.

These three old stagers from an earlier generation would prove to be the main guiding characters in my life over the next three years with the County Council. During that time they would persuade, bully, cajole and, more importantly, encourage me and my fellow trainees in our chosen careers. What they did not perhaps realise was that while they were sharing their knowledge and experience of the world they knew, that era that was quickly disappearing. Nevertheless, their eccentricities, as they now appear, firmly imprinted on my mind an attitude towards the law and the work which has determined the rest of my working life and without the likes of these and many others like them the story in this book would be doomed to failure and there would have been very little point in putting this pen to this paper.

The scope of the County Council's legal department extended to The Fire Service, Highways, Education, The Police Authority and, from the beginning of time almost, the old Quarter Sessions Courts. In consequence the offices were vast and, as a trainee I was a very small cog in a very large and efficient wheel that had established itself to serve the various communities throughout Buckinghamshire. I would of course glean much experience from these various duties of the Council in the three years that I would remain with them as a trainee.

The old County Hall Offices at Aylesbury

The Old Offices standing at the bottom of the Market Square had themselves suffered quite a tragedy shortly before I joined. They now quietly age without much of their story being known. Part of the main building housed the old Council chamber and also the old crusty quarter sessions court, which in my memory resembled those old photographs and films of pre-20th century courts.

Shortly before I arrived one young man appeared for trial at one of the many cases that had been heard in the courtroom. He was found guilty and duly sentenced to imprisonment. This incarceration was to prove more than just a heartbreak to his brother who didn't fully understand. Or perhaps did not begin to comprehend, the reasons why his wayward brother had been taken away from him. This poor unfortunate had special needs. And probably had some difficulty in understanding the relationship between crime and punishment.

Matters came to a head when the convicted young man came out of prison and shortly thereafter was killed, I believe, in a road accident. His brother never came to terms with this and from that moment on blamed the court for his brother's death. He would often announce his displeasure by visiting the police station located at the very back of the Council Offices and threatening to burn the court down. Each time he was politely persuaded by the duty sergeant not to be so silly and to quietly go away. However, one day he walked into the police station brandishing an empty can of petrol in hand as evidence that he had carried out his threat. Such a threat was confirmed when to his horror the duty sergeant indeed turned round looked out the rear window and saw great plumes of thick smoke rising from the front of that part of the County Council offices housing the Courts. Despite dramatic efforts from fire services from numerous fire stations in the area, fighting for many hours, they were not able to prevent the devastation of this ancient building or to preserve its glorious woodwork and interior.

Everything had to be restored, from the basement, which held original 18th century cells, up through the entire three floors of the building. Nothing had been untouched by the destructive fire, but every aspect of the building was painstakingly reconstructed by skilled craftsmen. The building was first stabilized and reinforced with steel girders and once the shell of the building was in place, the wood carvers and plaster moulders moved in to finally put the building back to its former glory. Much of the work depended on the memories of old Councillors and the information from old photographs many of which were tattered and faded black and white photos. Nevertheless they did successfully build up an accurate picture of the old Council Chamber and Court Room with their old wooden columns, the old benches in the judge's section, the witness boxes, the juror's seating, and even the public gallery. Veneered oak style beams boxed in the steel girders, which now held up the three floors and took three years to complete. The restoration was pitifully slow but when finished even included the old chamber pot, which had been recovered in a black and charred state, but once cleaned and restored and placed back into a little cupboard strategically located in front of the judge's chair for those "difficult moments" during a long trial when nature called, it seemed that no detail had been missed by the restoration team.

One issue, which came up unexpectedly at the last minute, pivoted on a disagreement between the Listed buildings officers and the Fire Brigade. As a listed building, the County Offices had to be put back more or less as it was with all its imperfections and one of these included huge iron bar railings across all the windows at the front of the building facing Market Square. The Fire Officers saw this as a risk to public safety in the event of a fire, one which could have caused fatality at the time of the original fire and was therefore wholly unacceptable for reinstatement. The Listed Buildings people took a different view and neither side was willing to compromise. And so the lines were drawn the arguments continued until someone finally and creatively proposed a rather simple solution. County officials collectively breathed out a great sigh of relief and so the offices opened and are as the public see them today.

The solution, which will not be immediately evident to most passersby was to replace the iron bars in the appearance of their former glory, thus satisfying the listed buildings experts, but to build the bars on hinges, so that in the event of a similar catastrophe anyone caught on the inside would simply open the windows swing the bars out of position and climb out. I always smile at this when passing the building that the solution to these entrenched positions, which for a time jeopardised the re-opening of the building, was so simple.

Dunstable College

Part of the terms of my contract of employment was that I should attend college and try to qualify as fully-fledged Legal Executive. This meant that I would have to travel to the Dunstable College once a week a distance of some 20 miles from Aylesbury. One advantage was when college finished at 4.00 pm I did not have to drive back to Aylesbury but could drive straight home some 15 miles north to what is now Milton Keynes. Another bonus was that my Mother who worked in Dunstable finished work at 4.30 pm so I could drive down to wait for her outside the gates and give her a lift home. As a result she could be home slightly before my father who also worked in Dunstable but was normally tied up with traffic during the rush hour. Dunstable in the early 1970s was a huge hub of industry. AC Delco, where my Mother worked, supplied Vauxhall Motors with spark plugs and other components. Lucas was another component company based in Dunstable and the entire Vauxhall van factory was located further into the town. As such the whole town employed thousands of workers and was indeed a thriving and lucrative place to work. Now to park outside the old gates of the AC Delco works at the end of the working day was itself quite an experience. We often see on old films how the whistle would blow and from what seems to be a deserted location suddenly fills up in a matter of minutes with thousands of workers pouring out of the gates. Blue collar workers mingled with white collar workers, management and trainees came out of the gates shoulder to shoulder, all trying to scurry to their buses and lifts to get home as quickly as possible.

During the several years I attended college I became acquainted with a number of fellow students. One in particular, who would follow me through my career to present times, and who I would describe as a particularly "confident" teenager and who became a bit of a friendly rival, is well remembered.

When we both first started at college I was on £15 per week, as I mentioned earlier. Local Authorities at that time seemed to be paying higher wages than the equivalent in private practice, and my young rival, who was in the private sector, was only earning £12 per week. However, as time progressed his weekly salary increased at about the same rate as mine until eventually when I was earning £19 per week his salary was only £16. We have kept in contact over the years, and at times his salary exceeded mine and vice versa. In the end he outstripped me. He is a partner in a well-established local law practice, and is responsible for several offices with an enormous staff. The fruits of his large income today are evident in the Porsche that he currently drives, and whilst my simpler life style is expressed by my Land Rover Defender.

Office Training

Throughout my three years with the County Council I was to work my way through various departments and therefore covered the wide range of the Council's responsibilities. For example, I was involved with debt collection, assisting in the setting up of the courts for the quarter sessions, and in minor conveyancing matters. My two trainee colleagues, Gill and Margaret and I, reported to the person put in charge of us, Robert Earl. Although Mr. Earl was probably only 10 years older than us, at the time he seemed absolutely ancient and he ruled the workplace with a rod of iron. What he said was expected to go unchallenged and anyone of us who tried to argue, disagree or fail to carry out the task set for us, quickly learned that they were up against a much sronger-willed man.

As Trainees we were made responsible for the diligent preparation of the departmental coffee, which had to be made ready to be drunk at 11.00 clock each day promptly for the head of department, old Fred and Mr. Howes the manager, Robert and we three trainees. Promptly at 3.00 pm our essential services were required once more but instead of coffee we had to lay on the departmental tea. Biscuits were also served, on china plates with the tea. Sometimes we would be allowed to stand and chat for a few moments sharing the day's events. My favourite was old Fred who was a very experienced Law Clerk. He had done war service but he remained very faithful to his trade. It was he who shared the secret of sewing up the old documents and deeds, producing (unclear) green tape (known affectionately as china grass) and a long needle. The tape had to be three times the length of the document which then had 5 holes, one in the middle one at each end and another two in between and all approximately half an inch in from the edge. The secret to sewing the document was to make sure that there were no creases and that all sewings ended up in the middle so that the two ends could be tied together around the line that passed underneath. On several occasions Fred would produce the taper, and the solid red piece of wax, light the taper, melt one end over the two ends of china grass to prevent any future tampering or fraud. This was a piece of art now long since forgotten. I was to offer in later years to anyone in my department a bottle of wine if they could sew up some pieces of paper but nobody took up the challenge. Old Fred also produced various seals that the Council had to insert onto the part of the deed that had to be witnessed.

Our working lives at this point were stable, disciplined and regular and indeed conformed to the boundaries set with everyone knowing their place. Our daily routine whilst staid proved structured safe and comfortable as well as successful and every day I went home I with a sense of achievement I had achieved a great day. However, in every organisation there is always the practical joker, the one that is always laughing and bringing everyone together with his or her sense of humour. Ours was in the form of Richard B. who was a good looking six feet plus rugby playing larger than life character who always had that twinkle in an eye that was ready for mischief. Richard was some 9 or 10 years older than me and being in his late 20's made him very ancient to my young eyes. He had a lovely family with a long-suffering wife and several daughters whom I understand numbered to a total of some 7 or 8 before producing the long awaited son into the household. Now Richard could never be trusted not to formulate some scheme or other to wind up his fellow workers. As one of the youngest, I was often the target. One day after returning from an outside appointment I discovered that my section of the office had disappeared. My desk, my chair and the remainder were nowhere to be seen. I eventually found everything in another room and had to lug everything back into its place. I once came back to find my well loved and cherished ex army trench coat lovingly retained from my "weekend hippy" days appropriately wired up on my chair to look like a person was sitting at my desk, complete with arm stretched out holding a biro and with a balloon for a head wearing a very sill grin, and a paper hat perched on the top.

These antics carried on over the three years of my employment with the Council. Richard even managed to telephone a young innocent assistant to the careers officer sitting right next to him in the adjoining glass walled office whom we could all see taking the call and being completely wound up by Richard oblivious to the fact that the man she was talking was less than 8 feet away with the rest of us falling over with laughter. However with all office jokers there comes the point of retribution. Working with us in this large room was an assistant articled clerk who like myself was a long-suffering victim of Richard's pranks, tricks and tom foolery, and had reached a point where we had rather had enough and decided to plan a practical revenge. Now Richard drove in each day in his rather clean Morris 1100 which he always parked in the same position, alongside the judge's chambers in the forecourt located just below the third story window that looked out from our offices. Richard made the mistake of never locking his car, believing that with others parked in front and behind there was little to steal and certainly the vehicle could not be removed. So on this particular evening Richard had finished for the day and headed for his car to drive home. Only when he opened the door he was greeted with a rather unpleasant surprise. Someone had placed inside the car a live chicken. It was perfectly safe as it had air to breathe but, as with all animals when slightly distressed, it had a very unpleasant bowel reaction which it managed to distribute virtually everywhere inside the car which not only was most unpleasant to see but also had the most unfortunate odour as well. Richard however took it all in good fun and with his usual cheeky smile gave a waved fist gesture to us all looking down at the discovery. I could never understand at the time of working with this practical joking team how anyone could drink tea or coffee that was not hot. Richard had this habit of still asking that his morning coffee or afternoon tea be made and left on his desk irrespective of whether he was either in the building or outside on visits and very often his beverage would be stone cold by the time he got to drink it. However drink it he would despite the grimaces and winces of his fellow workers even announcing how enjoyable it had been when drinking down the last of the dregs from the cup. Now again a further act of retribution was this time being hatched by another member of our little office group by the name of Peter who was himself part of the careers team. Realising that the morning coffee had all been drunk and the member's mugs still sat on most of the desks including Richards full cup of now very cold coffee. Peter proceeded to empty the cup of cold coffee and replace it with the dregs of everyone else's left-overs. This comprised not only coffee dregs but also tea some with sugar some without to make up this hotch-potch brew which was dutifully placed back on the table of the unsuspecting Richard who finally appeared went to his desk picked up the mug and with exaggerated gesture devoured the contents in his usual manner smacking his lips and saying how lovely that was. It was some time after that Peter did in fact confess his sins after much laughter and merriment of how someone could be fooled in drinking basically a cup of left over slops.

County Council Debt Collection

Assisting with the Council's debt collection work was one of my first tasks. It was necessary for me to draft various formal letters inviting debtors to settle for an array of debts and sundries owed. One action in particular was brought against an individual who had his private boat moored on the River Thames, which for some reason had filled with water and this required the local fire brigade to bail out the water and send him the bill for the charges. Others seemed reluctant to settle paying for private school fees, and indeed one chap had a tree that was so dangerous the fire brigade had to cut down branches over hanging the public highway. My initial problem was that up until my working life commenced I was only expert in drafting letters to members of the family by way of "thank you letters" to aunts and relatives for birthday and Christmas presents and so it came as a bit of a culture shock to have to write rather stiff and formal letters to members of the public followed by even more formal court proceedings in issuing summons judgements and executions. What also proved difficult in the early days was the use of the telephone in a formal and business like manner. My family only owned one telephone between us all and this was used very rarely for special reasons, and so telephone manner was again not practiced or perfected. At this time many homes were without a phone and many of the older generation were in fact frightened to use the thing at all. I remember my own Nan who I knew was often going to be at our home around 4.45pm and so I would telephone home knowing she would have to answer. She was terrified of the instrument, believing that it required shouting at to let the recipient know she was there and what she was trying to say. Eventually she did manage to treat this new device with the same ease and manner that I did, but only when she thought I would be at the other end.

Within the Council itself we had quite a number of members of staff who had served throughout the various wars and were very regimented in their attitude and approach to others. The ranks were still regarded as being very much alive and well, and one had to be aware of his or hers pecking order within those ranks. I do recall with horror one such character who worked in the Council's Treasury Department and was in charge of that departments wing of the debt collection, which rather put me in contact with him more often than I would have desired. I never actually met the chap face to face either during my stay at the Council or indeed afterwards, and all our conversations were through the medium of the telephone. He absolutely relished his job as a debt collector which I still shudder to this day as this seemed then as well as now to be the most boring and tedious job anyone could wish for. However, one still had to respect one's elders in those days and as discussed you were always called by your surname, never Mr. unless you had done something dreadfully wrong. Christian names did not even exist. I must confess at this stage one incident that still haunts me even to this day. I had to make a call to our friendly debt collector and for some reason my mouth appeared to be way ahead of my brain.

What I meant to say was, "Hello Mr. Smythe - Ainsworth here!"

What actually came out of my mouth was "Hello Smythe, Mr. Ainsworth here!"

As soon as I had finished my sentence the brain caught up with the mouth with a huge thud, and my whole body went into palpitations as the recipient went into sullen silence. The silence seemed to last an eternity till finally, a rather crusty, cold and gruff voice responded with "I think you had better call me back! " and the line went dead. By this time my knuckles had gone white as I clung to the phone my brain racing to avoid sheer panic not believing what mortal sin I had just committed. Was I going to be shot at dawn deported off to some French colony or simply locked up in old dungeons in the bowls of the earth below the old Quarter sessions never to see daylight again. After what appeared to be a total lifetime, seeing my working career as a potential lawyer disappear before it started, I eventually plucked up the courage to telephone my tormentor back and resume my pre-conceived message. The recipient carried the conversation as if nothing had happened. Of course, looking back now I feel sure that Mr. Smyth must have been still chuckling to himself in the background and indeed had a good hearty laugh to himself long after he retired!

Quarter Sessions

The quarter sessions days were pleasant and memorable. Meeting all sorts of characters to include the jurors summoned in from around the entire County and the court officials, the solicitors the barristers and those characters standing trial, was always of great interest to me. It was part of my duties for a while to set up the desk in front of the judge, where the Clerk of the Court would officiate, making sure that before the Court commenced all the books, pencils, water, precedent law books and bibles were laid out. At the time, and still being a teenager, this all seemed so very important. I was to be later promoted to sit alongside the Clark of the Court taking notes, and having the responsibility of actually approaching the jurors once the trial had started and in front of the entire court to formally swear in the jurors and thereafter as each witness entered the witness box to stand and ask them to take the oath.

During this time I was able to meet folks from all sorts of walks of life. Occasionally, to my surprise, some of the members of the Jury were unable to read and write and I learnt very quickly to quietly approach them at the beginning of the new quarter session to try to discreetly identify anyone who was indeed likely to be openly embarrassed in front of the open court and ensure that we could over come those difficulties. Instead of handing them the bible to hold in their right hand and a card in their left hand to read from, I would discreetly hand them the bible to hold in their right hand retain the card myself and simply ask them to repeat to me the words that I would read to them from the card. This way nobody in the court realised that the person had any such problem and thus we built a very good relationship with the members of the jury at that particular session. Now at that time we not only had the card from which the jurors would read but also various witness cards that would cater for not only the Church of England and Catholic faiths but also other religions and even the occasional agnostic that would be sworn in. Unfortunately I never did get to use my favourite card which provided for the swearing in of an oriental religion that required one not only to read from the card but also to smash a small plate uttering their oath that if they were to tell a lie their spirit would be broken for ever like the plate they had just smashed. What a pity! That really would have been a tale for the grandchildren.

As the original courtrooms were still being restored to their former glory due to the fire discussed earlier in this chapter some of the ordinary County Council offices were converted into temporary courtrooms.

A few brushes with the arm of the law

I need to digress for a moment back to my earlier youth for the purposes of the next tale forming this chapter of my life. As a youngster in my early teens it seemed that I was haunted by the local policeman who would often appear from nowhere and then detain me while thoroughly questioning my whereabouts, activities and intentions. This policeman always ended up with the same comment that I would never be any good and that one day he would catch me out. Indeed one evening I recall being passed by what was the then new style of police car what was later to be affectionately known as the "Panda Car" while I was riding my bicycle into town and resulted in me having to brake severely to avoid riding into the back of the car as it swung into my path while displaying what I thought was part of its breaking system with the word "stop" being lit up in the back window. I did manage to avoid sliding into the back of the car by swerving out into the road. I continued my journey until, only one a hundred yards up the road, the same erratic behaviour was repeated by the Panda car. The driver leapt out and made all sorts of accusations about my failing to stop and no explanation about not understanding the "stop" sign seemed to pacify him. I was then lectured on the fact that I had been "speeding" on my push bike, that he could prosecute me if he chose, that if he caught me again there was no limit to the legal options open to him. By this time it had all become a little farcical.

After years of this prolonged aggravation and persecution I was now able to start work in a different town and thus to all intents and purposes able to stay out of the local policeman's way. To my dismay and horror who should be approaching me across the forecourt at the back of the Council Offices as I was making my way to one of the Offices that had been dedicated that day to stand as one of the court rooms, but the very policeman who had been haunting me for years and who having recognised me immediately approached me and with great pleasure and a sneer asked me,

"Oh they've got you at last – so what have they caught you for?"

I had the utmost pleasure of replying that in fact I worked for the Quarter Sessions and was a trainee legal executive and was on my way to help set up the courtroom for that day's particular criminal trial. Fate was to play an even happier card that day as I was asked to attend the very criminal court trial where the policeman was giving evidence. The years of torment were to be fully exonerated on that one day when I was to be rewarded by sitting in and listening to this police officer, who was trying to give evidence against six so called hooligans who he had apprehended some months earlier and who he alleged had set upon him causing actual bodily harm when he had tried to question them in the street as to their behaviour and intentions. (main clause needed) However, each of the

16

defendants was separately represented by his own barrister and each one took it in turns to question the Police Officer and after hours of continuous questioning finally managed to bring out the true facts that in fact it was the Police Officer himself that had struck the first blow at these lads and the boys themselves were acting in self defence against the policeman. Needless to say the criminal action against the lads was immediately dismissed, much to the sigh of relief of the accused and their parents but of course meant that the career of the Police Officer was finally over. I learnt later that having left the police force in disgrace he returned back to Wales where he came from the set up a security business, which in itself failed. In addition with the help of Face Book recently it seems that whilst I felt at the time that I was the only victim being selected for continual harassment that he in fact repeated his methods with quite a few of the youth of the day throughout the town and who were all greatly relieved by his timely disappearance.

To my misfortune this was not going to be my only brush with the law during my early career. In fact one Friday evening about a year after I had started working for the County Council I had driven up to a small town some 25 miles north of home to a pub that had a side entrance leading up to a large room where a blues style music evening was held each week with the well known celebrity John Peele manning the door and selling tickets. Several cars travelled up with various mates and the evenings always proved highly successful. Afterwards we would make our way back to the infamous Newport Pagnell Motorway services where we knew a back way into the services to avoid driving along the motorway. Here we would end the evening with coffee and possibly fried food before heading home. This particular night I had met a young lady at the venue and having dropped her off home tried to catch up the rest of my mates who had left previously heading for the services café. As I came into Newport Pagnell I spotted a pair of headlights behind me, and believing this was one of the group I accelerated, not wanting them to pass me in my youthful vigour. Unfortunately I didn't realise that there were roadworks further ahead with traffic lights showing red. The next moment I was being confronted with a torch light held by a policeman who had been following me behind.

I was panic-stricken at the prospects of possible prosecution for speeding and so tried to be as co-operative to the officer as I could, answering all his questions as to where I had been where I was heading and that the car was mine. He seemed particularly interested in the back of the car and when I stretched round and wound the rear window down his arm went into the back of the car and in a flash pulled out this long black coat asking me who this belonged to. I realised that the young lady I had taken home must have left her coat in the back which on the one hand was an irritation as I was now going to have to drive all the way back to deliver it to her and on the other hand trying to keep the Police Officer happy with my story. Unfortunately it did not seem to work as he directed me to park the vehicle the other side of the road works and accompany him back to the Police Station in Newport Pagnell.

On arrival I was ushered into this large room while the Police Officer still armed with the girl's coat disappeared. I was left sitting there for what appears to be ages. Eventually the duty sergeant came across to me with the Police Officer and proceeded to be rather curt and sarcastic asking the Police officer if I was the pervert who went around stealing girl's coats which remark rather had me sitting on the edge of my seat. He then threw other insults at me saying how they didn't believe me that "someone" had gone into the local youth club earlier that evening and went into the girls changing rooms and stolen a girls coat. Despite all my protests they just wouldn't believe me. By now the time was well into the early hours of the morning but despite that the Police telephoned the girl's home, woken up her parents and repeated my story, which was confirmed. The police were still not satisfied and asked the parents to describe the coat right down to the buttons which of course they were unable to do so they were forced to get the girl from her bed to then describe in greater detail her own coat.

While this was going on the duty sergeant was still giving me a hard time even asking me who I thought I was (I was wearing trainers that evening) and whether I was a long distance runner. I replied no just a bit of a scruff at weekends to which he got quite nasty told me not to be funny with him and tell him what I did for a living. My answer that I worked for the Thames Valley Police Authority (one part of the County Council) at the County Hall in Aylesbury. This drew an incredible reaction. Suddenly I was believed There had been a huge mistake. "Sonny," suddenly became "Sir" and that I of course must understand they were "doing their duty." The sergeant then told the officer that he would make sure I got back to my car safely and took me back in this huge squad car still protesting about police duty of care. When we arrived at the car I turned to the sergeant and pointed out that I could have been any unsuspecting member of the public, that the treatment I had received was beyond acceptable and that be rest assured I would be lodging my own complaint with the head office on Monday Morning, to which I got a very, very polite, "Thank you sir and good evening sir." Needless to say I did put in a complaint, not the fact that I had been stopped and taken to the Police Station but by the way I had been handled and the way I had been spoken to assuming that all youths were layabouts and no goods instead of getting the facts first before coming to conclusions.

The old ways

In my early days the office equipment that we used was all rather basic with luxuries such as computers or even electric typewriters being beyond the wildest imagination. In fact the photocopier was jealously protected against misuse by the office manager who had a set of rules on how to operate and never to interfere with its supply of paper or ink cartridges for fear of damage. Legal documents themselves were still produced on old parchment type paper. As trainees dealing with contracts, road agreements and deeds we were expected to sew these documents and could be completing any number up to 7 to 12 each a day. I was very lucky in so far as old Fred had taught me to sew and although each document was time consuming I have to admit they did look rather lovely when finished. However we three trainees did finally revolt and with unanimous backing from the head of the department managed to persuade Mr. Earl to accept a very modern piece of equipment called an Eyeletter. This revolutionary piece of office equipment, which looked like a pair of blunt scissors, would first of all punch a hole through the collection of paperwork held for that purpose. A brass eyelet was then placed into the hole and squeezed to form a permanent rivet type object, which held to document together and acted as a deterrent to the document being interfered with or altered. However, it was still written in stone that this new device could only be used solely and strictly on those documents that had a restricted life such as a contract for sale. Any other documents of substance would have to be sewn and in some cases sealed on the ends of the green chord by either waxed seals or by the newer sticky seals.

The remainder of my career with the County Council rather passed in a secure and comfortable haze. Living at home with parents and travelling the twenty odd miles each day to work, being "let out" early during the various power strikes "suffering" the various postal strikes which meant another early release to go home. Being sent off as a junior to complete purchases at the offices of the seller's solicitors, which involved being armed with wads of papers and cheques. Very often I would be sent off on the train from Aylesbury into London arriving at Marylebone Station to either discover London by taxi or by underground or, even better, to walk thus to enjoy a whole day of freedom in our capital city at the expense of the Council. If there were papers to be delivered to one of the quarter sessions judges who lived on my route home, or if a completion was needed where the solicitors officers were in the North of the County I would be sent off early which to my delight meant getting home earlier than expected. All in all I was cocooned in this wonderful secure Dickensian system where everything worked well, everyone knew their place and role in life and when I didn't seem to have any of the domestic or professional worries that were awaiting me further in my career.

I remember one such trip that took me to a completion to the old town of Woburn. There in the middle of this small town that bordered on to the Duke of Bedford Estate was this small law firm called Holborn of Woburn which seemed to step right out of a Dickens novel. The door off the street led into this very musty dark and dismal office full of old wooden furniture, high shelves stacked with dusty deeds, discoloured papers and files. I immediately thought of the televised Scrooge when I saw these offices. The clerk of this particular office sat on one of the high-legged chairs and as I entered came down to the client counter to see what I wanted. When I announced I had come over to hand over a cheque from the County Council and pick up some deeds and documents I was ushered into a tiny office, which was equally as cluttered and shown a chair next to an old desk, again full of papers and a file tied up with a piece of red cotton string. Inside I was to find what I was looking for, a completed, signed but undated deed and the original deeds, part of which we were purchasing. I then unrolled the copies held in my brief case, and thumbed through each page corresponding with the originals and checked they were true copies, marking each page that was a true copy until I had gone through the entire bundle. At the end I was to date the deed hand over the cheque and then I could escape to make my way home earlier than normal. I can still remember the smell and the layout of that old office that depicted everything one imagined an old nineteenth century law firm to look like. All that was missing were the horse and carriages outside and folks dressed in Victorian clothes. The partner of the old Holborn of Woburn was again himself of very old school, typifying the image by the surroundings and who I would meet again many years later in completely different circumstances.

The last day with the Council was as memorable as the first. The County Clerk had his offices at the front of the building and as a very high ranking officer was duly undisturbed by mortals such as trainees. In fact, in the three years I had served with the Council, I had only attended his office once to deliver a rather important document for him to produce to the court that day as Clerk of the Quarter sessions. However, I was summoned! (the buzzer on the desk went and a voice boomed out, "Mr.Ainsworth can you come to the Chief Clerk's office") I arrived outside his office door and waited for the red light (enter at your own peril) to go out and the green light to come on to then walk into this whole different world. The coal fire was lit inside the office, with its own coal scuttle of highly polished brass which stood to attention dutifully holding a full load of coal ready for use, the two King Charles Spaniels laying gracefully at the side of this huge leather topped desk behind which the Chief Clerk sat and eventually looked up at me through his half-rimmed spectacles smiled and handed me my leaving present. I was extremely nervous but thought afterwards that for all his importance and the tradition that he followed with all the Chief Clerks over the year, he actually turned out to be a lovely man.

The archway into the County offices. My office was behind the left hand window.

2 Moving Home

In order to make progress in my career I needed to leave the protected world of Trainee and move on into the outside world. After three years with the county Council, that time had now arrived. I had started courting and really needed to establish myself as a Legal Assistant rather than a trainee legal assistant. After handing in my notice I took up a position in my own home town working for a private firm of solicitors as a conveyancing assistant. My mentor Richard B had by now left and joined a branch office of a local firm of solicitors near where he lived. John had also left to join a private practice in Oxford and I really felt the time had come for me to also move on. I applied for the job and was accepted which meant I would only take minutes to reach the office and would be dealing with local people.

As things turned out this new post only lasted 9 months as the pay was insufficient and to be honest I was a little out of my depth in the volume and type of work that was demanded of me. However, for the 9 months that I persevered within this private practice I did find it far more satisfying acting for real people rather than departments, and actually seeing the fruition of my labours with clients moving into their new homes was very satisfying. The partner, Giles, who ran the practice was a tall man and a very charismatic character. He seemed to spend more time in the office than going home and enjoyed life as much as he enjoyed work. Being so tall he would lean his arms against the top of the door frame when looking down to talk to you and the only car that seemed to fit him was his Jensen Interceptor, which took his long legs, and which he drove as fast as he possibly could. What was always interesting was when he occasionally turned up driving a little Mini Minor in which he had to literally unfold his legs out first before his arms and then drag himself out, rather like an octopus leaving a rather small pot. The staff were always amused by these contortions who stood and watched him disembark himself from the confines of his little container on wheels. I heard recently that he had in fact passed on, but true to form, he was still working on his computer the day before his illness finally took him to the great law office in the sky.

Living in Milton Keynes in the early 70's we were all affected by the great changes that had been imposed upon us with the introduction and development of the new Town of Milton Keynes. It had been a close call as to who would take charge of the project given that the Buckinghamshire County Council had lost Slough, a huge industrial town, in the Local Government re-shuffle of 1970, in the process losing a mammoth-sized annual revenue into its coffers, so there was an even greater incentive for the County Council to create another money spinner to replace Slough. At the same time, the local Council were not going to step meekly aside and revoke its own power and possible fortune to outside influences and they applied for their own plans to be implemented, which basically provided an outward ripple of the existing town of Bletchley in much the same way as the developments were taking place in Stevenage Harlow. Eventually central government decided, wisely and correctly to award the task to a specially formed Corporation, giving them their unilateral powers to acquire land and to plan and develop the new town.

This arrangement, although the best overall, did no favours for the locals seeking accommodation. Anyone coming into the area to work could automatically be sponsored for new housing on one of the new estates being developed for that purpose. Youngsters like myself who were either born in or spent most of their lives growing up in the area were directed to the Local Council who had little to no new housing stock and would simply add names to the already overstretched waiting list. It seemed very unfair at the time. I was personally advised that if I cared to "move away" and come back in say 5 years time then the Corporation would be able to help us as outsiders moving into the area. So many of my friends and schoolmates did that very thing and scattered beyond the boundaries of Milton Keynes, many of course never to return. A few did and a couple of those were lucky to indeed be re-housed but the majority were not so lucky.

I was courting at the time and I was now at the age where I needed to leave home and establish my own home; unfortunately the pay that was being offered in private practice was insufficient for me to fulfil my aspirations. Even so, I felt it was time for me to spread my wings, leave the nest and find my own home. Salaries were such that I could not afford a mortgage even with house prices at that time only being around the £6,000 mark. The only alternative was for me to go back into Local Authority work where local authorities offered accommodation. I applied for several posts and was lucky to be selected to go and work in Amersham for the local council. This posting came with a two bedroomed flat. I therefore reluctantly handed my in notice and started making plans to move lock, stock, and barrel down to Amersham.

3 Days in Amersham

As I was still living at home my total possessions consisted mostly of my own clothes. Luckily a friend's parents were buying a brand new home and didn't want the old furniture and donated most of it to me, including an old sofa, coffee table, bed and bits and bobs which I stored ready for my move. At this time, during late October/November, we were still suffering strikes and lockouts and the dreaded petrol shortages with the threat of actual petrol rationing just round the corner. We had been issued with coupons for petrol albeit their use had not actually come into force. It was a good 40 miles from parents home to the new flat and so the convey of vans and mates cars set off with the hope that along the way, the petrol stations would be open and just as importantly actually have enough fuel that they could sell to us to reach the new destination. After many stops we did eventually arrive in Amersham, where we unloaded the furniture and other items and limped back to Milton Keynes. I then had to drive in my car from Milton Keynes via as many petrol stations as I could find back to the flat ready to start work on the Monday morning.

Elmodesham House. Home of the Amersham RDC. My office was on the top floor, 3rd window from the left

To say the day had been eventful was an understatement but liquid compensation was found in a local hostelry after the job had been accomplished.

Jean Archer and Local History

When I arrived for work on Monday morning I was shown my desk on the top floor of this grand old house that was used for the Council Offices in those days. The actual office was shared with two others with the deputy solicitor in the little room next door. The floor itself was so rickety that one day one of the lads I shared the office with got an empty milk bottle and put it on its side at one end and it simply rolled by itself to the other. For my own work I was to share a secretary with the Town Clerk. Her name was Jean Archer, a middle aged single woman born and bred in Amersham. Jean turned out to not only be a wonderful warm and lovely lady and a very capable and experienced secretary. She was also the local historian and a book writer. She and I would sit talking for many an hour over the years I worked there, and I was able to feed on her local knowledge of the area. One of the books that she wrote, a short paperback still sits with pride of place on my bookshelf at home.

One of the many old glass negatives found by Jean Archer and her colleagues.

One day Jean and one of her historical society colleagues managed to gain access to a very old house opposite the Council Offices, which they suspected had once been the local corn exchange. The owner had died and they asked the executors for permission to gain access to carry out a thorough investigation to establish if their theory was correct. Once inside the layout and the style quickly confirmed that they had been correct and it was indeed the old corn exchange from many years past. However a greater treasure was about to be uncovered. Opening one of the cupboards they noticed what appeared to be a stack of very old very dusty broken glass window panes. On closer examination these panes turned out to be very old glass negatives. Many had been damaged beyond repair but with the blessing of the executors the panes of glass that looked like they could be saved were carefully removed for further inspection by a more qualified and trained eye. Apparently the method used to recover the images was to take a new photo of the negative and re-produce that as a modern photograph. What appeared from these old relics was totally beyond imagination, hope or belief. It seemed that one of the first gentlemen in the country to actually own a camera lived close by. Realising the sheer potential of his acquisition he took it upon himself over the years to take photographs of just about everything that moved or seemed of some historic value. He photographed the first gas mains to be laid, the men going off to the first world war, the annual fair, and one photograph shows all the postal workers stood outside the old post office. In their finest 19th century uniforms waving flags for what they believed may have been the relief of the siege of Mafeking. One photograph really brought Jean to a quiet repose. It was that of a young butcher boy, probably taken at the age of 13 or 14 riding the butcher's cart up a very dusty hill towards upper Amersham and looking back towards the Photographer. The young teenager turned out to be in fact Jean's great Uncle who had died at a very grand old age. I was so fascinated by these photographs that were finally mounted onto A3 cardboard and when I finally left the Council she asked me if there was one I particularly wanted. I chose the scene in the lower village of Amersham where the children from the local orphanage were posing in the centre of the square. In the top left hand corner the post coach can be seen arriving from London on its several day journey to the north; on the right hand side is the butcher's cart with the butcher leaning against a window, wearing his top hat and carrying his wicker basket while selling something to the occupant. The photograph still shows the old scaffolding around the Church which is recorded as finally being restored in 1894 thus dating the actual photograph some year or so before the final restoration date. The photo is signed by Jean and still takes a pride of place amongst my keepsakes.

Jean and I would chat for many hours and it was probably her more than anyone that kindled my interest in history. Not the history for kings queens revolutions and dates but a history of ordinary people of ways of life working conditions and stories attributing to those people. We talked about the Lollards, a religious reform group in the 15th century, who were persecuted and many of whom were taken to Blood hill to be burnt at the stake. Indeed the famous Quakers order was founded within a few miles of Amersham and fearing much persecution had famously left for the Americas. There is a large mansion on the side of the hill looking down into the Amersham Valley called Shardaloes and many mistake this building for Chequers, the weekend home of the Prime Minster but was in fact a private mansion. On the other side of the valley and further down stands the Amersham Church and there was supposed to be an passage that ran between the great house and the Church. Why such a tunnel was constructed can only be guessed at.

However during the late 1700's early 1800's the son of the owner wagered a bet with his friends that he could stay underground in this passage for two years which bet was gleefully taken in the spirit of the moment. However the young man not wishing to lose his bet did indeed venture into the passage and indeed remained there for the period of the wager his family never seeing him during this period but knowing he was still alive by the food and drink that disappeared. At the end of the two year period his friends descended into the dark passage to find the young man and confirm he had won his bet and to bring him out and back into normal life. Apparently when they found him he had gone completely insane and remained for the rest of his life institutionalised in an asylum. As you can imagine this and other stories kept me fascinated and in Jean's Company for many an hour during my time with the local Council.

A Christmas Tale

These days folks seem to relate any changes in normal climate behaviour to global warming rather than in most cases a simple freak of nature. I always recall the second Christmas that I worked in Amersham and on Christmas Eve afternoon sitting at my desk, with the sash windows pushed as high as they could to let in the afternoon sunshine of what was a gloriously warm sunny afternoon, thinking that this hardly seemed appropriate for all the advertised expectations of Christmas eve with no signs of snow or any other winter impediment. At that time we had an elderly lady working for us, who with her sister had been born and raised and lived most of their lives in the far east, then part of the British empire only returning for a short spell during the war and going back to the far east shortly after the war ended. As such both this elderly lady and her sister, once they become widowed and without family and very few friends left decided to return to England to live out their days. The problem was that back in the early 1970's the welfare state was less generous than it is today and they quickly found that as they had not contributed anything into the system then they were not entitled to any benefits, not even a pension, and this left the two of them penniless. One of the sisters was unable to work due to her age and physical condition, so it was left to the other, then in her mid to late 70's to earn money by taking a job offering secretarial services at the Council offices. At her age she really should have been sitting in a cosy armchair indoors during the afternoons after having her lunch for a quiet snooze that comes with the privilege of seniority, but instead that afternoon nap came upon her and she fell asleep at her desk. However her circumstances were understood and this was tolerated, allowing her to earn the few pounds that came her way each week for the little bit of typing and secretarial assistance she was able to give.

Now that Christmas approached we were all poised to disappear off to our friends and family. I was all packed and ready to return to the flat where I was living to pick up my bag and get myself back to family to celebrate the Christmas period. The two sisters unfortunately were not so lucky. They had nobody apart from themselves and this was rather a bleak time for both of them. However, it turned out that they did have a distant relative somewhere over in Hertfordshire who had offered them accommodation for the Christmas period. The problem they had was neither drove and nor had the money to pay for a train to London and then back out again. Feeling rather sorry for these two sisters, one of which I had grown fond of with all her stories of the Raj days, I volunteered my services to drive them over myself not thinking it would take very long. We closed the office an hour earlier than expected and so collecting belongings and two elderly passengers set off from Amersham, via normal main roads, given there was no M25 in those days to try to drive across country on Christmas Eve to the middle of Hertfordshire. It was an interesting journey with loads of traffic and problems and what I calculated as being perhaps three quarters of an hour maximum found us arriving just before 5.30pm. Now one might wonder how after forty plus years I could be so sure as to remember the actual time that I would be arriving at this rather busy hectic little town in the middle of Hertfordshire on a Christmas eve so long ago. Well it was about this time that I notice that my temperature gauge had risen quite considerably above the normal level and that steam was coming out of either side of my car bonnet. Pulling over, still with my two charges on board, and popping the bonnet to my horror I discovered that the top hose of the car was emitting rather dirty steaming water. Now how on earth I was going to get the car sorted, dispatch my two passengers and be able to get out of this strange town and home for Christmas eve suddenly became a panicky priority. By sheer luck I had just passed a Halfords car shop that were literally about to close their doors for the Christmas break and upon diving through the door discovered that they did, luckily, have a top hose for a Vauxhall Viva HC, which I purchased, along with a few bottles of water.

I returned to the vehicle and within several minutes had refitted a new hose, topped up the radiator to get me at least to a garage to fill up properly and discharge my two charges. I guess someone or something was definitely on my side that afternoon which could have ended up extremely embarrassing for my Good Samaritan's deed. I finally limped home keeping a very close eye on a temperature gauge and several hours later, having been on the road for over four and a half hours joined my friends in the local hostelry to commence the Christmas good cheer and celebrations. This was not going to be the last time that my Samaritan urges would take over Christmas plans.

Typewriters and colleagues

Now one of the skills I had learnt when I was still at school and which I had hoped would see me into my dashed career as a journalist was that of a touch typist. I had left school with various Pitman exams under my belt and had reached a speed of fifty-eight words a minute, as I mentioned in the first chapter. This was on an old manual typewriter on which it had been calculated by some statistical brain in a moment of boredom that the average typist would in fact during the course of the day move the equivalent of some two tons by the physical efforts of hammering the keys of a manual typewriter. However, the use of the typewriter had been very useful and indeed I used the typewriter somewhere to enable me to type receipts and memoranda about old deeds. Most transactions in those days were unregistered and when bits of land were sold off some record was required and memoranda endorsed on the original title deed. This was normal process. Now during my time in Amersham they had purchased a long carriage electric typewriter, which looked like an ordinary typewriter but the physical effort was minimal. I thought this was a complete revolutionary tool compared to what I had been use to. The secretaries at the time unfortunately wouldn't use it as they said it kept breaking down and making typing errors. So as time went on I inveigled this new wondrous machine into my office so that I could use it first hand for my production of such necessary receipts, letters and memoranda. It was very, very useful because the long carriage that would take large A3 deeds sideways, which enabled me to endorse the memoranda required. I never did find anything wrong with it and certainly it did not break down or make errors and I felt this was put forward as an excuse by the established secretaries who didn't want change, didn't want this new fangled device and were happy bashing away on the old style manual typewriters. When I eventually left Amersham I asked the secretary to the Council if I could buy it off them. I was advised to take it and if ever they were questioned then I may get a small bill. It was some ten years later and two jobs on that I finally got an envelope through my door for a request for ten pounds for the machine, which I had gladly paid. The old faithful typewriter remained with me more or less up to the advent of computers and printers and it was a long time in true loyal service.

At lunchtimes during the working week quite a few of us used to meet up at the local pub on a Friday at the end of village for a lunchtime game of darts and a couple of pints. One day a character came in sat at the bar and ordered his pint. I noticed that not only did nobody bother to talk to him, which was a bit strange given how friendly the pub was but also the atmosphere seemed to go sullen. Finally he finished his pint and as he stood up to leave declared so that every one in the pub could hear him that as far as he was concerned, "This is the most unfriendly pub I have ever drank in and I will never come back in again!" After he left there was a quite buzz about the state of this character's departure and much hilarity. I discovered later that this chap was in fact the local gamekeeper. What he, or indeed I, never realised was that he was drinking in the local poachers pub and most of his opposition were in there with him!!

At this time I worked with a rather tall lanky chap called Steve who wore these bottle thick glasses and had a rather basin shaped hair cut albeit that his hair was quite long which made him seem even more geeky, even though in his own right was a real character always falling over and being extremely clumsy. He was ridiculed from morning to night without it ever upsetting him or deterring him from his trail of total chaos and mayhem. I asked him one day just why did he have a pair of flying duck stickers prominently placed on the side of his little Vauxhall viva which was another point of ridicule by his work colleagues. In confidence he announced it was the only way he could find his car in a packed car park.

31

I asked him to explain and he confessed that he had in fact passed his test purely by fluke as he was in fact colour blind. In fact during his test he approached a set of traffic lights and luckily for him he was in fact in a line of cars and simply followed them hoping that the traffic lights would not change before he went through. He got away with it and passed his test and nobody apart from his immediate family knew of his secret. By having the ducks on the side of the car he could distinguish between his and all the other Vauxhall Vivas that were so popular at that time in the car park. Steve had this one "talent" which was playing darts. In the local pub where he played for the local team the ceilings were particularly low and while he would stand there looking totally gormless he had a secret card up his sleeve because when it was his turn to play he had mastered this ability to actually throw his darts so they used to bounce off the low ceiling and straight into whatever number, being single double or triple he wanted. It was absolutely mind-boggling to watch albeit infuriating if you were playing against him and I think he stored up all the punishment individuals had given him and had his revenge against them on the dart board. As a Trainee though he didn't earn a great deal of money so during the summer he would work locally in the retired folks gardens earning I seem to remember a £1 an hour cutting mowing edging and weeding for them. When it came to late autumn and through the winter he would then turn his attention to a little bit of decorating and painting. He couldn't have been that daft as he eventually gave up his post as Trainee in the legal department and went off working full time working with old folks. He eventually got married and as tall and lanky as he was Sue his wife was small and they did look a rather odd couple at the wedding but they were totally suited to each other and with his earnings he was able to secure quite a high deposit for his house from the money he had saved from his little part time jobs.

Election Day

One of the tasks given to most Council workers and indeed was considered a perk of the job was to help out with the local elections. The council staff could always earn a little extra on polling days, either by being the presiding officer, the assistant or if all else failed, as counters at the end of the night. On polling day itself the presiding officers would try to work it that the stations were closed at the earliest opportunity so that the voting boxes could be driven back to the Council offices ready for counting. It became an unwritten custom that the last person back would stand the last round of drinks before we were summoned to the counting. Poor Steve mentioned in the previous paragraph always seemed to be destined to work at with the most outlying village location and stood no chance of getting back before anyone else and always seemed to stand the round of drinks as demanded.

I was presiding officer for one particular election and I remember an elderly lady assisted into the polling station by her rather overzealous middle-aged daughter. I handed the mother her ballot sheet and still aided by her daughter she asked me which of the candidates took the order on the sheet as she had left her glasses at home. Her daughter became quite irritated and demonstrative and told her mother her not to be silly and just put her X in the box at the top. I then become a little assertive and remonstrated with the Daughter, pointing out that the ballot was private and that voter's wishes had to be upheld and, if anything, I would have to accompany the mother to the ballot screen. The daughter was fast proving to be a bit of a nuisance and I was forced to ask her to leave. Even as the daughter was walking out of the station she was barking her orders back at her mother with instructions to mark the top of the ballot paper. When we reached the privacy of the booth the Mother then asked me again for the order of candidates which I painstakingly did making sure that each time I read out the names I started from the other end so as not to seem biased and making sure that I described each candidate and his party in turn. The daughter had of course directed her mother to her candidate at the top of the page. The mother then asked me again where a particular candidate was located, which was not at all where the daughter had instructed, and she quietly made her mark, winked at me as her daughter led her away still clucking as to "what all the fuss was about!!" However this was a little lesson to me as well as any one else that the lady was entitled to her dignity, respect and understanding and to be given privacy to ensure she was not being brow beaten by outside influences with regard to her affairs and decisions.

The Flat on White Lion Road

My flat located along the White Lion road does I fear need a mention in itself. The flat formed part of a block, which consisted of several three and four storey blocks. Now the occupants were at that time shall we say rather lively to say the least. In fact the White Lion Pub across the road seemed to depict the flats. One side of the pub was very smart and frequented by very wealthy gentlemen driving very nice cars parked in the car park. They enjoyed very nice carpeting and general décor. The other side was rather "spit and sawdust" and was frequented by those they say broke into the other side's cars and most of whom lived in the flats. There were always strong words being screamed with the fights, loud music and general <u>tardiness</u> as would be expected in such an environment. To sum this area up, I had been out for a couple drinks with friends one Friday night before returning back to the flat to gather my bags to set off back to Milton Keynes for the weekend. I was actually stopped as I left the service road of the flats by police convinced I was actually on my way out to "do a job" and insisted on inspecting the car and the contents of my bag before allowing me on my way. However, to me this was my first home and once the front door was closed I was in my own little world with all my free furniture, TV and creature comforts. Now there are all sorts of visions of a bachelor pad and all the euphoria of its wonderful life of parties, loud music and good times. I must have been unfortunate to have been the minority of one because my day to day life was completely the opposite. Having returned from my weekends the first task was of course the washing. This was taken up on the time-honoured washday of Monday albeit in my case Monday evening when the twin tub was wheeled out. Shirts with cuffs and collars were scrubbed with a nail file and washing soap (the way my grandmother had showed me) then everything into the twin tub and then from there into the spinner that was probably less effective than beating it against a stone on the river bank. By late evening it was then introduced to the small balcony with its washing line going from side to side to dry. Tuesday evening was then set aside for the ironing and putting away. Wednesday was the evening for mundane housework and tidying up, so the only night I could actually get out before the weekend was Thursday and normally I was so knackered from the week's events that I just sat and watched TV and had an early night. Every Friday night I travelled home night ready for the weekend with my mates ready to start all over again from the following Monday - all in all pretty boring and mundane.

The Flats on White Lion Road

During my short career in Amersham we came across some very interesting characters and clients. I had to draw up a mortgage for a loan being given by the Council to a purchaser of one of the ex Almshouses opposite the offices, which were absolutely tiny, yet whilst 3 bedroom houses were being sold back home for around £7,000 this property was being sold for £17,000. I always thought the borrowers parents must have had a terrible sense of humour christening their child Christopher Robin especially given his surname as Wren. I should imagine he had a lot of flack from his school chums while growing up. We also had a very energetic and dedicated gentleman who took over the position of running the local crematorium who was so enthusiastic but could never understand others reluctance to share in his day to day joy. I think the penny did start to drop when after promoting an Open Day throughout the Council offices and the town and inviting attendance from all for a guided tour of the facilities, nobody actually turned up on the allotted day.

Every Sunday night in the old town there was an open folk evening. There an array of locals would gather in an old shed at the back of the shops and houses and proceed, unaccompanied in many instances, to simply stick their finger in one ear and launch themselves into song about some poor wench or lost soul. It was however so popular that even I used to leave the parents to drive back to Amersham early on a Sunday afternoon to attend this rather eccentric gathering. It was a refreshing difference from the normal gatherings of pubs that I was used to. I think this was the venue that really set the seed in me to follow folk music throughout my life and probably was one of the motives to recently take up learning the acoustic guitar along with the many wonderful folk songs that we used to listen to way back then.

The say all good things must come to an end and so my days in Amersham were drawing to a close. I was married with a first child on the way and certainly my current surroundings were far from acceptable to bringing up a child and was unable to buy a property in that area so it was time to once again move on. I applied for a couple of jobs advertised in the local authority paper and was successful in being accepted as a legal assistant with the Dacorum District Council in Hemel Hempstead. My starting salary was going to be £3,000 per annum some £1,400 more than what I was earning in Amersham. Now this really made a huge difference with the possibility of raising a mortgage and it meant that we could move back to our native town and be amongst friends and family when the baby was born. We duly walked into the local estate agents office, to be greeted by a local lad who I knew well and who turned to the filing cabinet took out this brochure, put it into our hands and announced that this was the best property for its price in the area. We visited and fell in love with the house and despite trolling all the other agents, and looking at dozens of other properties actually found that we kept going back to this first one and agreed with the Estate Agents comments. Little did I know that the chap who owned it was OCD in a big way although at that time this condition was not known or recognised. He apparently washed his car on a Friday night put it into the garage and on a Saturday morning often took it out and washed it again. The lawns were immaculate as if he had gone over after the lawn mower with a pair of scissors and inside was just as equally spotless. So we approached a lender for a mortgage and started the process. I had just completed the purchase when my notice expired so with a larger lorry this time we moved lock, stock and barrel from Amersham back to our home town ready for me to start work in Hemel Hempstead the following Monday. I was rather annoyed to say the least with the seller's solicitors at the time who really did not start off on a very good foot by advising me that I should seek the services of a proper solicitor to do my conveyancing for me despite me being a Conveyancing Assistant. He would prove to be one of a handful of lawyers that I would end up disliking for the remainder of my career.

I should add at this point that shortly before I started my new career there was a huge pay increase across the board within Local Government Departments and my salary scale for my own particular new job meant that my salary increased not only from £1,600 that was earning in Amersham to £3,000 but before I even started my first day that had increased to the sum of £3,600 which was considered then as an absolute fortune.

4 Move to Hemel Hempstead

For the next two and a half years I commuted from Milton Keynes over to Hemel Hempstead where I worked with a team of Legal Assistants heading out the mainly conveyancing work for the Council. My time passed reasonably quietly but it gave me an opportunity of working with a great bunch of guys and I was able to hone my drafting skills and prepare all sorts of one off agreements contracts. I remember one for the sale of Ice Cream for the local Italian ice cream vender in the local park during the summer months. Another enabled church-goers to use a car park and a private piece of ground to walk over to gain access to the church.

My Colleagues at Hemel Hempstead

The head of the conveyancing team was a great guy called John who was not much older than myself. His wife was pregnant more or less at the same time as my ex-wife although when we ever tried to discuss anything to do with injury, health, or accident of childbirth, he would start to look squeamish and ask us to change the subject. He was in fact rather nervous about the whole thing, especially childbirth and the thought of being present for the birth caused him to go weak at the knees. However, on the day that his wife gave birth he was rather caught without warning. His wife had been taken into the maternity unit to give birth and after the preliminary examinations and preparations was advised that the actual birth was some time off. John was beside her holding her hand and giving the husbandly assurances expected. When an "inspection" was due John stood and faced the wall till the coast was clear to so speak. In one of these so called examinations the nurse suddenly announced that her timings were in fact hopelessly wrong and that final stages were in motion and the child was close to being born. Needless to say she had little to no time to worry about this statue facing the wall and so the midwife and the nurse proceeded to carry out the operation of child birth while John had the formidable problem of having to face a wall holding his wife's hand and listening to events as they unfolded. Apparently he was okay until almost the end when imagination must have got the better of him and his slid down the wall into an immoveable heap on the floor. Nobody really had time for secondary care so as long as he was breathing he was left until after the child was born, at which stage he was helped out of the delivery room till be recovered from his ordeal. Needless to say he was rather reluctantly embarrassed to re-tell the tale.

Another great chap in our team was in fact a Barrister who had qualified in Uganda. However, being an Asian he and his family had suffered the humiliation of being run out of the country with literally the clothes they stood up in. Luckily for them they were brought to England and re-housed in Hemel Hempstead where he set to the task of finding employment and succeeded in finding a job within the Council's legal department. At this time most folks were still waking up to eating ethnic foods along Chinese and Indian lines. I had been brought up to at least try all sorts of foreign dishes so was not averse to getting the food beyond my eyes into my mouth. At this time our Ugandan Asian's wife used to make him up a plastic bag of mixed spices, which now most supermarkets sell but in those days had never been seen. The other members of the team were rather reluctant to try any but I certainly used to dive in and grab a handful for myself whenever the opportunity presented finding them incredible. In the end he used to ask his wife make up a bag for himself and a bag for me whilst the others looked on in sullen amazement.

The Rogue Land Rover

One lunchtime shortly before Christmas, several members of the team and I were walking back from one of the pubs in town where we had been enjoying a celebratory lunchtime beer. Suddenly we heard from behind us what sounded like a load of dustbins being kicked over. When we walked to the edge of the pavement and looked down the high street we spotted a rather tatty short wheel-based green Land Rover cruising slowly along and going in and out of the sides of the cars parked along the side of the road. Just as we were about to try to get the number plate the Land Rover disappeared off to the left up a side street so our opportunity was lost. However, while we stood in amazement, trying to get to grips with what this vehicle had done, the very same Land Rover suddenly appeared from a side street and then proceeded back along the route again driving in and out of the stationary cars causing more damage. This time we did manage to get the vehicle's licence number. Once more the vehicle disappeared up another side road.

By this time we were able to locate a policeman and report to him what had been going on and he called for a police car. And before help could arrive the offender passed us for a third time again crashing into the sides of other peoples vehicles, by this time collecting all sorts of various colours from these parked cars paint work on the front bumper until eventually half way round the service road on his fourth circuit he was duly apprehended by several police cars arrested and removed to the station.

The driver turned out to be a farm manager, who had quite a lot to drink before driving into town to pick his wife up from one of the supermarkets. Because she was not actually standing outside and not knowing fully where she was he carried on driving round the block till he hoped she would appear. At his trial the defence tried to dispute that we were wholly incorrect that we had not witnessed his vehicle driving into other vehicles, that the paint collection on his front bumper was not there and we had all been mistaken. Unfortunately the jury did tend to accept the word of half a dozen lawyers and the driver was found guilty. He lost his licence and as a result lost his job which required him to hold a driving licence. The job also came with a tied cottage and because he lost his job he also lost his home and all because he couldn't resist having a hefty drinking session before unwisely driving into town to pick his wife up.

Case experiences

I became very good friends with Martin Davis the Homeless Officer for the Council. A real *life and soul* character who was well liked where ever he went. He was to remain a very good friend of mine right up till his death several years ago. During our working years we shared some very amusing and interesting cases together. If he suspected that one of his homelessness cases was going to prove difficult or perhaps could create an awkward situation either for himself or for the Council he would ask me to accompany him as a witness from the legal department. This could and indeed did prove a very useful weapon. One such case involved a homeless couple who had decided to squat in this house, in Hemel Hempstead. No electricity, no gas and no water meant that the during waking hours these two would get themselves out very early and visit the bus station, shops, train station and anywhere that would offer warmth. Now the house had been allocated to a middle aged woman who was divorcing her husband but taking three rather well built sons with her. So we had the task of trying to get this couple out of the house that had indeed been set aside for the mother and her sons. Given that this couple left first thing I made sure that I got to work extra early so that Martin myself and the contractors who were ready to go in change the locks and tidy the place up could move very quickly once the squatters had left.

Unfortunately whilst we had a police presence, they failed to actually talk to each other at the station. The homeless couple had been picked up the night before and spent the evening in the cells. When they returned first thing in the morning they saw us waiting. They made a dash for the house, shut the door and barricaded themselves in. This created a rather awkward situation as the mother was taking possession that day. We explained the situation that unfortunately we would have to postpone the move for another day, or even another week. At this point the three sons disappeared to reappear several minutes later to explain that they had "spoken" to the squatters, who had agreed that they would be better off somewhere else and were just packing up their belongings. Sure enough they disappeared up the road a short while later giving the Mother access to her new home with her sons.

We would not be so lucky at the next case, which involved squatters again, this time in Berkhamsted a small town north of Hemel Hempstead. Again I accompanied Martin on his visit to the house that had been taken over. Persuasion was not going to work and these two were adamant that they were not budging unless they were re-housed somewhere nice in Hemel Hempstead. It was then revealed that where these two had been previously housed that they had run up over £1,000 in arrears before they disappeared off to Ireland and had come back still owing all this money. They just looked blank at Martin who said if they made cleared their arrears they could be considered. Still stony walled silence. So Martin said as a compromise if they were to say offer to pay say £400 off the arrears it would help. Clearly we were having no success and so we left and returned back to work. The following day we were both summoned to the Chief Executives office to give our version of the events the day before as the Squatters had contacted the local press and sure enough it was to appear "Council Official says give me £400 Bribe and I will make sure you jump the housing queue". Needless to say the story was retracted on my evidence that I was in fact a witness and verified that this was not in fact the case. It could however have ruined Martin's whole career and life.

I was always taught that a certain etiquette when answering the telephone. When introducing oneself one would also refer to either simply your surname or your full name but never introduce one self as "Mr". With ladies this was different, as the recipient would never know whether they were talking to a married woman or a single woman and therefore to leave off Ms. or Mrs. was polite. However, with every rule there is always the exception. Working with us in the Treasurers department was a gentleman who fitted the normal description of what one would expect to find but his problem was that he did have a rather high pitched voice which he was very much aware of and took extreme exception to anyone who laughed at him or in any way pointed out his natural impediment. I will leave it to the imagination when one day somebody called his office, he answered the phone by just stating his surname to which the caller simply replied "Mr. or Mrs.". His wrath could be felt around the building for hours afterwards.

One of my embarrassing moments took place one day while in the office which I shared with John and two others. For some reason which I have never understood is that whenever I have worn a suit irrespective of texture or cost the first point of wear always seems to be in the crutch area. The particular suit I was wearing this particular day seemed to retain tradition and reputation when all of a sudden I felt a draft in areas normally better protected and with horror discovered that the entire stitching from fly to rear waist band had parted company with the rest of the fabric of the trouser. Now sitting in an office with three guys was bad enough but being in the morning I had the rest of the day to spend and no doubt at some point call of nature lunch and other circumstances were going to be called up for me to rise and even leave the sanctity of my now very loving chair. Having confessed my predicament to my fellow workers and after riding the roar of laughter and banter of jokes I was advised that perhaps the best course of action was to ask the ladies in the typing pool if anyone possibly possessed a needle and cotton. Now in theory that was a brilliant suggestion but in practice unworkable. Our office was at one end of a very long corridor with the typing pool at the other end. Somehow, with dignity intact, I was going to have to somehow make my way down this corridor to make my enquiries and if successful tip toe back to the other end of the corridor where the gentleman's toilets were situated to try to bring some domestic tailoring skills to my predicament. Eventually not being able to sustain the banter any more and rather face the fate that awaited to the merriment of my fellow tormentors I made my way, rather gingerly to the typing pool. Now being in my early 20's the custom at that age to retain dignity posture and composure was of the utmost importance. However this quickly disappeared when the entire typing pool came to a complete mechanical silence while these awful bunch of women decided to unanimously jeer cheer and generally poke fun at my less than tender position. Eventually a needle and thread was produced to which I then had to waddle back down the corridor and in the sanctity of the men's toilets remove my trousers undertake the necessary repairs and then return back to this den of howling females before going back to my duties in my office. I have never forgotten or quite forgiven the outcome of that day, but always had a bit of a titter at the way this 20 something lad had been made to feel so embarrassed.

After a couple of years working in Hemel Hempstead with a great bunch of work colleagues the journey daily backwards and forwards was getting extremely monotonous and expensive. My wife then had fallen for our second child and I had rather planned in the overall scheme of things that I would end up not only living in my home town but hopefully working there as well. I had tried several times to obtain employment with the actual Corporation itself but without success. However, this particular application was greeted with an interview and an offer of a job which meant the travelling would come to an end and I would only be some 3 miles from home rather than over 25 and I could pop home in my lunchtimes and be home in the evenings in only a few short minutes. John had by now left and gone with his young family back to Wales. My Ugandan colleague had joined private practice and so the team was slowly splitting up and therefore felt that perhaps now was the time to leave the party while I was still enjoying myself. I still have contact with one or two members of staff and still look back on those days with fondness.

The Offices at Hemel Hempstead

5 Return to Milton Keynes

The Wallpaper Charter

They say that the world is a small place and coincidences do not happen by chance. Before I commenced my duties with the Milton Keynes Development Corporation in the Autumn of 1978 my first wife's father, John, shared with me a true story that had begun many years ago in fact back in 1965 when he was working for the Foreign Office and was based in British Guyana. While there, he was approached by the local Catholic priest, Father Ellis, who had heard that my father-in-law came from what was being publicised as the New Town of Milton Keynes. Father Ellis asked John to pass on his regards should he happen to bump into Jock Campbell. Jock Campbell was appointed Chairman of the Corporation Board and was to oversee the inception of the new town, the recruitment of senior management and staff, the acquisition of land and all the policies that would underpin the future development. To be able to even get close to Jock Campbell in those days, and probably in the ensuing years would have proved nearly impossible. He was later to become Sir Jock Campbell was part of a very old and well established Sugar Plantation Dynasty based in British Guyana.

After his time in British Guyana John was moved to Pershawa in the North West Frontier, Jordan, Cyprus and eventually Austria and the prospects of his meeting Sir Jock Campbell were increasingly remote But after I joined the Corporation in 1978 the burden of passing on Father Ellis' message was dutifully passed on to my shoulders to deliver. By this time the message was 13 years old, and with my holding a humble position of conveyancing assistant the chances of ever passing this message on was highly unlikely.

The offices were built in three separate phases off the original Wavendon Tower building, the house that had been taken over as the headquarters of the new Development Corporation. The staff were located in these and the only time staff would venture or indeed be invited over to the Tower was for some very important meeting or function which normally involved the heads of departments. I think in all the time I worked at the Corporation I probably only went into the main Tower three or four times in total. As fate would have it I was literally on my last day of formal notice to terminate my employment, and while on my way back from one of the outer buildings where I had said my goodbyes to staff I spotted Sir Jock Campbell walking back across the car park on his way back to the Tower. At this point, and now some 18 years on from the initial message, I approached Sir Jock Campbell and plucked up the courage to stop him and say that I had a strange message that I would like to pass on to him. He looked at me with total bewilderment having never met me before in his life had no idea who I was from where I had come and exactly what I was about to relay to him. So I simply said to him that "Father Ellis sends his regards" to which he looked even more bewildered. I then went into the story of John and his post with the Foreign Office, my relationship with his daughter, my then wife and my post with the Corporation and the fact that this particular day was strangely my last day so that it was all very opportune to meet him in such a way and on such a day. Sir Jock was very attentive and very appreciative that the message, after so many years, had finally reached him and found the whole thing rather amusing.

However, I had not relayed the whole story to him and so to really authenticate my story I asked him if he could confirm whether or not the *Wall Paper Charter* really existed. At this point he threw his arms back in a fit of laughter and indeed confirmed that yes the *Wall Paper Charter* was true and did exist. So finally, after all those years involving folks from half way round the world in a string of remote connections, the message finally got delivered.

As for the *Wall Paper Charter* this derived itself from a story involving Father Ellis and the Campbell family back in British Guyana during the early 60's when at that time there was a great deal of unrest and trouble between the plantation workers and the owners. Some of the Plantations were being ransacked and some owners attacked, maimed, and in some cases even killed. During these uprisings members of the Campbell family had apparently approached Father Ellis for advice on how they could avoid strikes, unrest or even injury. As the story goes, Father Ellis was standing in the great hall of the mansion house belonging to the Campbell family and he listened with great intent. When they had finished he quietly turned and without warning caught hold of a crease in one of the long pieces of wallpaper in the great hall and commenced to strip a piece of the wall paper from the hall. Turning the piece of ripped wallpaper over, Father Ellis then started to write down a list of pointers that he considered important for the Campbell family to adopt and hopefully help to save them from carnage and mayhem. Apparently his advice was followed and thus the plantation was not ransacked nor was there any bloodshed. The ripped piece of wall paper was framed and hung in the hall to then be revered from then on and became known as the *Wall paper charter.*

46

Wavendon Tower

Working at the Corporation

By the time I had reached the Corporations Gates I had felt that I had acquired a varied and reasonably good insight into the workings of local authority type organisations. This myth was put to rest as I quickly realised that the Corporation was nothing like anything I had worked in previously or indeed was to the future. I was to be privileged to share an experience with a collection of highly intelligent, motivated and professional staff and board members who had embraced the task of turning 3 towns and 11+ villages into a New Town to be proud of. What they have achieved even today is a remarkable success story that I am proud to have been a very small part of. First of all, the Board and Staff in the early days had to overcome the prejudices they were facing not only from the County and Local Councils who both felt they should have been selected to create the new town but also the residents, businesses and media that were all out to create problems and criticism wherever possible. However, the Corporation adopted a stoic position and moved the project forward in a positive and assertive manner and over the years the project proved more and more successful, and growth continues to this day.

One of the first things that the Corporation realised was that with most New Towns created in England that the very concept was flawed because the planners merely expanded outwards the existing town or area.

At any point the expansion could be stopped due to lack of money or change in government. What the Corporation did, having acquired the land and resources to achieve its goal was to create its grid road system with roads running north to south and east to west with nothing either side of them. The Corporation then ran ribbon developments the whole length of a few of these roads which for some while appeared to be in the middle of no where with no facilities services etc. This was completely intentional. The roads themselves were complete with roundabouts, lighting and verges. Small estates were built some possibly a mile from the each other. Every time a succeeding government tried to bring Milton Keynes either to slow or even stop then delegates were invited down and actually taken to these isolated pockets of developments etc. and pointed out how that by stopping the growth of Milton Keynes would leave ordinary folks stranded. This strategy proved invaluable in allowing the project to be continued and New Town to be built

The Corporation by the time I joined had in fact compulsorily acquired a major part of the land within its designated development area which under the New Towns Act they purchased with compensation being paid to the owners of the land under the agricultural land price values that of course were far less than for land with full planning permission. However, once the land had been acquired, the Corporation, under its powers granted to them under the New Towns Act, was able to then grant itself planning permission and immediately the land would have Development Land Value. Rather than allow developers to simply buy the land from it and therefore lose control of the land, the Corporation entered into Development Agreements with the developers. These were long documents allowing the developer to enter the land, build the numbers of houses allocated under the agreement, and, in partnership with the Corporation, then transfer to the new owners. At this point the Corporation would be paid an agreed sum for each plot sold on a pre-fixed sale price.

As time went on and land prices increased, if the developer sold those plots for more than was agreed, then such sales would give the Corporation a percentage of such increased price. So the Corporation was into a win-win situation. The further reason why the Corporation did not part with the land directly to developers was to retain ownership of the land and therefore planning. The local authority disapproved of this, but proved very successful in the integration of various types of housing, local shopping areas and commercial units such as offices, factories and warehousing.

Another very inventive scheme the Corporation introduced from a very early stage was to set aside so much money per plot to be paid by the builder into a separate funds for landscaping and children's play areas. This again was a political decision taken by the Board. The Corporation was of course answerable to the central government departments who oversaw everything that the Corporation undertook. The Corporation had to submit each year the accounts showing these figures before it was given its budget for the next financial year. The sum earned always seemed to reflect the sum granted for the following year which did not leave much room for error or new projects, and so the scheme of squirreling funds away into the Landscaping fund and the Children's Play fund was devised. The Money was set up under a Trust fund with the trustee being the Corporation. What the auditors failed to realise year after year that they visited for their annual inspections was that of course no one person or organisation can actually set up a trust fund to hold money for himself or indeed itself. It is an anomaly of Law. However this was never questioned and never refused and so the scheme ran its full course and this is why Milton Keynes is regarded as being so successful with its landscaping and every estate has a children's play area. All this we adhered to when drafting the various development agreements for the various estate developments throughout the new town.

With each grid square being developed with its advanced works of roads, paths and services being laid before any actual developments took place, this enabled all the services such as gas electricity sewers to be introduced on site. Another insistence that the Corporation had stipulated since early 1970's was that all housing construction would be connected via the piped TV and radio cables to a central location, so that everyone within the new town would have the benefit of the various channels then becoming available. This also helped to prevent the unsightly introduction of television aerials stuck on the sides of houses. The piped cable system was also to have a further great imaginative possibility to be discussed.

As a Legal Assistant within the Corporation I was given responsibility for developing agreements for individual plot sales. This allowed an individual to build a house to his own design, either through an association or self build scheme. These self-build plots were all serviced plots.

Over the years I set up numerous sites throughout Milton Keynes for this very purpose. I also got to see various grand designs and styles of houses that were being planned. Some were very grand and all seemed to be way past my league of affordability. Once a development site was set up and the plots began to sell I would send out the pack for that particular plot. This included a 20-page development agreement containing the constraints of the plot, the price, the outline planning consent for the plans sewn into the agreement, and more importantly, a time constraint for completion. The period usually took 18 months.

Within that period the private developer could have the land transferred. If a completion certificate had not been issued within 18 months the Corporation had the power to take back the land, even with the property partly completed at a price they would decide. This acted a rather strong deterrent against delay. I would visit the various sites in turn throughout the working week to ascertain progress and see that nothing was amiss

One such plot owner, having dug out their foundations, proceeded to dump the entire stack of waste soil onto the next door neighbour's plot and left an awful mess. He was served Notice under the development agreement to have this pile of soil shifted immediately or face rescission of agreement. The owner contacted me somewhat distressed to see if there was a practical answer. At that time I had moved into a new property and was in the throes of trying to sort out the garden, so I offered, if they were to pay for the digger I would pay for the lorry to remove the soil into my back garden. It took 11 full lorry loads and subsequently five months of shovelling, carting in a wheelbarrow and levelling to finish this work! A nightmare!

Another plot owner, Dave, who was also a Corporation employee, was in the throes of digging up the street sign when I appeared at his plot I was most upset at finding all the landscaping along the border removed and the road sign removed. Dave was very laid back and his favourite saying, which he shared with me at the time was, "Don't worry about it!" That would prove to be his epitaph. He rode a motorbike at the time and unfortunately suffered a rather serious accident in which he was to lose his leg through amputation. As he was laying in his hospital bed recovering he was looking forward to a new life with a leg missing and even then all strapped up would simply say, "Don't worry about it!" His visitors seemed more upset and concerned than he was. Unfortunately his brave outlook was shattered as he contracted a blood clot, which killed him. He was 33 years old. He would always sign his work both at the Corporation and privately with a butterfly. His funeral was attended by a large crowd of staff, board members, and friends. There was a huge array of wreaths, all in the shape of butterflies.

During and after the ceremony there was not a dry eye in the church as everyone who came across Dave held him to their hearts as a warm and wonderful man and an example to us all. His memory certainly stays with me to this day and when life really is getting quite difficult I just think to myself his words, "Don't worry about it!"

The Corporation functioned with the same professionalism as that of a private commercial company. It held its standards high and its efficiency paramount. For this reason, as the new Town developed and business was encouraged to consider the area for its enterprise, the Corporation would go to great lengths to wine dine and win over such companies. Members of staff were sent to the various corners of the world to publicise and promote the new town and try to generate new business. We always knew the importance of the visitors by the lengths that the Corporation would go to when entertaining. If the guest was at the top of the ladder, they would be flown into Heathrow and brought by private plane to Cranfield. From there they were carried by helicopter to the Corporation landing strip close to Wavendon Tower where they would attend a working lunch. Once more the helicopter would over the proposed site for a over view and after further conference at the Tower would then return by the same means to their own country. This way many of the larger firms were won over.

If you were not quite so important then the helicopter would arrive with its guests again flown to the site and returned perhaps to the train station or to Cranfield. Those on the next scale down met at the Corporation offices and were taken by air conditioned mini coach to the various sites.

So we always knew by the mode of transport and normally the time of day whether we had to be on our best behaviour and the level of guest being greeted. For those that were extra-important and weather permitting the Milton Keynes hot air balloon was launched so that the helicopter could fly round it. I recall on one day some very important dignitaries were flown in from Germany on a very tight time scale. They arrived by the usual route and had the usual working lunch, inspections and discussions. They were back in Germany later that day and within the hours of the normal working day, so smoothly did everything run. This German Company later mad a substantial investment into Milton Keynes.

The local Council were a constant thorn in the side of the Corporation's efforts. Whatever project they would criticise it. They had become aware of this visit and they complained bitterly that the locally elected body was not represented at these talks. They said this was disgraceful and the Corporation should apologise and assure the council that this would never happen again. The powers that be chose to ignore the Council's bluster. These guests were high-flying company executives of a multi national business and really were, completely out of the league of the Mayor who was no more than a local coach driver. His limited etiquette and business manner and would probably have been a complete detriment to the whole exercise.

The Concrete Cows

Nobody with the wildest imagination could have possibly dreamt up the free and unexpected publicity that was handed to the Corporation and would have an outstanding effect in putting Milton Keynes on the map, and would be talked about 40 years later. I am of course referring to the famous concrete cows. Various stories have been created for these but basically what happened was that a young American teacher working with junior children had created during the school term a "family" of concrete cows which the children helped to make and paint. At the end of the school year the teacher returned home and the children moved up a year. The project was now redundant and some thought was given to disposing of the cows. The teacher approached the Corporation to enquire as to whether they could accommodate the concrete cows pin one of the play areas. The Corporation did scratch its head and found a site under development that was rather out of the way. The concrete cows were moved into their new site to await the completion of the development.

Out of context this seemed ridiculous and photographs of these concrete cows circled the world and foreign visitors arrived from virtually every continent to come and see them. The new town was ridiculed and even to this day is known as the town of the concrete cows. While this was going on the name Milton Keynes became internationally known and proved to be the most successful media and publicity move that was given to the Corporation.

Developing the New Town

While we were entering into development agreements with developers to build housing for people moving into Milton Keynes it was important that equal if not more concentration was given to create jobs in commerce and industry. Again incredible imagination was at work with the lads from the Commercial arm of the Corporations legal department. What they basically were able to achieve I still find mind blowing to this day. The

Corporation would basically sell the same piece of land twice, all quite legal and above board. How it worked was very simple. Large Pension funds and long term investors are always looking for land to invest over a long-term. So the Corporation approached various large commercial enterprises and offered them land right in the middle of what was going to be the central Milton Keynes shopping area. The land being offered was going to be freehold. Not only could the investors acquire the land but the Corporation, who owned the land could grant them planning permission for an office block to be built and cut through years of red tape The further carrot that was offered was that the Corporation would then offer to take back the completed office block, funded by the investors on a long lease. Now this seemed all too good to be true but the scheme worked perfectly. The land, that the Corporation had purchased at agricultural land value many years before, was sold as prime development land at the going rate for central grown development land with planning permission. The investors would then set about getting contractors to build the office block which when completed would then be leased back to the Corporation at a favourable rate to the Corporation. While these negotiations were taking place, the Corporation representatives, were sent off to the various corners of the globe were winning over potential employers by inviting them to bring their business into Central Milton Keynes. The Corporation offered them a brand new office block to their specifications, which they would have built at no cost to the new business. Once secured the Corporation would go back to the original investor present them with the size and types of building they required to be built by the planning permission they would themselves grant.

So the scheme worked brilliantly the land was sold, the office developments completed, the building was leased back to the Corporation who then entered into a lease/lease-back deal with the new business opening in Central Milton Keynes, thus profiting from the same piece of land twice. It is said that the profits made from the sales of the various developments around the Central Milton Keynes in fact paid for the entire Central Milton Keynes Shopping Centre, a price that exceeded over seven million pounds, and all without a penny coming from the tax-payers pocket.

At this time, while this was all being worked out and formulated, our friendly local authorities were up in arms with the prospect of the new "white elephant" and in fact run a campaign pointing out what money wasting exercise it was, that the shopping centre required a catchment area of at least a 50-mile radius, that this was doomed to failure because of the

53

other towns such as Northampton, Bedford, Aylesbury even Cambridge and Oxford being within the 50 mile circle of doom. This all proved a total nonsense. Once the shopping centre opened, coaches brought groups of shoppers in from as far as south Wales, Newcastle and all corners of England and all paid for by the incredibly imaginative scheme thought up by the commercial department of the Corporation. These are unsung heroes who to this day remain anonymous apart feom those of us who had the privilege of working along side them.

I mentioned earlier in my chapter that all developments, especially housing, were connected to the piped cable system offering television radio and telephone. This idea stretched beyond what everyone had come to expect. One of the developments taking place in Central Milton Keynes was a large office development known simply as the Central Business Exchange. However, this original concept was not going to be simply an office development. It was planned as a huge main-frame computer. The computer would enable every home, every business, bank, office and cinema to be connected to it. This way everyone living or working in Milton Keynes would have the facility of connection to such computer and its possibilities. It meant that we could all sit in our homes and by home computer connection could check our bank accounts, order cinema tickets, book our holidays and generally enjoy computerisation that was only restricted by our own imaginations. It would also put Milton Keynes into one of the most advanced technological areas in the world. Unfortunately nobody could see it. Investors could not jointly agree or see what a far reaching and revolutionary concept this offered. Nobody surely would ever want to or indeed be able to sit at home and connect to their banks, or undertake social or business functions via this new system and so it failed to get off the ground. Now all we see is a lovely large modern office block in line with the others surrounding it instead of something that might have put the City of London into the Victorian age with this far reaching concept. The sad thing is we all now sit in our homes with our laptops and computers doing the very thing that someone with incredible imagination had worked out nearly 35 years ago.

Leslie Wetherall

During my days at the Corporation I worked under the leadership of what can only be described as a rather wonderful old Dickensian Lawyer who I came to regard as a true friend and mentor by the name of Leslie Weatherall. Leslie was the real life "Rumpole of the old Bailey" character. He was one of those brilliant minds that had forgotten more than I would probably ever get to know and was totally dedicated to his job. Leslie

54

rarely took holidays and the only form of break he was persuaded to have was to leave the office on Friday lunchtime to take the afternoon off with the remainder of the weekend. Such practice he followed from more or less the day I started till the day he retired shortly after I had left the Corporation.

Leslie was a mastermind at drafting what I would call freehold commercial land transaction agreements which not only acquired large tracts of land from farmers and the great land owners of Milton Keynes but also drafted the very core of documentation which would stand the countless land developments for housing in Milton Keynes. Some of these agreements were so complex that it would be left to his mind and his skill to put in legal documentation the various ideas that he Board discussed and put into fruition. Many of the large developers and indeed their own lawyers, who were based around England would know Leslie and had high regard and respect for him. Very rarely did they question his drafting. The only drawback in my early years at the Corporation was that Leslie would have these lengthy documents, sometimes 27 pages long, typed out by his long suffering secretary onto engrossment paper, which came in A3 size to include the plans. It was considerably time consuming and demanded no errors whatsoever. Each document was then hand-sewn using the old china grass method I had mastered while I was at the County Council some years ago, formally sealed by the Corporation and the developer and then exchanged. In contradiction of this practice, the commercial department dealing in leases of commercial buildings would rely upon the new art of computerisation, which once typed, could be quickly spell checked and produced on printers on A3 paper and heat bound. The whole process was completed in a fraction of the time it was taking for the engrossments to be produced by hand. Leslie was not going to lower himself to this standard which he considered extremely scruffy, did not comprise double sided only one sided, and was not satisfactory to the standard and art to which he was accustomed. His documents looked professional, stood the test of time, reflected the art of the law, were properly sewn up with each of the capitals underlined in red. Each sentence falling short of the end of the line was finished off with red line and looked the part of the professional old school deed completed with proper seal and signatures.

I was put in a rather precarious situation. Although I was one of the junior members, I had become nonetheless quite close to both Leslie and his wife whom I held both with great affection, whilst still maintaining my utmost respect for them and Leslie's position of head of department. I was summoned by the Deputy Legal Director and was asked if I could somehow persuade Leslie to move into the modern day and adapt his departmental development agreements to be incorporated into computer-produced documents. I was not happy about this. Leslie was old-school; I was still wet behind the ears.

Here was a man who, when he invited you on the extremely rare occasions to take a beer with him at his local pub, you turned up without question or excuse, and when he asked you what you drink you simply replied, either beer, cider or wine and certainly under no circumstances ask for a pint for fear of rebuke with the words, "You choose the drink and I will choose the quantity!" a mistake I only made once.

No this was a man who told me the way of the world and not vice versa so how was I going to approach such a subject with such an assertive leader? After worrying about the subject for several days and knowing it was something expected of me I finally formulated a plan which involved approaching Leslie in the afternoon, after he had returned from lunch. This was invariably spent at the local hostelry next door where his pleasure was always a couple of Gin and Its. The day I chose he was in an extra remarkably good mood and "relaxed" so having adopted his own phraseology I was able to turn the tables on him by starting the conversation with his own immortal words when he wanted something from the recipient. "I am in terrible trouble," at which point he put his pipe back in his mouth took a couple of puffs and waited for what I was going to say. I explained that I had been asked to approach him to consider adopting the new computers for future documentation which would ease the typing, time pressures and all the other wonderful excuses I could think of. To my utter amazement he simply sat back took it on the chin and agreed that from now on he would allow for his agreements, which I also was drafting, for small self-build plots to be produced by computer. This came as a great relief to me, thinking I could lose my job over this very issue, and of course his secretary who was now going to be able to draft and produce such mammoth documentation with more efficiency and finally the deputy director who had not had to approach Leslie with such a difficult subject.

Leslie was unusually ill one particular week to the point where he just could not work and had to go home. This was extremely unusual as he would drag himself in to the office even while looking like death warmed-up. However, this did not stop him from feeling terribly guilty that he could not perform his duty and be at his desk. To make up for his guilt Leslie proceeded to draft on his own dining room table a scheme that was

56

so complicated that no other local authority or Corporation had in fact been able to draft such a document even though this scheme was being adopted on a National scale. He drafted what was to be a 24 page A3 Lease, which, apart from a few future slight alterations, was to be accepted by the Department of the Environment as their standard form of deed. When Leslie returned to the office the draft was produced in full size and glory and pushed across the table to me with his immortal words, "You had better go and learn this, as it is not going to go away and may even stand you in good stead in the future."

I am referring to the first Shared Ownership scheme lease which he had drafted while he was ill, at a time when most of us would have dosed ourselves up and taken to our beds. How true his prediction was. Very quickly the word went out, and we were getting visits from Corporations as far away as Runcorn in the North and most of the southern new towns who wanted to take away a copy of this precious deed which was approved as high as the D of E for their own use For my part I had the formidable task of having to peddle the scheme round the local solicitors, who by this time had been employed to act on Corporation sales of properties within certain areas, but I was to receive a very crusty and negative response with some firms even refusing to have anything to do with what they considered to be yet another politically orientated half-baked scheme. If only we were all to know at that time what an important piece of drafting this was. In fact shared ownership was to stay makes up quite a large chunk of bread-and-butter conveyancing in Milton Keynes. For that alone I thank Leslie for the legacy he handed to me.

Leslie had one particular weakness and that was in the form of his huge pipe. He would puff away on it daily, which now sounds quite unusual with no smoking allowed in all public buildings, including work places. One day Leslie was in quite a foul mood, which was rather unusual as he was normally very cheerful and jovial. It turned out that he had inadvertently left his pipe at home. The morning had turned rather difficult with his secretary getting on the wrong side of him and then other folks were beginning to notice that he was a little short tempered to say the least. Even the deputy head of the department had come down to find out if any one knew who or what had upset Leslie as he certainly was not his normal self. In the end I really felt that I could not just stand by but to try to sort this little problem out. So trying to be a little assertive I walked into Leslie's office unannounced I asked him if I could borrow his car keys (I had in fact cycled to work that morning) I got the look that announced by itself that I too was fast becoming well out of favour. I just told him I needed to pop out and needed his car keys. I then drove his old Rover back to his apartment and asked Enid, his wife, to let me have his pipe as the atmosphere at the office was going down hill. She handed me his famous dummy and so returned to the office gave him his pipe and waited while he lit it up and had a few puffs. The smile returned and very quickly normal service had resumed. I think I scored a lot of brownie points that day not only with Leslie but also with the entire department. After Leslie passed on Enid asked it there was anything of Leslie's that I particularly wanted as a small memento. Of course the one thing I asked for and which she gladly handed to me was the famous pipe. She also gave me the silver stand, and several pipes other pipes of his which remain in pride of place on my old roll desk and remind me of those precious days I served under one of the greatest lawyers and personal friends I would ever have the pleasure to have known.

Tales from the Office

I shared an office with another legal assistant, Bill Campbell, although he was more senior and experienced than myself. We shared the same secretary for the varied work we were both responsible for. Our secretary, Wendy, was a great girl, full of life and had recently met and was shortly to marry another Bill, the new man in her life. They were both very good for each other although they were if we were honest a little like chalk and cheese, but complimented each other perfectly. Bill was huge. He must have been over 20 stone while Wendy was a slim slip of a girl. At the time they bought this really tiny van that had been converted into a small camper van which given his rather large size always fascinated us how on earth they would spend a complete holiday in any form of comfort.

On one occasion our secretary came in and announced that she and her new man were taking time out as they wanted to take their new camper off abroad and in particular to go to Holland where they could marvel at the famous bulb fields. My room-mate and I looked at each other in stunned silence but not wishing to be impolite, wished them both a good trip and a lovely holiday. Time passed and eventually the pair of them returned to work. After some period had elapsed we were able to ask how the holiday trip went, whether the camper was a success and more importantly how they had found the bulb fields of Holland. I will say at this point we were rather tongue in cheek with our questions as we had feared the worst, that the trip had not proved to be such a great success. In fact the excursion was far worse than we had anticipated because when they arrived they found the weather had taken a turn for the worse, and all they had were drab over cast and foggy days. As for the

Bulb fields these really were a complete and utter disappointment and certainly had not come up to their expectations. At this point my room colleague and I really couldn't contain ourselves any longer and, looking at each other, asked whether she thought that to go to Holland to view the Bulb fields in September was actually the best month or time of the year for such a visit? We did rather laugh with them both for some time about this. They both took on the chin and I am sure still smile about their slight error to this day.

The Pig Farm

In addition to the setting up of land developments both for the individual plots and now the smaller developers I was also given the added responsibility of the actual acquisition of land for development purposes, as there were still areas of land still outside the Corporation ownership. Some of the land acquired would be sold to Housing Associations for their rental stocks. Each year the end of March was always critical being the end of the financial year. I was handed several projects including five Housing Association sites and various other purchases, including a pig farm.

The Pig farm was especially important as this had to be purchased with surplus funds which had to be spent by the end of March, otherwise the money would be appropriated back into central government funds and therefore the project would have to be scrapped. It was particularly important as it formed the last piece of the jigsaw for the major dual carriageway road that was to be built from North to South through the spine of Milton Keynes and later to be known as the A5D (D for diversion). I obviously had to work very quickly on this purchase and very hard to achieve the completion date. The added pressure that was put on my shoulders was that thousands of pounds worth of earth-movers were booked to commence on a particular day to move onto site to start removing and levelling the advanced earth works necessary. If my part was not completed then dozens of these very large and very expensive juggernaut earth movers would be standing idle, which was not going to be acceptable.

The land was purchased and the earth-movers started, but all of a sudden everything came to a complete stop. By scraping off the top layers of soil they had uncovered the remains of what appeared to be an old Roman garrison. Everything stopped for weeks while the archaeologists came on site to see what they could discover under the surface of the land. It did actually prove extremely rewarding and much of the findings were on display for some time in the local library and in parts of the new Central Milton Keynes shopping Centre.

With regards to the five other Housing Association Sites I was handed five bankers drafts, sent off to London and basically told not to come back without all five having been completed. It was on the afternoon I attended the London School of Law in Holborn so my time was a little precious. At one solicitor's office I had to come up with the ultimate bluff by announcing that I had till 3.00 pm for them to decide whether or not the deal was to go ahead or not. I had to leave in less than 15 minutes and suggested they contact their client urgently failing which I would be gone, 31st March would have passed and the deal would never materialise. Happily the bluff worked. I handed over the cheque and came back to work the next day armed with five files with deeds showing the Corporation's title.

Mrs Thatcher comes to MK

During my time at the Corporation Mrs.Thatcher had come to power. One of her triumphs was to pass the bill that gave all Tenants the right to buy their own homes. The Corporation by this time had a huge stock of rental properties and it was not long before Tenants were serving their notices for the right to buy. Given the volumes of suspected sales one of my tasks was to instruct pre-nominated local firms of solicitors, who had been designated certain areas and sales within those areas. I had the task of preparing the full sheaf of title documents, to include the title to the Corporation, the plans, planning permission and any other documentation relevant to that particular estate. I then presented the packages to the selected lawyers along with the standard form of conveyance, which the corporation approved or, in the case of a leasehold property, the approved form of lease. At this time Mrs. Thatcher herself had agreed to visit the new town of Milton Keynes and one of her tasks while she was here was to present a couple with the deeds of their new home. A venue was discussed and agreed and vetted by the security authorities the couple approached and agreed to the visit and so everything was set. The Solicitors acting for the buyers had concluded all their searches the Corporation had granted the mortgage and so the deal was pushed through with greater speed than normal. The actual deed to convey the land to the new owners was on the old style of parchment A3 engrossment paper which I had the task of not only drawing but also having the deed underlined in red for all capital words, lines not completely filled being finished in red line and for the plan of the property to be inserted, and, using my skill learned at the old County Council, have the deed properly sewn up with china grass and two small seals. The deed was produced to the board for formal sealing and signing, to be dated at the time of the presentation.

The day arrived, the dignitaries gathered in the street where the couple would welcome Mrs. Thatcher into their new owned home and all the press and spectators were there along with myself tucked into an obscure corner. The cars arrived, Mrs. Thatcher emerged, and went into the property for a few moments with the couple, and came out to give her speech about the importance of home ownership. She finally presented the couple with the deed that I had prepared and handed it over to the Corporation official to pass over to the couple. After the photos were taken and all the pomp and ceremony observed, and the cars disappear with Mrs. Thatcher, I had to quickly retrieve the deed and replace it with the mortgage signed by the couple previous to that day. This was held as security for future payments of mortgage to be made. My moment of importance had passed, unnoticed, and life went back to normal. You could say I was a legend in my own lunchtime.

Corporation Land and Housing

Another task I inherited was the sale of the surplus stock of corporation houses. During the mid 1970s the Corporation were desperate to acquire housing for staff to be enticed to come and live and work in Milton Keynes. By the early 80s construction was so successful that the surplus stock of purchased individual housing was no longer required. So as they became vacant were then sold on the open market, which actually gave the Corporation quite a large profit on its original investment. I would receive the instructions from the local agents to prepare documentation and see the transaction through to completion. Sometimes on a Friday afternoon I would take myself off to carry out site inspections of some of these properties on a security basis, which also worked as a bit of a skyve out of the office.

For some reason I had a premonition about one property on one of the estates north of the New Town. When I arrived about 3.30 pm on that Friday afternoon I was somewhat surprised to see a couple cars on the driveway of what should have been an empty property, curtains up at the windows and, as I approached on foot, a rather homely smell of fried food cooking. Opening the side gate I saw sat in the garden this chap, in his deck chair surrounded by children's toys, reading a newspaper. When he saw me he jumped to his feet and challenged me as to who I was and what was I doing in the garden? I politely asked him who he was and he announced that he was the owner and lived here. At this point still retaining my composure I announced that in fact he was not the owner but my employer was the owner namely the Corporation. I also pointed out to this now deflating character that not only had we not completed his purchase and therefore had no entitlement whatsoever, but that we had not even exchanged contracts, and thus he was wholly trespassing and occupying the property as a squatter. His attitude quickly altered to being very submissive. I pointed out that I would report his taking possession without consent of my employers, and I suggested he speak to his own solicitors first thing Monday morning. I suggested further that they should contact me to discuss a satisfactory outcome, failing which we will require him to vacate the property immediately and look to him for the costs of all damage. On the Monday I was indeed contacted by the solicitors who did not have knowledge of their clients premature occupation of the property. We very quickly established that we required exchange of contracts within the next few days or their client would be required to vacate and the transaction would be cancelled. Further we required interest to be paid from the day we discovered his occupation to the day of legal completion, which of course they gladly paid for fear of eviction and liability to costs.

The Corporation had acquired all sorts of anomalies with their compulsory purchases of large tracts of land and farms. Most of the individual farm houses and buildings were sold off either as individual homes or for conversions into homes. However occasionally there were odd buildings that the Corporation really did not know what to do with. One of these buildings was located some 100 feet from the main road and was an old church located in what was to become parkland and was unlikely to ever be developed. To this day sheep and wild life enjoy the now well-established parkland surrounding our little barn-sized church building. At the time however there was much deliberation as to what this building could be used for or sold for. It did not have any services and clearly nobody would want to convert into a home. So the idea was put forward of perhaps turning the building into some form of music centre for musical organisations for practice and meetings. The only problem was, as previously mentioned, the building had no services whatsoever. which rather rendered the building useless. However, this was easily resolved with the suggestion that a JCB dig a trench from the building to the main road and thus the necessary connections could be brought in. The digger duly arrived, started at the door of the building working its way backwards towards the road. Then suddenly all digging stopped as the driver realised, to his horror, that churches tended to have graves and those graves also appeared between the church and the road. What the digger driver had managed to achieve with his bucket was to actually dig a trench through one of the dearly departed graves and worse still had managed to cut the skeletons clean in half.

The driver realising the possible outcome and reprisals for such action switched his machine off and disappeared. During his absence and by the next day when the officials appeared to examine and possibly repair the damage someone unknown had visited the site, gathered up all the bones of the one half of the skeleton that was now laying in the bottom of this freshly dug trench, and had very neatly piled them all up on the top of the trench. Now at this time we were all very aware of adverse publicity and the fear of the press for these types of stories was paramount. The one thing that everyone was dreading was the arrival of the local paper that week and on the front page a nice crisp photograph of a pile of bones and the exposure of the scandal.

The end of the week arrived and to everyone's sigh of relief no photographs or indeed any mention at all of this disaster. In fact nothing was ever exposed. As for the pile of bones of the dearly departed, well they were returned into the trench, which was then quietly filled in and the site left alone. As far as I know the building, which still stands prominent has never had services connected to it to this day. I still smile to myself every time I cycle past and look out at the little building and its secret that it has kept for the past 30 plus years.

My experience of how small the world was has already been highlighted with the story related to the *Wallpaper Charter*. However another story would surface before I departed the Corporation's employment to highlight once again this doctrine. During my time at the Corporation I was attending college to try to complete my legal executive training examinations. This involved travelling into London once a week on a Wednesday afternoon. It was a journey that I did not really enjoy in either direction but which was necessary to try to further my career. The train I would catch would be the lunchtime train, which stopped only at Milton Keynes on its journey down from Glasgow to Euston. This particular day I boarded the train and sat down opposite an elderly but well-groomed and articulate lady who turned out to be travelling down from Glasgow where she was living with her sister to visit other relations in London. As our journey together progressed and we got talking about general topics and the conversation became focused on Milton Keynes itself. The lady asked me if I lived in Milton Keynes and when I answered affirmative she asked whereabouts? Knowing she was from Glasgow I really didn't want to try to highlight exactly where as she would not really have a clue as to the various grid squares making up the new town or indeed the names given to each of the grid squaresSo I simply reflected that I lived in the north of the new town, not far in fact from the railway station where I had boarded the train. She pressed for a more detailed location saying that she was familiar with Milton Keynes so I referred to one of the villages known as New Bradwell (pronounced New Brad'll to the locals) which originally was located some 2 miles from Old Brad'll down a country road that no longer existed. She confirmed that she knew New Bradwell and asked me was I near the old public house the *Jovial Priest*, so named after the rather eccentric vicar who would ride the long hill from the top of New Bradwell down to the lower stretches where his church was located. I said yes in fact I was only a few hundred yards from that pub on a new estate that now cut the old road in half which used to connect the New Bradwell and Old Bradwell. She seemed to be lifted with this bit of news and asked me if the terraced houses were still there with the huge "W" shaped eves and roofs. I said indeed in fact where they finished, which originally took travellers straight into the countryside, was literally yards from my new estate and where I lived. At this point rather relieved that the houses had not in fact been knocked down, she sat back gave a sigh and announced that the second from the end was in fact the very house where she was born, and had lived there till leaving home to get married herself. I was completely taken by surprise at this that a little old lady who I had every chance of never meeting, sat in front of me on a train coming from so far away to then announce she had such a local history and knowledge which we had shared for such a short time in our lives. We said our goodbyes once we reached Euston and I was to never see or hear of this lovely gentle lady again.

The Closing Days of the Corporation

During my days at the Corporation as a Conveyancing Assistant I was able still to help our closest friends with their conveyancing which had to be conducted in their names but could be charged for my help. One such move was my dear friend Martin Davis who I have mentioned in the previous chapter and with whom I had worked at the Hemel Hempstead Council. Martin lived and travelled from Luton to Hemel Hempstead every day but with a young family he felt that Milton Keynes would be a far better place to raise his family. He found a property to buy and approached me for help. I was happy to assist him on the basis that, although I could not charge him, he would take my wife and I out for a rather nice meal. The transaction progressed through the usual stages and eventually completed. They kept their promise and we agreed to meet at a local village pub, which in those days was way out in the middle of nowhere. It was a rather nice carvery restaurant. To add a little flamboyancy to the evening Martin and I agreed to dress formally. We took the ladies to the carvery, which was reasonably quiet and to our table. While we sat there I spotted a customer who had arrived at the bar and who I knew very well. I excused myself for a few minutes stood and went over to him to chat. While I was talking to Brian, a young couple walked in clearly looking for somewhere suitable to eat. I certainly looked the part of a waiter and the young lady looked at me and asked if they could have a table for two.

"Most certainly," I replied and winked at Brian. I then asked if the couple would like to follow me, and remarking that it was quite quiet that particular evening and the choice of tables was quite extensive, suggested a table that was reasonably secluded which they agreed. Having placed myself behind the young lady and helped her with chair as she sat down, I then proceeded to hand them both their menus. By this time my own table had fallen into silence looked at me with mouths open. Undeterred I then ventured to say that they would shortly be attended to by the waitress who would take their drinks order and wished them both a most pleasant evening and hoped they enjoyed their food and visit.

I then returned back to Brian shook his hand asked him not to "give the game away" and then returned to my own table where I sat down and resumed my conversation. At this point the mists of confusion started to clear as the young lady looked across to us and started to realise that perhaps I may not have been a waiter after all. That conclusion was quickly confirmed when the waitress, who had asked us previously for our own drinks order returned and asked us if I was ready to order our food. I rather loudly announced that this was the second time that evening that I had been asked that and promptly looked over at the young couple to whose attention I now had one hundred percent who now also seemed to have gaping mouths whilst going a strange colour of pink. Throughout the evening the banter continued till as we left I asked once again, whether they have had a nice meal, wished them a pleasant evening and duly left. My duties as a one-off evening waiter had been accomplished.

I had now reached the grand old age of 30. Leslie my mentor was becoming worried that the days of the Corporation were becoming numbered. He was now in his late 60's so he could work his time out to retirement. As for me he suggested that it would be best if I thought about finding a job, perhaps in private practice, with all my connections with the local firms as he feared that I could end up being made redundant if the Corporation was to wind up. So I took his advice and started trolling the employment magazines and enrolled with a few legal agencies. It was not long before *Legal Opportunities*, a large legal recruitment agency found me a job in Plymouth. They applied on my behalf and I was given an interview for which my wife and I to attend. I had never been to Plymouth before so we made it a three-day trip. The interview went very well and with what I had seen in Plymouth, I thought that this would be a great opportunity So I accepted the job subject to being able to sell our house, hand in our notice and move to Devon.

This was agreed, and we returned to Milton Keynes and the house was put on the market. I advised my employers and they wished me well. My days at the Corporation had been incredible and I had felt so happy and settled, but like all good times they had to come to an end I was not really overjoyed at moving all the way to Plymouth, but then felt that if this was a good career move and good for the family, then I should jump at the opportunity. While I was waiting for the house to be sold my job and responsibility continued as normal. Each Friday afternoon I took it upon myself to deliver and documentation that had been sealed by the Corporation to the lawyers instructed by me to act for the Corporations sales and as a P.R. exercise ascertain if there were any problems any thing I could help with.

One of my visits always included two firms now based at central Milton Keynes. One office was above the old Halifax Building Society Branch in Lloyds Court, Central Milton Keynes. At that time it was occupied by a branch office of a well-known firm of lawyers and on the other side of the walkway giving access to the middle of Lloyds Court was another branch office of another large firm of lawyers. I normally visited the branch office above the Halifax Building Society first. The partner in charge of the branch was always so charming and pleasant to deal with and always made me feel welcome, and should I say, important given my age. and the fact that I was simply a legal assistant with the local corporation bearing in mind that status was still very much up held amongst the old school lawyers that still remained in practice. I would in my career bump into this respected and well-liked lawyer later in my career in different and rather sad circumstances.

However, after sorting out documentation, I then left his office and walked across to the other practice branch office. Here I met one of the most influential characters in my working career, Pete Collier. Pete was held the utmost respect from all the partners that he worked for and indeed amongst all other lawyers and professionals within the legal profession in the area. He was one of the most hard working, dedicated and practical lawyers I would ever meet. Peter had finished a huge stack of Friday completions and therefore had time to sit down and have a chat. I told him that I would not be seeing him much longer as I had taken a job in Plymouth, subject to selling the house was about to leave and set up home and career in Devon. At this point, Peter threw his hands in the air, told me that I was not going to Devon, but instead was going to come and work for him. I was rather taken aback as this was not the reason for the visit but at the same time quite honoured that he thought enough of me to consider asking me to work under him.

However, I politely shook his hand wished him a pleasant weekend and left feeling rather humbled by this powerful lawyer and what he had just offered me without any consultation to any of the partners of the actual firm. I went off for the weekend never thought any more about it until Monday morning when took a call from the senior partner of the practice who asked me if I could pop up and see him after work that evening.

This I did and when I arrived the senior partner and Peter Collier took me into the board room and within the course of a few minutes I was offered a job with a fantastic wage rise and a company car. By the time I got home I was rather reeling with joy. I politely contacted the employment agency and the practice in Plymouth to tell them what had happened and apologised for the inconvenience I may have caused. I received a lovely letter from the practice in Plymouth wishing me every success and if ever I was to change my mind or have a turn of circumstances not to hesitate to contact them. Although I would never actually contact the practice again the thread of coincidence would weave its web yet again in years to come in relation to this particular practice.

6 My First years in Private Practice

With the new job about to start at the new practice of Gerrard Neale Fennemore, later to become Fennemores, came the opportunity of popping along, before I started, to one of the monthly meetings. This would give me the chance to get to meet all the partners and the other lawyers that make up the team (who we call "fee-earners" in the profession) before I actually started work with them. The practice at that time was a very leading and respected local law practice. Although I was still working out my notice at the Corporation, I finished my normal days work and drove to Central Milton Keynes. Here I saw first hand the inner workings and systems of this future thinking practice. After the meeting had finished, the senior partner, Roger Fennemore, who I was later to admire as being probably one of the best leaders and motivators I have ever worked for, invited all the members to a local pub for drinks. After a few beers some of the partners and fee earners drifted off home with the few remaining wanting to go for the customary post meeting meal at one of the local curry restaurants. I was invited to leave my car in the car park and Andrew Ray, one of the younger partners would take me with him and drop me back afterwards.

A convoy of cars slowly left the car park with us following on from behind. As we backed out there was a strange loud grating noise coming from the back of Andrew's car which then suddenly stopped. A quick examination out of the windows didn't spot anything peculiar so off we went. After a lovely meal in the company of this great bunch it was time to get home. Unfortunately young Andrew, the partner, had drunk a little too much to lawfully drive so he suggested I drive his car back to the pub with him as a passenger, and then he would get a taxi home from there. There were only a few cars left when we arrived back to the pub, which included my little Astra and what seemed to be a strange object on the road in front of it. When I got out of Andrew's car and examine this strange object was it turned out to be the entire spoiler section from the front of the Astra. What had happened was when Andrew had backed out of the car park, he had inadvertently caught the underneath of the spoiler. As he drove forward this forced the spoiler to detach itself from the car. So it was to say at the very least a little embarrassing having to put in an insurance claim to my new employers, before I had even started, for the damage caused and the repairs necessary to my car. I found out afterwards young Andrew was even more embarrassed and actually thought it may have put me off joining them altogether and that I would turn the job down.

On my first day with the practice I was not terribly surprised to find that I was about to inherit some 29 files for clients who were trying to purchase under the new, shared ownership scheme. At this time few people really had come to grips with the scheme. In many cases they did not really want to know about how it worked how it was going to form probably thirty five percent of future conveyancing here in Milton Keynes. All the conveyancers thoughts and beliefs were that the scheme was going to fail from the outset and therefore there was no real point of really trying to get involved. The twenty-nine new clients themselves were not really interested in the legalities. What they were sold on was the idea of being able to own their own home for a fraction of what it would have cost had they bought in any other town or in a freehold situation. So I set to work not only working with the first of my clients purchasing through this wonderful scheme but also what led to many evenings spent with Estate Agents Building Society Managers and lenders to explain the fundamentals of the scheme on the first generation sales but more importantly what was just around the corner and that was going to be second generation sales. The general turn around time of owners in shared ownerships is probably eighteen months to two years. This proves the success of getting folks onto the first time ladder and within such a short period they would wish to move upwards to either freehold or larger properties which would not only release a good stock of first time buyer properties but would also help the larger property market and also the new homes sites.

One of the developments that was being sold under shared ownership was a very nicely designed estate located in the sleepy village of Woolstones, close to the pub and church but also only a mile and a half from the central Milton Keynes. The design the brickwork and general layout proved to be very popular and it was not long at all when all the properties were reserved albeit not yet completed structurally. On those files that I was acting on we completed our preliminary enquiries and searches mortgage offers arrived and we were then able to exchange quite quickly so making sure that the commitment had been made and once the houses were built the new homes would belong to my clients. We exchanged the purchases in the autumn with the anticipated completion date taking place long before Christmas.

However my clients waited patiently as the weeks ticked by and started to get a little concerned as autumn drew into winter. The houses themselves all looked completed but the Corporation who were having the houses built under contract were refusing to accept the keys from the contractors as they were arguing that certain specifications had not been completed to the Corporations satisfaction. The street lights came on each evening and went off each dawn and still the Corporation refused to budge. Time was now fast running out with Christmas fast approaching and one or two clients began to have a moan that whatever the holdup was really was no reasonable excuse not to allow people to move into their new homes.

Eventually the mystery was discovered and it was simply that the contractor had in fact put what was in the building trade a standard bath edging round the baths whereby the Corporation had stipulated some half baked idea and so the argument ensued for several months so much so that it got to the point where clients were threatening adverse publicity which eventually forced the Corporation to give in, accept the keys and structural completion and thus allow folks to start to legally complete and move in but by now days from the Christmas festivities. Unfortunately, by this time the public utilities had got pretty fed up themselves and the new owners suddenly started finding that the electricity meters and the gas meters had in fact been removed. So there was a mad scramble, not only to get into the new homes by Christmas but also to try to persuade the utilities to return with the meters, which got a little fraught to say the least.

What fun we all had in those ensuing five years. We would work hard (very hard) but play hard as well. We all knew our positions within the practice and of course had a very strong leader in Roger as our Senior partner. He invoked such a strong team spirit. We all looked to each other for inspiration as well as looking out for each other. The monthly meetings were written in stone. We would have to sit through what I called our blame apportioning time. We had to admit any mishaps to any of the company cars, any problems with clients or within the office, report the number of new files that each had opened, and of course the most important as to the amounts of monthly fees earned. Then we always went off to the local pub for a beer and followed by a curry. In later years we would meet at Wicken Hall a previously privately owned Hall now converted into a hotel where afterwards we could enjoy a drink in the bar. Every Christmas and Easter were even more special times with parties and events being organised by the Partnership. In England at that time in late autumn there was always the traditional annual Nouveau Beaujolais run that was unofficially staged. This is where drivers and their cars would travel down to the region and at certain unearthly hour of the night bid in an auction of the that years supplies of Beaujolais Nouveau. Then the race was on to see who could get their bottle or case back to the UK first

71

to be served in a local pub or restaurant. Roger, our senior partner, always seemed to have friends that either did the race or had contacts with the race. As a result he always made a point of making sure there was a bottle of Beaujolais Nouveau sitting on every fee earners desk when they arrived the next morning. At Christmas Roger would team up with the head conveyancing fee-earner, Pete Collier, and between them they would organise Turkeys for all the staff. Peter would turn up in his great big Ford Granada Company car which would be down to the axles with all the weight in the boot. He had been to a local farmer client of his on his way to work, and acquired a car full of turkeys. These were distributed amongst all the staff whether secretaries, fee earners or administration staff, as part of their Christmas presents from the practice. Another way of making everyone feel part of a special and loyal team.

Peter Collier

I should take time at this point to talk a little more about Pete Collier. He was one the main conveyancing non-partner fee-earners who had I had spoken to shortly before leaving the Corporation for a job, as I thought, in Plymouth. He joked at the time that I wasn't going to go there but was coming to the practice to work for him. The phone n call from Roger on the Monday morning inviting me to an interview proved Pete was not only serious but that he held a well respected position in the practice. Pete was a character larger than life itself. He was extremely good at his job, had a large client following in both domestic and commercial law. He was already established as the mentor for many in the practice and certainly was not long before he became mine. Pete was loved and respected by all fee earners young and old, partner or not. Pete came from a military background with his father an ex regimental sergeant major. This reflected in Pete who stood over six feet tall and had a hard granite shaped chin and looked like someone not really best messed with when cornered. He always dressed immaculately and was always a man's man. Pete always set the example, would put himself at the front of every task or problem making sure he led from the front. He always showed everyone how to make a success and how to achieve. It was he that educated me, among other things, that every good lawyer carried a pen. He also explained that the annual practice Christmas party was not for us, the fee earners, but for the staff. In his words we were taken out every month and wined and dined. The Christmas party was therefore a time, he would say, when each fee earner made sure they had plenty of money in their wallet to buy not only their secretaries but also their partners, drinks throughout the evening. We were to make sure that they felt as an important part of the practice as we were made to feel.

As I have said we worked hard, some of us were in the office just after seven thirty in the mornings and never ever left before six in the evenings at the earliest. The rewards were worth it and working with such a highly motivated team meant you felt you belonged from day one.

Some Unusual Transactions

Another client I had at the time had decided she too was going to move into her new home before Christmas with her teenage son. The only problem was she insisted that due to work commitments it would have to be the morning of Christmas Eve. Now most lawyers as far as I remember try wherever possible to avoid Christmas eve at all costs for a host of obvious reasons but the main one is that if anything goes wrong, money doesn't arrive, doesn't get sent or doesn't arrive then the client is left in limbo for the whole of the Christmas period when neither law practice or the Corporation were in fact going to be working. To make matters worse we were closing at lunchtime and the Corporation were only working the morning so that they could have their office party luckily in the offices themselves.

So all in all my client was not particularly popular either with the staff of the practice I was working for or the Corporation for whom I had managed to persuade that if we could get the money to them in time would they be prepared to release keys whilst enjoying their party which they had agreed. Anyway as the morning dragged on, the money was telegraphed off and it was then a waiting game for it to arrive, and not to hassle them too much but to make contact regularly to see if it had arrived. Literally at 12.30 the phone rang to say that they had indeed receive fund and the client could pick the keys up. I rang the client and then released my staff to go off for their last bits of shopping etc. for Christmas.

I was myself one of the last to leave and turning all the lights off making sure all was secure arrived in reception where there was literally just me and the receptionist with her coat on ready to lock up behind me. The phone then rang off which was the dilemma should it be picked up or ignored and we clear for the Christmas break. Part curiosity and partly fearing a problem I picked it up to find my insistent client who had collected the keys, gone to the property with her son and then discovered a smell of gas and what was I going to do about it.

Now I did happen to carry the Gas Board emergency number in my head at that time which I promptly gave her, suggested she ring them tell them that she was a woman on her own, with her "young" son moving into brand new house for Christmas, and I have felt guilty for years thinking of some poor chap, having to drive all the way over from Oxford, some 50 miles away to sort out a gas leak for a rather selfish inconsiderate and impatient client when he himself was probably looking forward to getting home to his family to start Christmas.

As with all builders as the time approaches towards Christmas they try where ever possible to start winding down so that any properties that were not going to complete without a positive and meaningful push would be left to the New Year which in some cases was going to be several weeks. I had an elder couple moving over from Leighton Buzzard to a brand new and rather expensive development literally at the end of my road where I now lived. Now we had exchanged contracts on both their sale and their purchase simultaneously and for some strange reason for which I have never been able to fathom out at the time or indeed succeed in repeating on any other new development since, the builders agreed to a fixed complete date rather than one on formal notice. That fixed completion date was only a few days before Christmas.

Now having been involved with builders and their structural time scales and seeing the particular builder dragging his feet I was not at all confident driving past the estate of houses each morning that these were going to be ready in time for the fixed completion date. I was right come the day of legal completion when my clients were having to move out of their home the house was no where near ready and would not be until after Christmas. However we had a fixed completion date. So I had engineered with the clients that the best way to get the builders attention was that themselves and their removals lorry would turn up on site on the morning of contractual completion. I then notified the builders solicitors that they were in breach of contract and that in accordance with the contractual remedy my clients would have to put their furniture into storage and move into a hotel until such time as the house was finished and all at the builders expense which was going to be very costly if it was to extend into the New Year. The builders were totally horrified at their mistake first of all of agreeing a fixed completion date and secondly at the hefty bill they now faced. The clients on the other hand, being primed previously had chosen a removal company that indeed stored as well as moved furniture and again who were pre warned what was about to happen. So after turning up on site, delivering their bombshell the removal lorry dutifully drove off to the depot so that everything could be professionally stored and the clients cleared off to be pre booked small hotel for a few days rest at the builders expense.

Meanwhile back on site floodlights were installed round the house, and contractors worked into the early hours night after night until got the property completed. Apologies were bountiful as the new purchasers were invited back to inspect the completed house, all sorts of incentives were given in addition to the settlement of the removals and storage and so finally with tongue in cheek the happy clients moved into their new home in plenty of time to settle down ready for the Christmas break.

Some time later after my happy couple had moved into their home they asked me if I would indeed act for their daughter who was about to embark in the purchase of a shared ownership first generation property from the Corporation. No problems and everything went normally smoothly, through to just before exchange when I invited the daughter to pop along to go through the contract papers discuss the shared ownership scheme and if she was happy with our meeting to get her to sign the contact pay her money and we could then exchange. However, at the meeting she was accompanied by a young man who when asked who he was turned out to be her boyfriend, I asked if he was going to be living with her which he confirmed he would. I asked why he was not a joint purchaser to which he confirmed he was out of work and didn't think he could join in. This I confirmed was not a problem and arranged for the contracts to be amended to show her and his names and a fresh mortgage offer to be issued. We then met again got signed up and exchanged. We now merely awaited constructional completion so that we could arrange to complete their purchase and get them in.

Unfortunately it was not going to be quite as easy as expected. Between exchange and completion the couple turned up and announced that they had in fact got married. So, before completion took place we had to arrange for yet another twenty seven page A3 shared ownership lease to be produced in duplicate for the second time along with a fresh mortgage offer in their new married names. These were duly signed and a sigh of relief that a problem had been resolved before completion. Again, shortly before completion I had yet another visit from by now was a very sheepish looking couple with yet another "confession" to make. This time they pointed out that their married name obviously had adopted his surname of "Murphy" and she had lost her own maiden name of "Pelmear" which was an established yet unusual name and would in fact now die off as the parents had only produced two girls, the elder already having got married. The question was therefore posed as to "how difficult" it would be to prepare deeds of change of names, new leases (twenty seven pages long in duplicate) another mortgage offer. The situation was now becoming a comedy but the Corporation duly obliged and all the documentation was now changed for a third time. Finally, we got the transaction completed the couple moved in to live happily ever after. Six months later the young man was back saying they had split up and could we act for him in his divorce.

Sometimes the boot is on the other foot and I would have to try to make my excuses on behalf of my client the builder. One such builder was developing a new estate on the edges of the city where again the houses were completed, there was no reason why they could not complete before Christmas and indeed the buyers and the buyers solicitors were champing at the bit to try to get their clients formally completed wanting as many days as possible for notice to be given by me so that they could apply for funds and carry out final searches so that their clients could achieve their goal of being in their new property before the festive season.

Day after day passed, no final certificates were forthcoming and it was getting tighter and tighter to try to complete. In the end the developer confessed to me that the whole estate was being held up because of a pumping station problem with the water authority. On investigation it turned out that this was a sewer pumping station that literally would dispose of waste from the homes situated in a dip up and over the hill and away into the main public sewer system. The pumping station had been organised rather late and the water authority was being particularly dilatory as to its provision construction and completion and we suspected that the water authority, like the building trade was rather hoping to have the project finished in the New Year.

We therefore made our apologies to all the buyers through their solicitors, who then had to make arrangements for temporary accommodation over the Christmas and New Year period until the whole industry started up again in the New Year could get the pumping station completed and thus the houses connected to it and once tested and passed would allow the legal completions to take place. Strangely this happened very quickly once the building industry started up again and the water authority was able to carry out its connections. Notices were served and completions started to happen from mid-January. Soon after, all transactions were finished.

Once the dust had settled I eventually spoke to the area manager about the pumping station to tell him how embarrassed we were. The whole public relations side had been a bit of a disaster. I saw the manager look at me rather sheepishly out of the corner of his eye, and I suspected there was another side to this story. Indeed it turned out that the developer had achieved a really successful year and had surpassed all its expectations and was in fact well in profit and way above its targets for the year. It was therefore decided in the higher echelons of the client that perhaps they should find a reason to slow down the number of completions being achieved and thus the profit made. The idea was to put the blame on the pumping station which was so feasible that even I had swallowed the story hook line and sinker and had in fact advocated the work that had caused the delay in completion of the station and prevented all these people moving in before Christmas. The whole thing was a collaboration to which I had been an unwitting part to which I was indeed not best pleased.

When I had been employed at the Corporation I had been involved in the self-build project and responsible for the setting up of the development plots for individuals. I had to get the legal title set up along with all the documentation for the sale pack. The form of contract had to be drafted which included the development agreement for the constructions of the various house designs on the plots. I was always impressed at that time with the size and design of some of these wonderful houses that I would see from drawings to the final construction. Something I would have loved to have achieved for my self and my family but thought I could never have afforded.

Our Own Home

A friend of mine, Paul Griffiths, who I have known before we could even pronounce each others names as toddlers, still worked at the Corporation. Paul and his fellow team were responsible for the advanced design and subsequent implementation of footpaths roads bridges and general layouts of certain estates within the new town. In one of our telephone conversations he confided that if ever I was looking to move house, I should look no further than this particular estate he was helping to design. His explanation made it all sound really wonderful. The Estate was also to include full serviced self-build plots. The plots themselves were all going to be close to the canal, close to the linear parks and close enough to be able to walk to the central Milton Keynes shopping centre. Now it was rather coincidental that the offices that dealt with the marketing and reservations of these particular plots was situated right across the courtyard from where my office was located. I trotted over there one lunchtime, picked up the brochure and looked at the various constraints, price ranges, and sizes of the plots on the estate in question and got rather interested.

One afternoon, shortly after I had collected the brochure, I noted that across the forecourt people were beginning to gather with their chairs flasks and blankets. The queue had started to form for the following morning`s release of the plots. Realising this was my only chance to possibly secure a plot I excused myself from the office, shot home to get changed and returned with my own camp chair/bed and joined the queue that was now some 20 to 30 people long. During the evening various members of the families of those in the queue came and went with food drinks pillows and warm clothing and we settled down for what was going to prove a very long night.

However, looking back it really was great fun and certainly a way to get to meet all your neighbours before actually moving into a house. The next morning, without having achieved much sleep we all lined up and slowly worked our way forward to pay out deposits and secure one of the plots available. I was a little disappointed in not being able to reserve the plot that I rather fancied from the plans. As it turned out though the one I ended up with was in fact a far better location. Having reserved my plot I went home showered changed and got back to work for my normal days requirements and tasks.

That evening however, Monica and I decided it would be a good idea to perhaps go and find this particular plot in what was described as being in a wonderful corner of Milton Keynes. I was really disappointed when we arrived in the road that served the plots along each side. We felt that this whole area was in the middle of nowhere. It all seemed miles from the nearest housing, shops, or any amenities. All we had was a working farmhouse, with herds of cows walking up and down the road each day dropping mud and debris everywhere to and from the fields for milking. The vision that came to mind was of having to build a railway station in the middle of nowhere and waiting for the railway to actually arrive.

Having secured the plot my next task was to employ someone to actually design a house for us that would be acceptable to the Corporation planners. Their constraints were very strict on the types of bricks, roof tiles, windows and materials to be used. An ex-Corporation work colleague Richard Petty, who reminded me of the ultimate nutty school professor with his wild hair cut and flashing eyes, and scruffy appearance, agreed to help us and one Sunday morning we took a drive all round Milton Keynes. We looked at other people's doorways, windows, roofs and all sorts of strange sections of houses. after several hours we returned home and with a piece of A4 and a pencil Richard then sat down and drew the roof windows doors etc that I had said I had liked. Lo and behold there was the house of my dreams that had been locked in my head but just needed a genius to pull it out and put it onto paper. I still have the drawing of the house as it was scribbled and now as it has turned out and where I have lived now for some 30 plus years.

The new town of Milton Keynes did indeed slowly catch me up, pass me by, and the house now forms part of a large developed and well established part of Milton Keynes. Paul was proved right with all the wide spaces between the houses, the landscaping, canal linear park and Paul's forecast did come true as it is indeed one of the nicest areas of the new town to live.

More Cases

One of my developer clients was later to acquire from the Corporation the large tract of land at the very end of my own road for his development. The site was surrounded by canal on one side, fields on the other and had only a single access road. It was so remote and so boggy that the first winter the developer put a blade, or large bulldozer on site, it sank into the mud and remained there throughout the winter before it was finally pulled out in the Spring. Somehow unwanted visitors to the site were still being able to get into the properties and steal all sorts of materials. It got so bad that the developer asked if the bathroom sets to fitted to the houses could be delivered and left in my garage. He would then ensure these were not fitted till the last day before completion of the sales for fear of getting stolen.

One late evening one of the bathroom suites was collected from my garage by the director and site foreman, after all the other site workers had gone home. They took the bathroom suite to the new property carried it up the stairs and into one of the bedrooms out of the way. The next day when they arrived for work at 7.30 am, to their total surprise, the entire suite had gone. How the perpetrators knew it was there, how they got in and how they got the entire system away is still a mystery. The couldn't carry it across the canal or across the fields so they had to bring it back down the road yet I did not hear any vehicles that night.

One afternoon at the beginning of this particular week I took a phone call from a gentleman who said that he was from the Coroner's office in

Northampton and could I confirm that I had acted for this particular chap. We had been receiving various phone calls from all sorts of bogus people pretending to be anything other than what they really were which more times than not turned out to be debt recovery agents trying to obtain information by any means. I did rather give this chap short change and suggested that if he gave me his number I would in time ring him back. Having rang him back the number was indeed genuine, that the chap was in fact a Police Sergeant assigned to work with the Coroners Office to put together the facts and story of one of my clients whom I had acted for previously and had, rather sadly, been found dead in his home face downwards on his sofa with no one claiming any knowledge of him or his background. I was asked if I could in fact tell the Police Sergeant anything about this character and the reasons behind the purchase etc. I confirmed that I had indeed acted for him and that he had migrated down from London to purchase one of the new, shared ownership scheme houses uniquely being offered in Milton Keynes. I confirmed that when he came to initially instruct me he had attended the offices with another couple who he introduced as his cousin and his cousin's wife who would be living close by and also a lady that he introduced as his wife. Having acted for this gentleman in his purchase, I would later be introduced to his niece who I also would act for in a similar transaction.

With this information the Police Sergeant went off and didn't hear from him for several days. However, he still did not have any joy so I confirmed that he should contact the Milton Keynes Development Corporation from whom he had purchased the property, and the Nationwide Building Society from whom he had obtained a Mortgage. A few days later, the sergeant was back still no joy. The so-called cousins only admitted that they knew of him but were not related, no sign of any wife in the property and certainly no one knew of a niece. The Corporation were unable really to supply much information and the Nationwide produced his application but all the details, references etc. seem to have come from a hotel address in London which proved later all to have been forged by fictitious names and references so that he could buy the house. As a last resort the Police took the deceased finger prints and sent them off to Scotland Yard in the vein hope that they may have some record of him. This proved very successful as our friend who had called himself by one name in fact had several names and indeed had spent time at her Majesty's pleasure in one of her hostelries for naughty people, in fact he had done time for being a con artist.

With all this information the main task was still not achieved, finding someone that could inherit what small estate and more importantly could arrange a proper and fitting burial. The Coroner quite rightly merely wanted to get this poor chap off the slab and into the ground. At this point the Sergeant pointed out that in fact I was probably the last person to see him alive and admit to it and was probably the only person that could identify him.

"Now we have taken some Polaroid photos that are not very nice," he said. "Could we send them to you so that you could have a look and confirm that it is in fact the same person?"

Oh joy! What fun! I had not seen a dead body up to that stage and now I was going to see one, on the slab, un shaven that had been lying about for a fortnight!! Now we used to open the post as a team in the mornings, so I pre warned the team that these photos were going to arrive at some point over the next few days. Gingerly each day the post was opened, contents inspected sideways and nothing arrived.

The weekend then came and went and on the Monday morning everyone really had forgotten what were on their way. There was a huge scream as Kathy threw the envelope up in the air to be showered like confetti with these photos as she disappeared out of the room and the comments "we take it you have found the photos then."

The photos were taken back to my room and after plucking up the courage to open them and have a good look sure enough whilst not very pleasant as the chap had not been cleaned up at all, it was definitely him. I signed the back of the photos returned them and as far as I know the chap was duly buried. The Authorities tried to find any relatives but unfortunately nobody came forward and so sadly the chaps estate went to the State. He was still haunting me years later as whenever his title came up I would get phone calls asking me had I acted on the sale.

Another site that I was involved in was situated very close to where I lived. It was a small development of two and three bedroom terraced and semi-detached houses designed for the young families and couples just getting together. One evening I got a phone call via my parents house where I was having evening dinner as I was myself in the middle of my divorce from my first wife and the site office was on the phone asking if I had in fact got a key release for one of the plots that apparently had completed that day and the young couple who had supposedly purchased the property had turned up rather late with their young baby and lorry full of furniture and belongings. I had not as far as I know had a completion that day but drove back to the office just to double check from the file. This was now 6.30 and nothing recorded that any completion had taken place, and no money had been sent. I rang the site office, who rang the area manager, who tried to reach his boss, who was on a golf course unavailable (before the advent of mobile phones), and so we had no authority to allow the young couple who had travelled down from London with all their furniture and young baby, access to the property till the next day.

I only lived round the corner from where they were moving too and so as a gesture of good will I suggested that I left the office went home and met them with their lorry for them to leave the lorry on my driveway for the night, feed and change the baby who was extremely wet by now, and return to London to stay the night for whatever happened the next day. Needless to say I was fuming at my time wasting, my clients time wasting and embarrassment that this had caused. I sent a fax to the other side's solicitors and certainly did not mince my words pointing out that they had let their client down, had let the profession down and do they realise what turmoil they had caused. I then received a very sheepish phone call from the gentleman at the practice acting for the young couple who was extremely sorry for all the inconvenience, appreciated my point of view thanked me for all the assistance I had given this young couple, that he had forgotten all about the completion but would complete that day, and what made matters worse the young couple were a "freebee" as a favour to the senior partner who was friends with the couples parents and had received my fax before he had.

Practical Jokes

As in every work place gags and jokes were played on each other and certainly during my career I have been the target of quite a few and indeed perpetrated one or two myself. At our practice we had a young qualified solicitor, Neal Francis. Neal was a very handsome looking debonair young solicitor who was also super fit and actually represented his county being a member of the national Hockey Team. As a team member he went to international games round the world. This particular season, shortly before Christmas he was away in Australia playing for his national pride. Now while young Neil was representing his country the rest of the work force were busy earning a living and serving the public in the various aspects of the law.

Now at that time, our reception, on the ground floor boasted a very modern telex machine. Kim our receptionist was rather proud of this

82

machine and operated it with great enthusiasm and skill. It would send out any messages instantly with a green printed record of the message sent and a red message being received. I was curious to learn whether it was possible to "cheat" by perhaps having a sent message actually look like a received message. ie printed on red. Apparently this was possible although the actual intricacies were rather baffling to me. Anyway, we "conjured" a message from our international player to a fellow fee earner who was supposed to be caretaking his work in Neil's absence. The message was kept simple and to the point and simply read "Guy, having problems returning to UK please hold Fort, will contact you again after Xmas," signed Neil. The telex was then dutifully put on young Guy's desk.

Guy Brookes was a young very hard working and conscientious litigation lawyer but was clearly getting affected by not only covering his work but also that of his colleague. What we did not know was that Guy had been trying to locate Neil in Australia without much success to enquire when he was likely to be returning to take back his own work load. With this "news" that Neil was now going to be absent till at least the New Year. Guy immediately rolled up his sleeves, and set to and try and catch up with some of Neil's work and bring the work-load back up to date. I suppose his conscience was also pricking as he had let the work load slip a little on the belief that Neil would be returning shortly.

What we didn't know was that Guy had in fact booked that very afternoon to meet his then Girlfriend, later to be wife, for a spot of Christmas shopping. He had a long list of presents still yet to buy for family etc. Needless to say the girlfriend was not best pleased to learn that her boyfriend instead of accompanying her on her hunt for presents was going to be locked up in his office for the rest of the day, and evening.

At some point later that particular evening/night, Chris Hilton-Johnson the partner in charge of litigation, as he was leaving the office, popped into Guy to see if he was all okay, and really to ask why he had cancelled his afternoon leave. When he learnt of the reasons why Guy was now locked into files and dictation he just shrugged his shoulders, smiled and as he closed the door simply said, "You do know this was just a hoax!"

Neil did in fact return prior to the Christmas break was very appreciative of all the hard work Guy had put into to keeping the work load up to date. It took poor Guy up until the Christmas office party, and quite a few free bribes in the form of free drinks before ascertaining that the culprit in this terrible hoax played against him was in fact – Me!!   He did get over it by the time we resumed the New Year office hours.

Now I suppose that fate always pays back its debts but not in money! I was about to be paid back for the terrible tricks I had played on poor Guy. I had already mentioned that I had been smitten by the Christmas Good Samaritan Bug several years before when I drove two elderly sisters over to their distant relation one Christmas eve so that they could spend their Christmas at least with a family member and the bug I am afraid bit me once again. It was coming up to Christmas and we were all getting excited that the Christmas holiday was approaching.

As Fee Earners we were attending other business parties; luncheons; evening get-togethers and the feeling of Christmas approaching was reaching climax. The girls in the office were all busy buying friends and family presents and the organisation that goes with the festive season. The office party itself had been and we had all had a super evening.

However, unknown to us all one of the secretaries was not quite as lucky as the rest of us and her circumstances meant that her Christmas was not going to be as comfortable and festive as the rest of ours. Ann had recently left her husband for rather sad reasons and her and her two boys were now reduced to living in the Women's Refuge for homeless or battered wives which at least they found a little peace from their previous and often harsh lives although the living conditions was at its best only suffered temporary before wanting to move out and obtain your own space especially if children were involved. It was very sad. Dallas my secretary felt a particular sadness as her and Ann shared an office space together and without really giving much away Ann had confessed enough for Dallas to really feel the pangs that Christmas joy was not going to be enjoyed fully in one particular family.

It was the day before Christmas eve when Dallas came to me quite a bit upset and when questioned advised me that she really was feeling for Ann who not only was living in the Women's refuge but that the refuge itself was closing for Christmas and for three days her and her boys were in fact going to be homeless. Now I had already suffered a miserable Christmas with my previous marriage break-up and I think having gone through the emotional trauma really couldn't see this happen to someone as close as one of our own secretaries.

It did rather bring me down to earth with a bit of a bang so going home that evening was with a rather heavy heart. I mentioned the family what I had discovered during the day and there was very little discussion before the unanimous decision that Ann and her boys would be invited to join us for Christmas if she wanted to accept the invitation. The next morning arriving in the office I summoned Ann to my own office sat her down and asked her if she would like to be our guest, with the boys from Christmas eve until Boxing Day afternoon when my own children would be joining us and when we would have to take her back to the Refuge. She gladly accepted and it was agreed that I would pick them up from the Refuge that evening at about 7.30pm, which would give us all enough time to get home from the office for us to make our Christmas Eve preparations and Ann could do her packing. What she didn't realise was that my new family were all out buying little bits and pieces that they could afford to give the boys something to open Christmas Day and even a few bits and pieces for Ann herself so that they all felt they were part of the family rather than outsiders watching us all have a lovely Christmas.

The evening arrived and I drove from home down to the Refuge to pick up our guests and found two very excited boys and a rather grateful mother all packed and standing by the door. A quick loading and we set off and arrived home fifteen minutes later. The children were shown their bedroom and their belongings unpacked for their stay. Eventually the excitement turned into tiredness and off they went to bed ready for Father Christmas to arrive the next morning.

We had a lovely Christmas Eve sharing stories and drinks till we too were spent and retired for the night. The next day was a typical family Christmas day. the boys were up early and we all sat round the tree sharing presents and surprises. Ann I remember had a new pair of slippers and the usual girlie perfumes etc. Lunch came and went and soon we were all sat in front of the log fire and a cosy Christmas night again swapping stories and wallowing into a very Christmas cheer.

Before we knew where we were it was all over and I was driving Ann and the boys back to the refuge ready to pick my own children up for what we affectionately called "Christmas 2". As I dropped Ann off she was so grateful that we had taken her into our home for Christmas and I told her that there was no way that we as a family enjoying the pleasures of the home and trimmings were going to see anyone that we knew to be homeless on that special time especially with two boys. Ann looked at me a little surprised and then announced, "But we were not going to be homeless. I could have gone to my sister's in Wales but didn't want to travel all that way so we were offered a house on the next estate which we could have borrowed over Christmas to go back the Refuge this evening." Now had I been able to get hold of Dallas that evening ...... words would have been swapped. I had been well and truly kippered!! We looked back after Christmas and had a smile or three but we did secretly feel that we had given a small family a special Christmas.

First Impressions

They say you should never judge a book by its cover. Similarly you should never judge your clients by first appearances. At this time I had built up a good relationship with numerous Estate Agents, Building Society Managers, and Bank Managers. One of the Estate Agents was managed by a very conscientious young man, who I met on a regular basis for lunchtime and evening beers. On one of these occasions he asked if I could help out with a rather tricky situation, which involved the marital break-up of his girlfriend's parents. I offered without hesitation and suggested that if they would like to ring me at the office I could make an appointment for them to pop in and see me and as long as we could all work together to get the job done then there wouldn't be a problem and afterwards everyone could "get on with their lives" so to speak.

The day arrived and this extremely well-dressed, slim, very good looking gentleman, in a very smart dark blue suit, with dapper shirt tie and shiny shoes, turned up with what can only be described as the most plain nondescript woman I have ever seen. Talk about chalk and cheese. These two just did not look like they had anything in common in the slightest even though they had been married for several years and had several children. For my part, whilst professionally I could not take sides, I took an instant dislike to this chap and felt really sorry for the wife who clearly was going to now spend the rest of her life very much alone and unloved.

We went through the procedure of instructions, forms funds etc. and I promised to open the file and commence the conveyancing work for the sale of the matrimonial home. As they were leaving, he quietly doubled back and asked if I would be happy to act on behalf of himself and a "female friend" in a joint purchase. My dislike for him increased even more although I agreed. Later that day he reappeared with this very attractive lady a lot younger than himself, but very intelligent and very well dressed and, I must confess, a bit more suited to him than the ex-wife even though I found his behaviour quite distasteful.

Anyway the conveyancing procedures were undertaken, the day came for the two to sign contracts on the sale, and later that day by way of separate appointment he returned with his young "friend" to sign contracts on the purchase. Exchange took place and so did completion with the husband and wife sharing a matrimonial split of proceeds and the husband and young "friend" both putting in funds to complete the purchase.

And so the transactions were completed and the husband and wife could get on with their lives albeit that I was still feeling very sorry for this poor woman and her looming life of solitude. So much so that when I met my young Estate Agent friend again for a drink I could not help bringing to the surface my disgruntlement at what was a very difficult transaction as far as my professionalism was concerned, being tested by the husband with separate meetings, not being able to speak about the wife or the other "friend" at any of them, and being made to feel very uncomfortable especially as I felt so sorry for the poor wife who I appreciated could not help her looks or demeanour but would be very lonely now.

My young friend listened to me waffling on then burst into fits of laughter. He then announced that I had the story so completely and totally wrong. In fact it turned out that the husband was in fact doing the "honourable thing" by allowing the sale to go through as in fact the wife had been caught having an open affair with the "friend's" husband. And in fact after the sale and she had her money, she the wife and the husband of the "friend" moved in together where they enjoyed a very erotic life together for the short time that it lasted till the "friend's" husband got bored and went off with someone his own age. In the meantime the husband asked the friend rather than be on her own if she would like to house share with him purely platonically but at least they would not be homeless or one their own which is exactly what they did. I certainly never judged another situation till I knew all the facts!!

Charity Boxing Night

I discussed earlier in this chapter how at Fennemores we all worked hard but we also played hard as well. Throughout the year there were various events that we would attend and which we would invite guests to say thank you for the fact that they had supported us during the year.

One particular event that came around every November was the annual Charity Boxing Night. Various businessmen throughout Milton Keynes would book tables at the local leisure centre for a Gentlemen's evening. Every man would be dressed up with dinner suit, dicky bow and all looking very smart. We would be allocated to our tables with our guests where a full three course meal with wine was served and after the toast to the queen, cigars were then lit, and the evenings entertainment would begin. This entailed up to 12 to 14 separate boxing bouts where two boxing clubs would put forward boxers to come into the ring located in the middle of the floor, and go through a highly professional amateur boxing bout with proper judges scoring etc. at the end of the evening all the gentleman would make their "merry way" home probably much the worse for drink but having had an absolutely superb evening where everyone felt a million dollars if only for a few hours.

Now this particular evening because of the size of our practice we had to organise two tables one for what I called the senior table and one for the junior table. The senior table housed my friend and mentor Pete Collier, the Partners and their guests, who were all a little older than myself. Each table held about 20 sitting in a circle. The evening progressed as expected, with bottles of wine, superb meal, queen's speech, followed by cigars, and various rounds of boxing starting with the junior level and progressing up to the senior and more experienced boxers. At about half way through the evening the lights came on and various items were auctioned off to add to the over all total of the evening that would go to a local charity.

Amongst other items being offered for auction was a cricket bat that had been signed by the entire England cricket team. After very fierce bidding another of the partners, Alistair Brooks on the senior table succeeded in out bidding everyone else and became the proud owner of the cricket bat much to the pride of the two tables.

The boxing continued and at the end the boxers were presented to the audience to great applause and then the gentlemen began to collect their coats and with their guests slowly drifted off home. I had booked taxis for my own guests and so having successfully got them all together we came out of the leisure centre, I ushered them into their taxis and got home myself to what I still remember as a really great and enjoyable evening.

The next day being Saturday, we did not have to work, which was just as well as we were all feeling a little under the weather. However I was rather surprised to receive a call from one of the guests from the night before who announced that the partner who had won the cricket bat on the grown ups table was in fact now on page 3 of the Sun Newspaper and not as a model. Needless to say it was a hasty trip to the newsagents to see what the story was all about.

It seems that just after we left the hall, there was a member on the senior table of ours that had in fact, during the evening got more and more obnoxious as the evening had progressed, but had got even more out of hand to the point where other tables were beginning to notice and he was drawing attention not only to himself but to his table where he was in fact a guest. So, Alistair had apparently lent over and tapped him on the shoulder with the cricket bat with the request that he calmed down and behave himself. Instead of taking the advice and calming down he took the other approach by exploding into rage accusing Alistair of hitting him from behind with the cricket bat and then commenced to go round the table towards Alistair striking each guest as they got in his way.

As he approached my mentor Pete Collier who was built more than capable of looking after himself, stood up and was happily going to take on this maniac in a tuxedo. However a chap on the next table who clearly considered himself far more able than he actually was stood in front of the drunken guest and Pete offering to sort it all out, at which point the drunken guest hit him so hard he sent him clearly over one table and into the next breaking the chaps leg and causing all sorts of other damage. Needless to say the headlines the next day, of which Alistair often boasted that he had appeared on page 3 of the Sun Newspaper read "Boxing Match Commences Outside the Ring."

Expenses

As part of the responsibility we always had to make sure that we looked after those that supported us and we had a budget for expenses each month to so do. I always made a practice of trying to find good local pubs and restaurants that we could visit and have an enjoyable lunch plus a couple of pints but be back at work within the hour and try not to spend too much money as the budget had to last the week.

Unfortunately one of the young partners could never quite work this out. He could only afford to go out a couple of times a month and would hit his target whereby I was out three or even four times a week without going over budget.

My secret was that I found various pubs, one in particular that I still visit today that used to do the most enormous Steak Sandwich (which in fact was a piece of stake with onions etc. inside a large round bap) with all the trimmings for just £5. You can see I lived very well for the £100 that I was allowed to spend each month.

However I did meet my match and some. There was a client who was from one of the French colonies who clearly enjoyed wine better than I. It was the time when the Beaujolais had arrived and the client asked if I would like to join him this particular lunchtime at the wine bar located not far from the office. I was and have always tried to be conscientious about my time spent in and out of the office and certainly could not meet him at his suggested 12.00 o'clock but instead opted for 1.00 o'clock the start of most of our lunchtimes. By the time I arrived my French guest had just about finished his first bottle. Not being up to his liking we decided to take a taxi to another location where between us over lunch we were able to "sample" another three bottles by the end of which words were taking quite a long time to form and by the time I got back to the office was certainly in no fit state to attend clients or anyone else so I made my excuses and went home.

My French friend, who I still admire to this day where ever he may be, got in a taxi and went off to meet his friends as they had several other bottles that they were going to sample throughout the afternoon and evening. As already discussed it was always the senior partner's view that it was important that the fee earners were well looked for all their hard efforts as shown by the end of the month meetings and the curries that followed afterwards, it was also considered important that each fee earner on the celebration of the Beaujolais arrivals that every fee earner would have on his desk one bottle to take home for himself and his family as another gesture of good management and good will.

More Tales of Clients

My workload formed part acting for builders and part acting for private clients. There was a chap I acted for who was ex-military and stood some six feet six inches tall had fought in the war and was a real old character. However, his health was failing and he had to sell his house to move into a smaller home. I had the unenviable task of ringing him on the day of completion to ask why he was digging up the paving slabs in the back garden especially as he was moving into a flat situated on the second floor of the building. He told me he could sell them for fifty pence per slab. I suggested it would be a good idea if he could put them back as it really did form part of the transaction.

Another chap used to travel up from Slough to Milton Keynes on his motorbike to instruct me and see how progress was being made. I felt very sorry for him as he was told just before exchange of contracts that the price he was paying For his new home did not include the central heating which he would have to pay for as an extra which was all a bit of a ploy on the builders to promote the avoidance of purchasers having to pay stamp duty. He of course did not have the two thousand pounds extra for the central heating as was completely devastated that he had been duped into this purchase. We had not choice but to abort the transaction but I suggested to him the new Shared Ownership scheme that the Corporation whose offices were next door were promoting, and that he should enquire if they had any properties under the scheme for sale of which he was able to secure. He was so pleased that he had no longer to wait for the second property than that of the abortive house and worked out far cheaper for him and built to a much higher standard. Sadly shortly before he moved into his new home he was diagnosed with Cancer and died six months later. Very sad.

Another couple I had the misfortune to represent were buying a brand new home. They were very arrogant and brash and to my concern after exchange of contracts I discovered through my final land charges searches that he had various entries registered against him. I called them into the office and asked him did he know that he had entries registered against his name. He seemed little concerned at all so I pressed the question as to whether the entries were in fact relating to him, rather than just someone else's name the shame as his and was he in fact bankrupt. He confirmed he was and then wanted to know, "What was I going to do about it?" to get them their new home.

Now, an undischarged bankrupt cannot enter into a contract for the buying or selling of property so I knew he was in rather large trouble. Being a little troubled to say the least by the situation I rang the builders solicitor a chap called Fred Wilkinson who I knew had a very good strong professional relationship with my old mentor Leslie Weatherall at the Corporation. Now Mr. Wilkinson, like Leslie was a absolutely brilliant lawyer albeit old school who had forgotten more than I would ever learn. I told him my plight and asked him if there was anything I could do. There was the long silence that seemed like an eternity then finally his voice that simply uttered "Forms and Precendents – Volume (so and so) page (so and so). I think you will find your answer there," and hung up. I flew to the bookshelf took down the volume looked it up and if I could have kissed the guy I think he would have been extremely embarrassed. There was the answer, the contract had been entered into "in error" the conveyance from the Corporation and the builder by the direction of the bankrupt was to go to his wife and so all would be wonderful.

One problem though that the wife was the lower income of the family and there was a joint mortgage. No problem, she contacted the lenders who were in Scarborough for a fresh offer to be made whereby she suddenly promoted from being a secretary on something like £7,000 per annum to a personal assistant on some £18,000 per annum. When she drove to Scarborough to pick up the new offer, as time was of the essence with notice being served and legal completion looming, we used the magic telex to send the lenders a message pre-warning what we suspected.

Despite our warning the lenders decided not to take our advise issued the offer, and we duly completed a few days later. I had occasion to visit the two of them shortly after the completion date, to find pure opulence awaiting me in the shape of new cars, new bikes for the kids dumped across the new front lawn, lights on every room, and guests attending a flamboyant dinner party to which I was announced as their "lawyer" and they wanted to "instruct me on Monday" to sue the carpet fitters for a shabby job! I was not surprised at all that six months later, Guy in our litigation department was instructed by the Scarborough Building Society to press for possession proceedings as the couple had never made a single payment on their mortgage.

There is an old country saying that basically provides that when someone is trying to offer unsolicited advise they are simply told "you farm your way and I will farm mine" and so I was to receive a telephone call one day from my own father who himself was a professional white collar worker and a supervisor over quite a large group of staff working for EDS assigned to Vauxhall Motors. During our conversation he drew to my attention that he had been at one of his lodge meetings earlier that week and one of his lodge friends had remarked that they thought I was far too friendly for a lawyer and rather over familiar with my clients.

Now being in my early 30's needless to say I was rather in awe and therefore took this advice very seriously and decided to try to be less friendly towards my clients and be more reserved and so from then on for quite a few weeks I tried be more "professional" and aloof. Something I hated as I had prided myself in the relationship I thought I had built with clients some of whom had returned to use me again in other transactions. However, eventually the end of the month arrived and all the fee earners gathered for what I used to call the "Blame Apportioning" meeting where we would once again go through our "confessions", as to how many damaged company cars there were, overdrawn expenses accounts, and then the monthly figures of how much each fee-earner had actually brought in for the month, how many files had been opened and any other business relating to the month's activities.

At that time we had some five offices spanning not only Milton Keynes but also Northampton Stony Stratford Bletchley and Luton. In all the offices we covered all the aspects of the law including conveyancing, litigation, matrimonial, and probate. When it eventually came round to my turn to announce the number of files opened for the month I was rather pleased with myself not only to find that I had in fact opened the most numbers of files for the entire practice but had also brought in the highest amount of fees above all the other fee earners including the partners.

The following day I phoned my Father back relaying back to him what he had told me and also then informed him about the end of month meeting in which I had excelled above all other fee earners, that I had achieved it by my own way, using my own skills to win over clients hearts and minds. I then suggested that whilst he was successful in his own field, not to ever again interfere in my field or the way I actually work.

Many years later my daughter rang me in a state saying that she was being accused by others that she was too friendly and not professional, which all began to ring a bell from my own past. I let her complete her tale of woe then relayed back to her what had happened to me all those years previous and told her to follow her own instincts and keep to her own path, to work the way she knows best. This she did and not only has she excelled in her job but has been promoted several times to become area manager herself in charge of two offices and their staff.

They say that Lawyers are the prophets of gloom and doom and seem to have a problem for every suggestion. I think that is because over the years lawyers, as indeed with any other profession encounter the problems and pitfalls that draw attention to the reasons why certain rules apply to certain applications. One of the rules that I learnt by way of default and chance and which I still maintain to this day clearly illustrates this point.

I was acting for two friends, and also neighbours who were selling their home due to a matrimonial split. He had found another person in his life and was prepared to sacrifice his wife and two boys for that alternate life. The sale progressed without any particular issue up to exchange when something prompted me to ask them both to put in writing that they first of all agreed the sale, and what the split of proceeds of sale was going to be after the mortgage had been paid off agents fees settled and the legal bill paid. At this point he was very much "on his back foot" and feeling rather guilty simply confirmed that all he wanted was £6000 the remainder to go to her to buy a home for her and the boys. The sale completed, he received his £6,000 and promptly disappeared. I then acted for her buying a little place not far away for her and the boys to live in which again came through to completion without any particular problems.

Not long after she moved in with the boys, but his money ran out, the new girlfriend had dumped him and he came back with his tail rather between his legs. She feeling rather sorry for him but not wishing to resume the relationship, agreed that he could move into the new home but on a lodger basis with him paying towards the bills helping with the boys etc. Whilst the relationship worked at first slowly it all got rather difficult and unworkable to the point, after 2 years that she had to tell him that really he ought to seek a new life for himself and leave the home. He, by now justifying his actions, promptly announced that he wanted "the rest of his money". When she asked what he meant he announced he only took the £6,000 as part payment so that she could buy her house, that half of it belonged to him and that he wanted it sold and his half given to him. It all got very bitter and very litigious. They both instructed lawyers who battled it out what the law did or did not provide.

She contacted me although by then I had left the practice that I had been with at the time of their sale. However, I remembered by default getting them to sign separate instructions on the sale proceeds and therefore suggested she got her lawyers to contact my old practice, seek out the old file and in particular the separate letters signed.

The last I heard was that the two pairs of lawyers met on the actual steps of the court house shortly prior to the hearing and agreed that the case be abandoned as clearly he did not have a case to stand up in court. I still to this day get clients to sign consents separately which I ensure are placed on the file.

I had referred earlier in this book my time when I was able to sneak off early from working at the County Council offices in Aylesbury to attend a completion in the old town of Woburn and visit the offices of Hoburn of Woburn, an old very well established Dickensian style law firm. Well sadly the firm had to close for its own personal reasons but the partner of the practice a Mr.Ornsby Issard-Davis that I had met all those years previous was not quite ready to hang up his hat quite yet and indeed joined our practice but working at another office as the Probate lawyer having many connections with local folks over the years and still handling many of the estates and Probates of such families in the area.

He remained with the firm for quite a few years till finally it was time for him to accept that the time had come for him to retire. A young very capable lawyer Stuart was brought in from his previous job in London to take over from our old chap who he befriended and carried on his tradition extremely proficiently and kept in contact long after he had retired and in fact the old gentleman moved down to Cornwall where he not only bred pug dogs but also was a judge at the Crufts Dog Show as continued a very close link up until he died recently at the age of 100 years.

We have always had to be extra careful who we spoke to and what information we gave relating to clients and clients confidentiality. There was a particular client who again was an old neighbour of mine and whom had got himself into all sorts of problems. One day I received a phone call from an international telegram firm who were trying to locate this particular client as they needed to deliver an urgent international telegram. Suspicions raised, I asked them who or what they were and could they give me more information. They declined saying it was client confidentiality that they had to maintain. I then asked them if they wished to deliver the telegram to me I would as a law practice pass the details and contents on to my client. Again they declined and instead tried to telephone back several times to speak to my secretaries and other members of staff to whom had all been primed and pre warned not to give any information whatsoever away. Again our instincts proved right as there was no such thing as an international telegram company but were instead a dept collection company trying to use foul means and fair to locate a client of ours.

Christmas Shopping

Since I was a youngster for some reason my Mother every year seemed to like to visit London for the day for her Christmas shopping. This had gone on for years and such venues as Shepherds Bush Market and into the west end seemed to be the annual pilgrimage which was never looked forward to or enjoyed actually doing. Equally was the change of venues many years later when Leicester became the target. Leaving early, doing the department stores and the markets and getting home way after dark, replaced the trips to London. I had long since left home establishing my own family when my father decided that enough was enough and put his foot down on the basis that he refused to take my Mother any more to Leicester for her jaunts. In defiance of him she rang me and asked if I would take her if she contributed to the fuel and offered a free lunch. As I was not really particularly busy that Saturday I agreed and her and I set off for her yearly ritual.

Arriving in Leicester we found the same car parking spaces she had used for years, and off we went to troll the market for her bargains, with the promise that at the allotted time we would return the shopping gems to the and saunter off for lunch. Now all the time I was being assured that where we were going for lunch was not the most exquisite of venues. It was clean and reasonable and the food was good and I had to look past the building and to the food and service.

The hour finally arrived when bargains were dumped in the car and off we wobbled to find this extraordinary restaurant that I had heard so much about. Needless to say the description surpassed its actual state and condition when we approached and started to climb the stairs of what appeared to be the fire escape of a very old dilapidated cinema. The only difference was these stairs seemed to carry us up several floors of bare brick walls and bare concrete floors which were very dimly lit. With each step my mother must have heard me grumbling and she tried to reassure me that all would be well and it would be worth it in the end.

As we approached the final floor the décor suddenly took on a change and instead of dim dark and dingy suddenly became very Christmas festive with red carpets decorations and a lot more cheerful. Then my heart sank, a queue. Now I am not very good with queues, at airports, at railway stations in fact at not many locations but worse of all when I am hungry and need to eat, but again the assurances that all would be well. We slowly shuffled up the stairs with all the other shoppers, loaded with bags baskets and children. As we neared the top of the stairs and round the last corner the décor again seemed to step up yet another grade, although the doors of the restaurant looked rather dark and foreboding. It was at this point I began to question whether my Mother was in fact in the right location and that this was definitely the restaurant. What I had failed to notice in my own irritation and the eternity it had taken to climb the stairs to our final location was that there was a rather lot of women in the queue, but those majority of women all had children. The children were also very young children. This awareness became acute when having asked my Mother for assurances that this was not a time wasting exercise and that we really were queuing up for our food that a fellow queue member promptly replied, "Oh no dear, this is not the queue for the restaurant. This is the queue for Father Christmas!"

My humiliation knew no bounds as we retreated past hoards of laughing mums and bewildered children looking at this rather red-faced grown up accompanied by his Mother departing from Santa's Grotto! My

Mother has never been completely forgiven and the shopping trips to Leicester failed to repeat themselves in ensuing years.

One of the several building firms I acted for had successfully completed numerous developments within Milton Keynes and had gained the reputation of one of the better builders in the area. For this reason they were given a very lucrative building contract to build seven houses on a small area of land close to a very prestigious village. The Corporation were looking for their first very large houses that would in fact be sold for over £100,000, which by today's standards is very small but then would be equal to the first million pound house being built and sold. These houses were huge. Built behind a very private wall there were three driveways serving clusters of four and three houses. Each house had a private section of driveway that could house up to six cars with large garaging.

Everyone at that time just raised their eyebrows. How on earth anyone could afford, let alone try to sell a house for more than £100,000? However the houses started to take shape the interest was phenomenal and it was not long before they were all sold before construction and now form part of a very exclusive area.

I should really, before I move on and close this chapter of my career and the reasons why I left the practice to pursue my destiny, pay tribute to my Mentor Pete Collier who meant so much to me then, as he does now even though he is no longer with us. Peter was a giant of a man who loved his wife his daughter and was proud of his family, including his brother, his parents and all his relations. There was nothing he would do for his family and his close friends. I was to be honoured by a touch of this generosity when during a very difficult and emotional breakup of my marriage, the three most unlikely people I ended up turning to and found I could rely upon was the senior partner, Roger Fennemore, who told me that he would not let me have any time off, that he was going to work me even harder than before, to get myself back to Mum for a few days because I would not even be able to make a decision about what tie to wear. The second senior partner, Chris Hilton-Johnson, who personally drove me to his friend and very good matrimonial lawyer and ended paying the matrimonial lawyer's bill to get me legally straightened out. Not to forget Peter who was there every morning, every lunchtime and every evening to make sure I was on the straight and narrow and able to cope.

One bitterly cold winter's afternoon, when staff were being released early to try to make their way home in the blizzard we were experiencing, he travelled exactly the opposite way to his own home in the villages. He was going to try to meet up with my wife the to see if there was anything he could do to try to save my marriage. Failing in his attempt he then had to travel back into Milton Keynes and then out into the country lanes driving in the dark around the snow drifts and abandoned cars. I will confess that every year, at midnight, on New Year`s Eve I quietly raise my glass to toast his name.

Peter and I would meet again professionally later on in my career for a brief period but would end very tragically. Shortly before I left the practice Peter had already departed with another of the partners and Cathy, who had found the photographs of my dead client. Peter had gone back to his beloved Leighton Buzzard, a market town where he had practiced many years before. He had gone back to seek out old clients and contacts and to continue his own success story. The senior partner, Roger Fennemore, also left the practice having been offered a most lucrative career in the new Docklands developments. Here he was going to be part of a large corporate team to develop part of the new dockland investment. Life without them all didn't seem to be as exciting or demanding as it had been. My mentor and partners that I looked up to had gone. Those that remained worked on.

Lloyds Court, Central Milton Keynes

Life became repetitive with time and seasons passing. At the end of the financial year I was surprised to be offered a "bonus scheme" instead of a wage rise. I tried to argue that I did not need a bonus to work hard. It was part of the package of being a successful conveyancer. I had a regular flow work, I loved my job and really all I needed was that little recognition of a small salary rise. This argument fell on stony ground and I was told that I had a target to meet. That target was set at £65,000. However, anything above that sum I would earn a percentage. From £65,000 to £70,000 it would represent a 25% bonus and anything above £70,000 would represent a 30% bonus. Needless to say, I was extremely disgruntled and very insecure at this new arrangement.

At this time I was representing both developer clients as well as private clients and one of my colleagues was struggling to cope with domestic conveyancing. He never really settled into Milton Keynes and wanted to return to the North. Eventually he threw the towel in and handed his notice in that August. It just so happened that by the end of September I reached my first milestone of £65,000. My colleague, being aware of the constraints on me, donated his files and his clients to me, so with this extra workload I reached my £70,000 by November and thus received my 25% of the £5,000. This could not have come at a better time as the washing machine had just blown up and needed replacing along with a new cooker.

I was steaming along and during December January and February my fees were going through the roof and one partner was actually overheard saying, "Don't give him any more work – he is earning more than me!"

Indeed! My costs went up to nearly £130,000 and my bonus exceeded my annual salary. So much so that I was able to furnish my new home that I was with all new furniture. I calculated that this year would be a one off and that next year's offer would not be repeated. I made sure therefore that I had spent the money wisely, that we furnished our home with everything that would last. Some of the furniture still exists after some 30 years.

Sadly my prediction was fulfilled. The end of March approached and the inevitable meeting with the personnel partner and the chief accountant took place. It was an uncomfortable meeting in which I pleaded my own defence that all I had wanted a year before was a reasonable salary increase and not a bonus. The scheme thought up by the accountant had caused bad feeling amongst the partners and fee earners had made me stand out to my detriment in the practice. I was then offered a small salary increase but advised that I would have to forfeit the company car.

This was a complete slap in the face and totally unexpected. At that point I decided that perhaps it was time for me to move on. I had been with the practice for a number of years. The best years, in my opinion had passed. The time had come to now move on. Keith Wylde, that rather brash young college mate I knew many years earlier, was now part of a large and very modern and successful practice. I had mentioned on the phone to him that I was becoming disillusioned and was summoned to a meeting. Within days I was offered a job to start before Christmas. I accepted and so my destiny was to move to the next stepping-stone.

7 Days in Northampton

Introduction to computers and Technology

For political purposes and unknown to myself at the time I was not going to end up working in Milton Keynes although this was really where I belonged. I knew all the estate titles and had built up a good working bank of clients and contacts. Instead my new practice wanted me to transfer to Northampton, a town that I knew as a child for visiting, shopping, leisure activities and theatre. I knew nothing about it as place to work. However I was happy to take up the challenge.

The Dunstable Office

Before an actual position was open I was to travel over to the Dunstable Office to help the partner there. Dunstable was then very much falling onto its knees, having lost most of the Vauxhalls industry along with AC Delcos where my Mother had once worked some 30 years before. Conveyancing was very slow and most of the local practices were based in Luton. In Dunstable there were a couple of firms, including the one I joined that had established itself through the hard efforts of the partner in charge. I arrived at the little office that I was to occupy only for a couple of months whilst caretaking the position for a conveyancer who was working out his notice from his job in Luton. During my time in Dunstable I was to enjoy meeting some of the characters that made up the town and its history.

One story that comes to mind was about a rather shady couple who were selling their property to buy a narrow boat. The sale proceeded through to exchange of contracts and then to completion. Funds were taken in, the mortgage re-paid and the net equity duly telegraphed to the clients. A few days later, the lawyer acting for the buyer rang in a bit of a panic. She had failed to put in hand her land registry search and horror of horrors the search revealed that a second charge had been registered against the title after the office copy entries had been issued. On our side we would not know of such further charge or registration and it was up to the buyer's solicitors to make sure adequate searches were carried out before completion. Then they would duly notify us so that we could clear any further loan. We were only aware of the one mortgage, which we dealt with and paid off. We were never informed of the other mortgage and by the time we had been put on notice it was too late. This left a rather bitter taste in my mouth so I chased this couple from one end of England to the other to try to persuade them to do the honourable thing and pay the money paid into the account to clear the second mortgage. Despite assurances that they would pop into the office to settle they never did and I am afraid this poor conveyancing lady had a very expensive lesson. The money would have to be claimed on the practice insurance.

Every Friday as part of the hearts and minds exercise for his staff the partner used to close the office for the lunchtime period while everyone went off to the local pub for a beer and some sandwiches. It created a bonding with the staff, and also was a way of getting to know if there were any problems. The system worked very well and the office was a close-knit and well-organised happy group. The litigation solicitor at that time was a chap called Ian, who was not a partner but an assistant solicitor. Ian was a really great guy although not very old. He had tried several times to be made up to partner of the practice but had so far failed. One Friday lunchtime, as we were all wandering over to the pub, he was coming back in the other direction from the police station where he had been called earlier that morning to represent a chap held on remand and represented under legal aid. When Ian was asked if he was going to be able to join us he shrugged his shoulders a little annoyed as he was going to have to go back to the station. He didn't mind losing his lunch hour but he was irritated by his time being taken with this particular "crime". The man has been caught in a rather "compromising position" with his own pet dog by a member of his family who called the police. Unfortunately I did not stay in Dunstable long enough to learn of the outcome.

What I did learn some years later more or less at the time I left the practice was that young Ian had been rejected yet again as a partner. A few days later, after a remarkable series of events, Ian ended up in charge of the office.

It was quite sad in later years because the set of offices that this practice had was to suffer the slump felt up and down the country and as a result some offices were closed, and a couple offered to partners in situ to avoid closing. The partner at that time was not fully qualified albeit that the arrangements gave him the partner-in-charge status. This meant that to remain open a qualified solicitor would have to take over responsibility and ownership. Now Ian had been trying for some time to become a partner but was always refused. Now all of a sudden, having gone home on a Friday night as an assistant solicitor, he came back on the Monday morning as owner of the practice and in reverse, the chap who enjoyed partner status on the Friday night suddenly on the Monday morning was demoted to the assistant. Which was all very bizarre. What was even more tragic to follow was that young Ian who really had the rest of his life before him to enjoy his hard-earned status suddenly died leaving a huge void and a problem without a qualified partner. I understand that the practice was taken over but the original chap in charge quietly disappeared into retirement. The entire practice has now gone and another casualty to the desperate times that have befallen the industry.

The Northampton Office

I finally took up my position in Northampton where they had installed a rather splendid computer file management system that I had not come across before. Certainly up to this point I had worked with the old regime of dictating my work, the tapes being taken away to be processed by one or two (in my later days at my last practice) secretaries who would then produce their work at the end of the day for checking and signing. Although I had always had my own typewriter on my desk and was capable of producing my own work in small doses here the stable door was flung wide open and an opportunity for me to produce whatever I wanted and at speed. Not even knowing how to even turn a computer on, the senior partner took it upon himself to give me some "soft lessons" while waiting for the technical boys to return from holidays. Each day I would pick up another piece of information and by the end of the first week I had definitely adapted to this new technological lifestyle. When the Technical lads came and started showing me even more useful tips and, although I did have secretaries, I was able to institute my *clear desk policy*. This is still my practice today. Everything that comes to my desk is dealt with the same day. The system was brilliant and I took to it like a duck to water. In the early days it was very much a typist's system working with DOS and a keyboard. Nowadays the system is more advanced and the mouse is an integral part.

However this was a good start on the road to what has been a major advancement in my career.

The staff at my new firm was very partial to practical jokes! It was a very young and friendly firm to work for but each day we all had to be on our toes for fear of what might be played against us. One January I was due to take the family and friends on a skiing holiday to Austria. We had booked a coach to take us at some ungodly hour of the morning to Stansted. I left the office at 5.30pm and drove home to get an early night and rise in the early hours. When I got home there had been a phone call from the Technical chap's daughter, so I rang back and was told that her

103

Dad was on his way over to me to pick up the firm's car, which was needed while I was away. She added that she wanted him to call when he got there. He had still not turned up by 8 o'clock despite another phone call from his daughter to ask whether he had arrived. By this time I decided I would get my head down for a few hours so without any further delays I climbed into bed and dropped off till the alarm went off in the early hours. I asked if John, the Technical chap, had turned up but he hadn't and so we cleared off for our fortnight's holiday. When I returned it was revealed that the whole exercise was a total wind up, a ruse to keep me up so I would be like a wet dishcloth the next day. Thinking very quickly on my feet, I turned the whole situation round to my own advantage and announced that whilst I thought it was all very funny and a good wheeze that it had in fact backfired rather tragically. My wife at that time had in fact stayed up in my absence to wait for John to turn up, and unfortunately because she did not get any sleep and suffering terribly with her neck and arms had ended up not being able to ski for days, had ended up in her surgical collar and the whole farce had cost her quite a few days of her holiday. Their faces were an absolute picture as they turned from a success story of yet another trick being played to realisation that they had created a total disaster. I had to make a quick phone call home as flowers were being ordered and all sorts of apologies being drafted and delivered and we were still "cashing in" on the "tragedy" nearly a year later at the office party when she met the perpetrators of the crime. Hopefully one of them will be reading this and realise that we, not they, actually had the final laugh.

One of the young lawyers in our office, David Ruddle, was a real man about town. Smart well-liked and always with a huge smile on his face. In the 1980s the word "yuppy" (young, upwardly mobile) was in fashion and David fitted the stereotype. He loved his job and the techie toys that went with it and was, I suppose, a bit of a young poser, although every one had such great respect for him. One day he had left his practice golf umbrella unattended. Seeing my opportunity I sought my revenge for the skiing incident and emptied the entire contents of my hole punch into it and then did the umbrella up and stood it back in its position. He collected the umbrella each day, went off up the town for his lunch, returned putting the umbrella back in its position. This went on for a week. The wait was agonising. Finally, at 1.15pm on a Friday lunchtime there was a muffled howl, followed by slight cursing and mild swearing as young David returned to the office red-faced but still grinning. He seemed to know who the offender was as he came straight to my office. He took the joke in the best possible manner as only he could but he did mention, as he left the office, that a rather attractive girl was coming up the street and as it had started to rain, he thought he would impress her. As she drew next to him he offered her shelter under his umbrella. At which point he popped it up to shower both of them with lots of lovely little coloured circles of paper! He was still chuckling with the embarrassment some hours later. He has remained friends ever since and occasionally does get the odd dig in to remind me what I did to him that day.

Castillian Street, where we had our offices.

Another young and rather well-dressed conveyancer in our practice was called Andrew Gordon. Andrew, although a really great chap, did not possess the same sense of humour as David so playing tricks on him was not going to be taken in quite the same sense of humour as he did rather take life rather more seriously. This firm held end of the month meetings in more or less the same format as the previous practice. On one occasion, we were all sitting about in the lounge area of the hotel before we went into the formal meeting and one of the fee earners asked me what sort of crazy stunt I was planning for myself in the near future. By this time I had gained a bit of a reputation of having a go at all sorts of sports, with sailing, water skiing, cycling, running, snow skiing, rough shooting and canoeing, to name but a few. I had in fact been quietly working on an idea, which would raise a little money for the Willen Hospice charity, located not too far away from my home. What I announced was that I was planning to cycle to work one Saturday (we had to attend the office one Saturday every fortnight) and then after work cycle home and hopefully if I could rally enough interest maybe we could raise some money from members of the practice as well as sources who we were in contact with. As we were discussing this, young Andrew, in the comfort of the hotel lounge and with the warmth of a couple of beers inside him volunteered to accompany me. The partner agreed that if we wore the practice's football strips he would ensure the partnership would contribute. The next day I set about telephoning a few Estate Agents and contacts to see if any one would be interested. Very quickly names were being written down and donations pledged. At this point I remembered our young volunteer from the night before, so instead of drafting one sponsorship form I drafted two, one for myself and one for him. During the day, and especially lunchtime I contacted numerous firms and individuals and by late afternoon had quite a healthy sponsorship on the two forms. At this point I thought it best if I perhaps went and announced my success to our young enthusiast. Walking into his room I told him that he was in fact doing very well with his sponsorship to which he looked totally blank at me. I then reminded him of his offer the previous evening and handed him his sponsorship form which had accumulated quite a few names on to which he went red faced, looked at me in total and utter disbelief and then announced that he had not even got a bicycle. As I left the room I just shouted over my shoulder that perhaps it would be a good idea if he found one as we would be launching ourselves off from Milton Keynes the following week Saturday. For my own part I took out my old Austrian Puche bike and over the ensuing evenings took myself off for a few test rides in and around Milton Keynes. I had been cycling now for many months so preparation really had already taken place. As for our young Andrew I learnt afterwards that he approached my old mate the cheeky lad from college days Keith Wylde and now one of the senior partners, who told him bluntly that he couldn't let me, the firm nor, most importantly, the sponsors down. He offered Andrew his own bike so that he could get himself fit! (I did say previously that the entire practice including partners were always up for playing a trick or two against one another and in particular their staff). Anyway young Andrew puffed and peddled his way round various courses over the ensuing nights to try to persuade his legs to move the pedals easily. He was not really very advanced into his super-fit aspirations when we met at 7:15am outside Newport Pagnell fire station on a rather chilly Saturday morning. We put on our football shirts and were waved off by a couple of partners and those that couldn't sleep and wanted to see first hand this strange spectacle. We set off side by side but after a couple of hundred yards I looked behind me and the promising young athlete was nowhere to be seen. I realised that he must have doubled back and taken the back route past the famous Newport Pagnell Motorway services and would pop out on the road several miles ahead of me. The only thing to do was to get my head down, get the legs moving and pick up speed. One sponsor had already said that if I could make the journey to the office in less than an hour he would double his sponsorship, so this was an added incentive. I pedalled my legs off to reach the point where he would pop out in front of me and no sign either up the hill leading from the back road, or indeed in front of me heading to my destination, so no choice but to carry on legs pushing as hard as they could to try to catch him. No luck, I arrived at the office in just under an hour and went to find our new urban Olympian to discover that he was not there at all! I couldn't have passed him so where on earth was he? Over three quarters of an hour later he appeared extremely red-faced and out of breath, managing to whisper one or two rather mis-descriptions of my good self. When I asked what on earth happened it seemed that as he set off his chain had dislodged, so he dismounted and quickly re-fitted it, but when he looked up I had set off at a pace and he never saw me again till he arrived at the office. Needless to say the return journey was not going to be welcomed with great warmth and enthusiasm for either of us but the witching hour arrived and off I went, again with no sign of our young friend. We had a pre-arranged meeting at a local pub in the middle of Milton Keynes. I was back again in just on the hour to a well deserved pint. Again some half hour plus later I recognised his car as it appeared round the corner and he confirmed that he had struggled to get back to home where he quickly swapped two for four wheels to complete his trip to the pub. We did collect over a £1,000 pounds for our chosen charity and were proud of our achievement, even though I still get ribbed to this day by the not so young Andrew. He decided to end his cycling career after that one occasion. AS far as I know has not been on a serious bike ride since. As for me I went on to other charity events to be disclosed later in this book and as for my cycling I have achieved the 100 miler and have swapped the old Puche for a modern 27 gear Spanish racing cycle that certainly would have been more than welcome back on that cold autumn Saturday morning, now so long ago!

Communicating without Mobile Phones

One thing I learned from my peers is that a client's appreciation curve climbs steadily to the day of completion and then quickly falls away. Whatever you have done for your client up to the day of completion will be quickly forgotten but what and how you handle the situation on the day of completion will be that which the client will remember. For this reason I always ensure that the crescendo slowly builds to the climax on the day of moving. I lead the client along to that day making sure that they settle the gas and electricity bills, have water meters read, agree agents fees, make themselves aware of the redemption figures from the lenders and drop keys off the day before completion. On the day everything should go as smoothly as possible, although there are always exceptions to the rule.

One I recall was a couple selling their home in Northampton and moving off to Wales. The gentleman had come into the office on the Wednesday to go through the final documentation and have the final procedures explained to him to avoid such problems on the day of completion. The day of completion, Friday, arrived and by mid morning the purchaser was dancing up and down demanding keys to a property that his solicitors had not yet paid for, and was most disgruntled because they were not being released to him. Lunchtime arrived as did the purchaser at our offices once more demanding his keys. He was advised that until funds arrived he could not and would not be having any keys. My client in the meantime had dutifully deposited keys with the Estate Agents, packed up and departed for Wales. In these days we had no mobile phones but had to rely upon the use of public telephones. Eventually at mid-lunchtime the funds arrived and so I telephoned the Estate Agents to release the keys. To my horror the Agents announced that they did not have any keys, and the client had definitely not left them with the Agents.

What on earth could I do? I was not going to be able to ring my client on his mobile for at least another 25 years. The purchaser was now justified to being on the warpath threatening to sue every one that was preventing him from entering his new home. The only course open was for me to ring the Estate Agents in Wales where he would appear for his own keys for his own new property and ask them rather oddly not to give him the keys for his new property till he rang me back. The Estate Agents must have obliged as the client rather mystified called me within the hour. I announced that we had a problem at this end as he had not delivered the keys to the Estate Agents. He pleaded innocence and proclaimed that he had indeed delivered the keys to the Agents; in fact he went there straight from our meeting on Wednesday. He then described his journey on foot from our offices, up to the top of the hill turned left in St. Giles Street, down St. Giles street to the Square where he turned left and then halfway down the hill popped into the Estate Agents and gave keys to the gentleman inside. I went back over his journey with him and when we got to the square I pointed out that he could not have turned left and down that road as this was Bridge Street and clearly he should have gone straight over the square and down Gold Street where the Estate Agents were located. No, he was most insistent. He got to the corner of the square where the bank was, turned left, went down and saw the large sign outside the Estate Agents went in and dutifully delivered the keys. The Penny dropped!! I understood what he had done. I asked him to hang on for a few minutes while I checked thing out. I quickly rang the Estate Agents and told them I now knew where his keys were. Could they possibly nip down the road from Gold Street, where they had their offices, to Bridge Street, where the keys were. Sure enough, half way down on the right was a huge sign of a Key. You see the Estate Agents then were called "Key Consultants." The Key the client had spotted was outside the hardware store. He had not noticed when he went through the door that the "estate agent" was dressed in a brown overall standing in front of screw drivers and hammers rather than someone in a white shirt and tie behind a desk,

The Agent burst in and asked the hardware man if a client had dropped some keys off to him Wednesday? The gentleman half turned, took some keys off the hook and handed them to the Agent announcing that a strange chap had come in and said that "his solicitor had asked him to drop them in to them to hold safe till Friday." He guessed there was a good story somewhere! We all laughed about this one for years after.

At the time of my career with this practice I heard of one cautionary tale. It did not happen to our practice but we were all aware of one case. On the day of completion a young couple had collected their keys and toddled off to move into their new home. When they got to the door they felt it a little strange that curtains were still up and the property still looked lived in. When they tried the keys the door wouldn't open so they knocked on the door and an old lady came to the door and asked if she could help them. They said that this was their new home, that completion had taken place that morning and these were the keys for them to move in. "Oh No dearies . . . this is not your house yours is the one a few doors down." The couple protested that the lady was mistaken, as this was the one that they had viewed and in fact had been back to look several times and the one they had decided to purchase. Oh no the old lady continued, you saw this one as it was in better condition than the one you have purchased but you have definitely bought the one a few doors down. A quick visit back to the conveyancer involved and indeed the property they believed was the one they were purchasing turned out not to be the one that the lawyers had bought for them. There was an awful row and litigation proceedings commenced against the firm for negligence.

Bidding up Your Own Bid

One of the clients we represented at that time was a personal friend of the senior partner who dabbled in buying old properties and land and successfully developing both private and commercial premises. We had acted on several occasions without too much fuss. One time he decided that he wanted to purchase a property but was a little embarrassed as he knew his own architect was also hoping to bid for the same property and didn't want to bid against him. He asked the senior partner if perhaps he would agree to attend the auction, and at a given point start bidding if necessary against the architect. The partner agreed and on the day of the auction they toddled off together to see if they could succeed in their conspiracy. Some hours later the senior partner returned with a huge grin on his face and he could hardly contain himself to tell the story.

When they got to the Auction sure enough the Architect was in attendance. The senior partner therefore separated from his client and worked his way towards the edge of the auction room where he placed himself strategically to be seen by the auctioneer. The auctioneer turned his attention to the property in question and the bidding commenced. It slowly increased to the given level that the senior partner had been instructed to join in and so he signalled to the Auctioneer and joined in on the bidding. He did not look at his client to give the game away or indeed to the gentleman sat some rows behind him who became more and more enthusiastic to outbid the senior partner to secure the bid. After all other bidders had been cleared off, and eventually exhausting the competition bidder, the senior partner secured the property for his client although he did have to go several thousand pounds above the agreed limit. Even so, he felt sure his client would be delighted that the little conspiracy had worked. After the auction he caught up with his client outside the auction rooms and was rather surprised to learn that it was not in fact the Architect that had been bidding against him at all. In fact the Architect had given up some time before the end. So who was it that was bidding against the senior partner and had pushed the price up to a larger level than expected. The client looked rather sheepish till the penny dropped with the partner who asked him jokingly that it was not him that had been bidding against him to which he confessed that indeed it was. But why the partner asked, he had secured it, and the property was already his. The client simply announced that he was having such fun and had got carried

110

away that he couldn't stop bidding even though it was against his own agent in the same bid. It takes all sorts I suppose.

My Car Gets Stolen

One afternoon I was at my desk working as usual when the telephone rang and the senior partner asked if I knew where my car was? I found this rather curious but said that it was parked in the usual place in the public car park further down the street. He suggested I check "Here we go again!" was my first thought but best go along with what ever scheme was being hatched. So I put on my jacket and wandered down to the car park to find that the company car, (surprise, surprise) had disappeared. I went back to the office to confirm that the car had gone. He then gave me a telephone number and asked if I could contact them and discuss the company car. I returned to my room I made the call to the "local police station" to be advised that the company car had been found in a car park in Bedford some 20 miles away. Going along with the story I gave them the details of the car and described what was in it and was then asked if I could make yet another phone call to the "Bedford police station" which I obliged them with the next call. Again we went through the motions of advising what had happened, giving details of the car, the make, the colour and registration. At this point the story was beginning to sound too true to be false and it began to dawn on me as the conversations progressed I began to actually realise that this was not in fact a spoof, that the company car that it had indeed been stolen.

It seems that I had been unlucky that my company car that had been chosen for a joy ride. On the other hand good fortune had a plain police car parked in the car park at the Bedford railway car park waiting for cars to be taken from the car park and was least expecting a stolen car to be driven in. There had been a spate of car thefts in Bedford. They were suspicious of the occupants and radioed the registration number, and learned that the owners were a firm of solicitors. The occupants hardly fitted that profile so the police brought in back up, boxed the car in, and arrested the occupants, who then confessed that they had indeed taken the car from Northampton. They had driven it to Bedford to find a quiet parking space, park it, and then abandon it. Unluckily for them they were caught. Whilst this was all going on I was completely unaware of the fact and it was pure luck that I had not finished work at 6.00 o'clock, walked to the car park and found my ride back to Milton Keynes had disappeared. I asked a fellow staff member to drive me over to Bedford, where we met the police. After careful inspection of the vehicle and noting that nothing had in fact been taken and only very minor damage caused, I was allowed to drive the car home. The only thing lost in this incident was that I was about half an hour late home from the usual time.

Back to the Office

Having learnt lessons from the couple selling in Dunstable a property with a second mortgage and of course my bankrupt purchaser some years earlier, I was always keen to make my searches against the land registry and against the purchaser as soon as possible after exchange. These searches often came back without any problems but obviously against common names such as Smith, Brown or Jones there were often entries that needed to be certified by the client to enable the purchase to go ahead. There is nothing particularly unusual in this for most conveyancers. However, on this particular day was a there was a pending action in Bankruptcy against the client's name. This set the alarm bells ringing. I noticed that the client's surname was that of a chip shop owner in South London. I posted the search to the client to ask him to kindly certify that it was nothing to do with him and expected it back in the next post. Instead I received a phone call from a very irate client most put out that I could suggest that this could be him and he did not own a chip shop in South London. I explained that this was a normal procedure that we had to carry out the search and I was sending it to him not to accuse him but rather to get him to certify it that it wasn't him. No this clearly was not good enough and he was not going to sign it because it was not him. We went round in circles for quite some time trying to get the penny to drop that we both knew it was not him, and to convince the world that it was not him could he simply certify the search. It took all my persuasive powers to get him to finally concede, and to understand what I was trying to say to him and to sign and return to me. Sometimes folks are very difficult to convince that you are actually on their side.

I had mentioned that I had at that time two secretaries covering my work. One was a rather emotional girl, and highly charged. She seemed to have all sorts of emotional problems in her personal life. I tried where ever possible to understand and to be her "best buddy" in times of issue even allowing her to take time off at short notice to enable her to go off to sort out what ever crisis had befallen at that particular time. However, it is often said that you cannot run with the fox and hunt with the hounds, and that doctrine did come back to bite me, because I was trying to be a best friend and an understanding employer. Yet for some reason she saw this as threatening and she was quietly complaining to my bosses about me behind my back. I was summoned to explain what was going on and while I had every sympathy up to that point my patience very quickly ran

112

out when I discovered what she had in fact been doing. Asked what I wanted to do I simply said that I could not have staff working for me that clearly were not working with me and undermining me and my professionalism behind my back. I was therefore given full authority to deal with the situation however I wanted even to the point of dismissing the offender. With heavy heart I returned to my office, called the secretary in and simply asked what I had done to upset her, and why she had turned against me with the things she had been saying to the partners. A whole different character then appeared before me. It was quite disturbing and I had not encountered this type of person before. After trying to discuss the situation it became quite clear that there was a real problem, jealousy or what ever it was, that prevented us continuing to work together so without further ado I asked her if she would please return to her desk and collect her belongings and leave. She called her partner who attended the offices rather sheepishly to collect her and her belongings and she left the office in a whirlwind. I hoped that I would not have to confront either her or that situation again. I was correct in the latter but not the former as I will explain further in the years to follows.

After what seemed to be a very happy few years based in Northampton working for what I considered was a very good firm with very modern ideas and practices, the bottom fell out of the domestic market and the inevitable happened. Estate Agents were closing, banks and building societies were shedding staff, and as we were primarily a conveyancing practice it was not long before the entire firm started to look inwards to cut back staff and offices. One office was closed altogether, others were offered to the partners in charge. such as the Dunstable Office previously discussed, and another, whilst our office and the Milton Keynes office struggled to keep afloat. This meant only one thing, that myself and others were going to be made redundant. My very good friend at the time Norman, who was working at a local market town office, was summoned to a very difficult meeting where he was given redundancy to take effect immediately. As he lived in the North he was released on full pay till the end of his notice. I was not long before I was called in and given the sad news. It was just so totally beyond my wildest imagination that a time would arrive when lawyers were going to be made redundant. It just never happened,: they moved on, retired or even passed away but never became redundant. However, I was asked to stay for the three months to work out my notice and in which time I could contact recruitment agencies and look for other employment. Within six weeks, after I had attended several interviews, I was offered the post of a commercial lawyer at a firm just off Oxford Circus. where based on my limited experience with building contracts and developers. I was therefore able to leave at the end of my notice period with full dignity and pride and was going to another job without the stigma of actually being out of work. By the time I left a staff of over 27 had been reduced to a mere half dozen, including the two partners. It was a very sad time. However, I was grateful to Keith and the practice to be able to learn all about computers and computer systems This has been a great benefit to me ever since.

8 Commercial Work in the Capital

Throughout my working career I had travelled into London on numerous occasions for completions, attending college and for a whole host of other reasons. I had got to know and love my Capital City, as a visitor. The thought of actually working in London had never entered my head apart from when I was about to leave school with a fleeting desire to follow a career in journalism. London had always been to me hours away on cramped and cold trains and London streets were always dirty, busy and unfamiliar so my first instincts about working in London were not positive. The first thing I had to get used to was getting to the station early to allow time to get to the office. My daily journey was now an hour and a half whereas my previous travel time to work had been an hour at most. This added an extra hour to the day.

The Offices on Oxford Street, London

I arrived on my first day and found the staff were all very friendly and surprisingly, after having my head filled with images drawn from films, quite normal. My office was quite roomy and overlooked Oxford Street, where life is quite full and entertaining. When you visit London for the day or a few hours shopping you don't realise that there is in fact a whole community that exists on the streets. Only by working there do you come to understand it. Every day you see the same street cleaners, window dressers, staff and workers. Every day the same street buskers take their pitch and ply their trade to persuade the public to part with their money. One day I was watching a new busker from my office window when the old busker turned up. An almighty argument arose because the new guy had taken the traditional place of the incumbent, as it were. Accusations that it was his place and the new chap should move on got louder and this in itself became entertainment for the passing shoppers. Inevitably the heated argument came to an exchange of fists coupled with swearing and cursing until the Police turned up and stopped the squabble. These two old boys were sent away still shouting abuse and curses at each other.

It's monotonous travelling into London every day. Nobody talks to each other, or even recognises that anyone else is on the train. A newspaper is all very well but day after day, in both directions becomes very boring and tedious. Do you buy a book? How many books can you actually read before again it all becomes boring.

Skiing in Italy

It was about this time that we had returned from a skiing trip at a small beginners resort high in the Italian Mountains. It became a regular place to visit for some years to come. We absolutely fell in love with the little hotel and the locals, so much so that I really wanted to improve on the few Italian words that I had learnt from a child travelling with parents to this wonderful country. John, an old regular visitor from Chelmsford and later to become a very good friend in the following years, also felt that this was the place he would be revisiting regularly. He too out of respect for the village and the hotel would show the courtesy of learning a few words to speak to them in their own language. And so, John and I swapped notes, and audio-tapes to help each other. He then told me about a book that the BBC had just printed called "Buongiorno Italia". So hot-footing into Regent Street and the BBC bookshop I quickly located the book and found my salvation. For the next two years travelling backwards and forwards on the trains to and from home I learned Italian.

I can now announce to the world that I have found the perfect place for studying. It beats any library or quiet corner and that is the commuter train. You see there is a secret code that you have to learn. Immediately you step on to the platform you must take your place at the same spot every morning, sit in the same seat on the same side facing the same direction and there is total silence. You don't speak to anyone, you don't acknowledge anyone and it is as if the whole carriage is empty and only you are on it. So with total isolation you have the perfect place for study without any form of interference, irritation or annoyance whatsoever. I started by reading a few pages, then going back and writing out the pages, converting what I had written with the English version below. After a chapter I would then go back to the beginning and start again. The more I got into the book the more the studying took over. The entire book was actually written around the very places that my parents and I had visited as a child. I have the fondest memories of old towns, churches, market places, camp-sites, fishermen and all the smells and sight and feelings of the northern towns of Italy. I was back there every time I picked the book up to read and write. Often I would arrive in London and find myself the only one on the train as I carried on writing long after everyone had departed. Each time I returned to Italy I would try out my new words and new sentences and quickly found a whole new world opened up once I was able to understand and be understood. By the end of the two years that took me to and from London I had in fact written out the entire book twice and could ask for punnets of strawberries, what time does the train go, which platform, ask for shoes, rooms, prices, and all the necessities required of a tourist in a foreign country. My high point came when while skiing my ex-wife had suffered a ski injury and was in the hospital at Sondrio, a town some 25 miles down the mountain. The buses had stopped running for three hours and I had to hitch a lift with a local and was able to keep the conversation going all the way to the doors of the hospital. When I arrived back at the hotel that evening, the week's guests that we had arrived with had departed and a fresh party had arrived. After the hotel owner had asked me in Italian how the day had gone, an English lady asked me what had happened and how things were in English and I found myself translating what she had just asked me into Italian and answered her back in English. Unfortunately my skill these days has greatly diminished as I have not been able to study quite as well as I did in my travelling years. Also when we do visit Italy the Italians seem to insist that they must to practice their English rather than allow me speak to them in Italian.

As for John, we kept in touch for many years after that. I normally telephoned him to ask if he was going to travel out to Chiesa that next year to which he always replied, "Of course!" It got to the point that he would fly out mid-December with his skiing equipment and leave it there for the season. He booked a season ticket, and usually spent Christmas and New Year at Chiesa, then fly home to do some work. He would gather one of his sons to drive back to Chiesa in February and stay as long as he could until the snow finally melted. He argued with the powers that be every end of season to allow him to buy his season ticket for the next season without avail. However, he did persuade the hotel to store all his equipment in the off-season and then he would spend his summer on the golf course until winter returned. Sadly John was on the golf course when he suddenly suffered a massive heart attack and died before he hit the ground. Knowing John as I did, this was probably one of the best ways to go. As for his family, one of them had the task of trying to retrieve his equipment from the hotel and the generous hotel owner gave them a free week's skiing as a tribute to John.

Some Big Commercial Deals

So my career had started in the great Commercial world in London. I did not have a clue what was expected of me only that I was going to be involved in leasehold commercial work involving factories, offices, shops and other commercial premises. Our main "client" was an ex-partner of the practice who had built up a huge portfolio of commercial premises. He had properties all over the country and soon found himself having to break away from the day to day running of his normal law practice and set up an office separate to ours, in Regent Street, to run this mini empire. The man had no personality whatsoever and ruled with an iron fist. He frightened many that came into contact with him including his own staff.

Once he was due to fly off on a Friday afternoon to New York to attend a party and having worked his girls double time through the morning eventually rumbled off into a taxi at lunchtime to head to Heathrow. His staff breathed a huge sigh of relief to at least finish one week in a more relaxed atmosphere. To their horror he walked back in at just after 4.00 pm as he could not justify going to enjoy himself in New York with so much work to do. He and his staff both worked late that evening.

He was a ruthless man and as a result of encountering men like him, I decided that I would not enter into any commercial work again after I left. However, this chap had a stalker, a female. We never really did get to know the full story but she apparently was totally besotted by him. She would send him presents, messages and phone calls. She would visit him and wait for him even though he gave her no encouragement. Quite to his disbelief and distaste. Unfortunately the ardour wore off and one evening after work, when the entrepreneur was leaving his office, she suddenly lunged out of the shadows, knife in hand, and stabbed him. He was injured but it was not fatal. However, there were obviously sufficient grounds for a restraining order to be issued against her, and although there was always the fear that this "bunny boiler" would reappear, such an event never happened. Life resumed some normality although care was taken when leaving the building and returning home.

A commercial transaction of huge significance and size was presented to us. It was a joint venture purchase of a huge commercial shopping centre in one of the new towns circling London at a price of some fifty million pounds. It comprised 50 separate leases ranging from small units up to a major supermarket and it was to be built with under ground car parking. I spent day after day, week after week, reading through leases, and jotting down on A3 sheets of paper, the dates of the leases, the lengths of the leases what the rents were, what break clauses were in each lease and what the planning uses were along with other minor details. Why I did this I had no idea but was later to find out. It seems that when a commercial property is looked at for purchase the price to be paid is worked out on the types of leases when the rent can be increased and just as importantly what the uses for those units are. If it is found that within a few years the rents are coming up for renewal then the rents are calculated and may become part of the capital gain for the purchase. If it is found that a unit has a specific planning restriction on its use, then that is not as profitable as a unit with an open planning use especially if the lease is shortly to come to and end and a new type of retailer can be introduced with a much higher rent. All this is taken into account when making the final decision to purchase.

Now having completed my pages and pages of information, having gone through the 45 pages of draft contract I was then to report to the ex-partner with my findings. He for all his faults had a brilliant mind and soon found all sorts of holes in the contract that he wanted plugging and re-drafting although he did find my research very interesting was very quickly able to confirm to his fellow joint venturers that this was a viable acquisition and well worth going for. At that time the Arab investments were becoming less and less viable and were slowly being replaced by the Japanese, the latest investors on the block. They were becoming quite a big financial and global player in the commercial world. In this particular venture, unlike previous, it was the Japanese that were being invited on board along with other smaller acquaintances. When the Japanese conducted business they had this peculiar habit of coming to a meeting with their lawyers and their bankers, so each time we met it was quite an event. Each person would bow to the other business cards would be swapped and it was all very formal, very polite and etiquette maintained at all times. The lawyer for one of these Japanese clients came from a very large law firm in London but resembled very much the late Roy Kinnear the comedian. He was the same size and build, thin on top and sweated a lot. What was mesmerising to me though was that the legal "Roy" spoke fluent Japanese and had mastered Japanese etiquette.

Over the months the transaction slowly came together. All angles had been looked at, the finances put in place, the joint venture agreement drawn up and all parties ready to sign the contract on this side of the Christmas break with completion to take place in January. We were all to meet in the ex-partner's offices in Regent Street for the final signing. The arrangement was that the sellers solicitors, who actually represented a local authority, would prepare the final 45 page contract taking into effect all the amendments (which contained some curious clauses) and would fax the entire document to us by 4.00 pm on Christmas Eve. All the members of this joint venture started to gather at around 3.45pm including the bankers and lawyers. Everyone bowed, shook hands and swapped business cards. Drinks were served along with nibbles while we waited for the final document to arrive. 4.00 pm arrived and passed so did 4.15pm. At 4.30 matters started to look a little shaky. Phone calls to the seller's lawyers were not being returned although promises were made that the contract was "on its way". By 5.00 pm nothing had arrived and extreme embarrassment had now set in. The ex-partner, who was not a man to cross at the best of times, telephoned the practice again to enquire as to why they had all been kept waiting only to discover that the law firm had no intention of concluding the transaction that day. They were not going to send over the form of contract as it was their Christmas party.

To say the ex-partner was furious was an understatement. He was close to committing murder. He had to apologise to the Japanese who made it even worse by being so understanding and graceful about the whole thing, to their lawyers, to their bankers and asked if they could all re-convene in the New Year. My client the ex-partner smiled very graciously but I knew deep down inside he had been presented with a most humiliating day that would not be forgotten or forgiven for some time to come. I was delighted because I had been let off having to come in between Christmas and New Year and could now get off home early and spend the Christmas with my family.

In the New Year it was business as usual. The contract finally arrived, it was checked for all the amendments, including one or two peculiar clauses that had been re introduced by the ex-partner, the joint venturers were summoned, the courtesies re practiced and the contract was duly signed exchanged along with the huge deposit payable on exchange. My job now was plain sailing and simply to get the searches done final statements prepared and collect the funds ready for the final completion date. When the date got close everything seemed to be very relaxed, in fact so relaxed nothing happened. No monies passed hands, no completion took place in fact nothing!!

The seller's solicitors were on the phone before during and after the contractual completion date but still nothing. They advertised to the world that they had no choice but to serve notice of breach of contract. We had a limited period to come up with the balance money plus a huge sum in interest of forsake the contract and the huge deposit that had been paid. Still no reaction and still no completion. The days ticked by the day of rescission of contacts fast approached and by this time I was having sleepless nights for worry. On the day of the actual rescission of contracts I was so beside myself I took it upon myself to go to the Regent Street office to try to find a reason for this laid back inactive attitude that this so switched on aggressive commercial lawyer had taken. He simply rang the solicitors who had been broadcasting to their clients, and everyone else how they were about to rescind the contract and collect all this money in interest and losses to discuss the situation. Now I had mentioned earlier that a couple of rather peculiar little clauses had been added to the contract. I have also mentioned that part of this fifty million pound deal included a supermarket. Their particular lease included three underground car parking spaces. For some reason the landlord, had insisted that that to part with the car parking spaces consent was needed of the landlord before sale. A very small clause had been added to the contract that the transaction could not be completed until such consent had been given to these couple of car parking spaces. The question the ex-partner asked was very simple. Could he please see the consent of the landlord to these couple of spaces before he completed. The chap at the other end representing the sellers must have felt his world was about to collapse. All he could admit to was that he had "forgotten" to which the retort was that his notice was invalid, that he contract remained valid, and that no interest therefore could or indeed would be paid. The guy at the other end simply stammered, "but that's my costs!", which amounted to some £42,000 lost in interest because he failed to follow just a couple of lines in the contract. When the ex-partner put the phone down, he showed a fleeting sign of emotion. He smiled to himself, and that said it all. "You embarrassed me in front of all my joint-venturers at a time when your Christmas party was more important that this huge commercial deal – and now is pay back time." I was just bowled over. I was reeling for days at the brilliance and yet cut-throat way this had been managed.

We did complete, eventually, after a very hurried licence had been gleaned from the freeholders for the assignment of the car parking spaces the balance of the fifty million was paid, without interest and the joint-venturers acquired their new investment. I earned for the practice thirty eight thousand pounds in fees, whilst the seller's solicitors earned nothing. My days of survival in the commercial world were numbered. I couldn't live with my conscience in such a world as this!!

Shortly after this transaction I sat down to use the same format in the acquisitions of several commercial factories and units up and down the country. One development entailed the acquisition of a whole warehousing complex that had been divided up into some 18 units. It was the property of a local authority, which had purchased it for future pension funding and were now cashing in to pay. Once more I went through the procedure of reading each lease and jotting down all the details as I had done for the shopping centre. I then compiled a long report for the client. As I came close to concluding my investigations, the commercial world had caught up with domestic markets. Prices slumped to the point where nobody was investing in commercial properties. One by one all seven transactions in this deal fell by the wayside. I got my abortive bills paid but it was devastating for the local authority pension plan. They lost a purchaser at the eleventh hour and were unlikely to be able to sell for quite some time, let alone at the price they wanted.

London Transport

One thing that annoyed me about working in London and which often raises an eyebrow or two with those uninitiated with life in London, is the inconvenience caused when the transport infrastructure grinds to a halt. First thing in the morning London resembles an ant colony. Thousands of people are darting into the tube stations, heading for buses, and rushing off purposefully in all directions. Everything is practiced, everything is well-rehearsed. everyone knows where to stand, where to walk, which side to stand on the escalators, which part of the platform would be opposite a train door. It was a practiced routine. Anything that hindered this well rehearsed daily routine was beyond irritation. I have seen sightseers and tourists shouted at to move over to the right hand side on escalators or to move out of the way in trains because busy commuters wanted to rush past. It all gets rather brutish and selfish. Apart from these occasional outbursts most commuter travel was done in silence, as it would almost be a crime to actually talk to anyone. That in itself would distract from the task ahead. The end of the day is similar. The objective is to return home without delay.

Oxford Circus was less than a hundred yards from the offices that I worked in and that tube stop was itself only three stations from Euston, my main line terminus. With daily practice it usually took me about 15 to 20 minutes each way if I was quick and able to catch the tube trains, especially in the evenings as leaving at just after 5.00pm meant that most commuters had not advanced as far as Oxford Circus. With this mindset one can imagine the frustration if there was ever a hitch. On occasion this meant a lengthy walk half the length of Oxford Street and then the length of Tottenham Court Road to Euston, up to three quarters of an hour late. I had to jostle with the huge crowds along the route and experience even worse crowding on the platforms. Trains became standing room only. It was hell on earth, especially in the middle of the summer. In those days there were still smoking carriages and if the only available place was in one of those, you really suffered. By the time we reached Hemel Hempstead and Berkhamsted a half hour later, commuters had filtered out, releasing seats. It was some relief because lungs were burning with lack of oxygen and fluids.

Having set the scene for the daily commute which I am sure readers having made the journey would sympathise, one regular occurrence that would stand out above all others, such as the regular strikes and breakdowns, was an announcement that the trains would not be running due to a Suicide. That may surprise you, but it was not infrequent. My reaction to these events, which were often just before I was due to catch the tube home, was not charitable. It was usually along the lines of: "Why oh why did this inconsiderate, selfish individual, who after all had all day to complete his mission, decide to leave it till 4.55pm, on the very line that I was travelling." It became so infuriating. I am sorry, but the first few times it happens you feel sorry for the individual, his or her state of mind, the family the friends, the poor spectators and even the poor chap that has to go scrape up the body. But after a dozen times you begin to get really annoyed and justifiably put out.

What did used to amuse me on the other hand was anything that caused the glum silence to be broken, when individuals would speak sing or just make a noise to the irritation and discomfort to the flow of silence enjoyed by the rest of the world. A group of visitors would get on a tube and start talking, or worse, a bunch of Scottish lads down for a stag party would start singing, and the looks of total astonishment and disbelief on the commuters faces was hilarious. Once I boarded the tube train and because of the volume of passengers moved to the other side of the entrance and turned to face those still trying to get aboard. At the last minute a couple dashed onto the train just as the doors were closing and they were both highly charged. It turned out that he had been the hero of the day and rescued this young girl from a bag snatcher. Neither had previously met the other. They were both laughing about how they had beaten off the attacker, when the offender suddenly appeared at the window screaming obscenities at these two, very much to their horror especially as he was waving his fist at the hero. Everyone on this part of the train started shuffling uncomfortably as this was completely beyond the norm. Suddenly without warning the doors opened and a fist belonging to the offender appeared over the crowd catching our hero on the top of his head before the doors closed again. Shocked, but unperturbed the hero regained his composure and his bravado and announced to the girl that it was "lucky for him the doors had shut, otherwise he would have made mincemeat of him." At which point the doors started to open again and this young lion suddenly turned to mouse and cowered back. Fortunately the doors shut again with this screaming face at the outside window. I am convinced there was a guard further down the train with a very wicked sense of humour pushing the green and red buttons just to wind the carriage up. When we arrived at Euston I was nearly in tears with laughter as the young hero left the train like a greyhound and cleared three flights of escalators like a gazelle on a mission.

I recall seeing on one occasion a "down and out" who found it amusing to walk along the platform, take the empty orange cartons out of the bins jumping on them to make a large bang, to his great amusement and a touch of anxiety amongst the delicate commuters. This was I suppose my entertainment for the boredom and tediousness of my limited time working in London. I did absolutely love my time in our vibrant capital, although to this day I shudder at the thought of all those poor folk having to suffer the misery of the trains to and from work. Once in London the whole environment becomes electric. At lunchtimes I could travel to all sorts of corners of the capital to markets, shops, and other venues and still get back within the hour. I visited all the famous spots, rekindling some of the adventures I had while a trainee at Aylesbury, delivering packages and documents to the capital. It was just so alive! My ex-work colleague, Norman Perry, from the previous practice, who was also a casualty of redundancy, had landed himself a cracking job in the city working for a large commercial law firm that represented such companies as Shell. I would when I could travel over to him at lunchtimes and between us we would visit some of the famous, and infamous, hostelries for lunch including the Prospect of Whitby in the East End. This

124

waterside pub gained some notoriety for hanging of pirates from the rails outside at low tide and letting the defenceless wretches drown as the tide came back in. The famous Sun Pub in Holborn that had one horseshoe shaped bar that was full of the country's real ales. We never did get all the way round even after several re-matches. Norman, my friend, lived in the North at the time and commuting daily to London was out of the question so he took lodgings and travelled back to the north at the weekends. Once, Norman was mugged, even though he had a large and formidable build. He did send the mugger packing but the experience did leave Norman feeling less secure so he gave up his lodgings and for the next three years commuted by train daily. Now that was dedication to work.

The Break-in

I arrived one Monday morning to find the entire office in chaos. All the offices were covered in thick dust and debris and there were police officers in the reception area. It turned out that sometime over the course of the Saturday Night/Sunday morning burglars had broken into the offices using the roof skylight. They came down the stairs to the very solid very thick safe that stood in the offices. Using the noise of Oxford Street to hide the sounds they proceeded with circular electric saws to try to cut their way through the ironwork of the safe, and then into the concrete casing in side, which must have taken them hours and hours. The dust that this created had spread throughout the various offices on several floors and the intruders must have been wearing thick masks and glasses as well as finding it very difficult to breathe. Once they had gained entry I am sure they were very pleased with themselves after all that toil and trouble. Unfortunately their elation must have turned quickly to that of extreme anger and frustration. The only contents inside the safe that was waiting for them was simply a bag of foreign coins. Their frustration was obvious as the bag had been thrown across the room splitting the bag and scattering its contents everywhere. Needless to say they left empty-handed and a nights "work" completely wasted.

Redundancy

Unfortunately fate was about to play its role yet again when I was summoned into the partner's office. He was a gentle man, very placid and very generous, but unfortunately the time had arrived when I was doing very little to nothing to earn my keep and so I was asked to accept redundancy with three months full pay. What a shock when only a year before this lovely man had doubled my months salary as a Christmas

125

bonus. I did however leave under a bit of a cloud as he wanted me to hand him over my rail ticket which he had helped pay for. I pointed out that I could not get home without it but he insisted that he would not give me my redundancy cheque unless I handed him over the ticket. So that I did, collected my cheque and left. It meant that I had to walk the distance from Oxford Street back to Euston as for some reason I did not have my bank card on me. When I arrived at Euston I simply boarded a train hoping someone would help me obtain some form of credit note but was in fact able to travel back to Milton Keynes without any checks or fines for not having a ticket. I now had an uncertain future ahead of me.

Oxford Circus: the view from the office door.

126

9 Days of the Unemployed

It is one thing to arrive home on a Friday night ready for a few days off for the weekend or even ready for that two weeks well deserved holiday. and the relief that there is no more work, travelling or worry for the next few weeks. However, to arrive home, having just been made redundant, knowing that there is no job to go to and no particular reason to get up in the morning is a whole different scenario. The sick feeling that this creates cannot be described to anyone other than those that have suffered it. After working non-stop since I was 13 years old when I first started my paper round, going into a vocation that always seemed safe and protected, I was probably in a state of shock.

I suppose I was prepared for the inevitable a couple of years previously when I was first made redundant but at that time was able to find alternative work while still in employment. This time it really hit hard. The first time round I was at least able to put my own finances in order, make sure that all loans, overdrafts and debts were cleared, credit cards destroyed and money only spent when actually earned. From a financial viewpoint this redundancy was not going to be as critical as it would have been when I was younger. However, there were no jobs around. Week after week I trolled the jobs available in my field and at one time there were just three positions advertised nationally, two of those being in Cornwall. The situation was completely hopeless.

I should also share the terrible emotions that unemployed folks have to endure with our social security department and the dole office. If there is ever a place to completely deprive the individual of all hope and self respect it is here. Anyone that has watched the television series "Bread" and the humour highlighted with Joey standing in the queue to be greeted by the sullen face of the girl behind the glass, can get a flavour of exactly what it is like in reality. I would have to suffer attendance once a fortnight for the next 11 months and join the queue that became "affectionately" known as the "shuffle club" where nobody spoke, nobody looked up while slowly inching their way to the front of the queue. There to be "greeted" by the attendant who without even looking up called "next", followed by "name?" "Have you worked in the past fortnight?" Stamp, stamp "Next!"

There was no human contact, no humour, no pleasant greeting. It was like cattle falling in line awaiting their fate. It was absolutely awful. In the beginning of my endurance of unemployed I tried to bring some form of humility into the situation by first treating the morning's signing-on as a possible treat or "morning out" and would after signing on wander into the local shopping centre for a coffee and possibly a cake. On arrival at the desk I would always say good morning and keep on till the assistant acknowledged me and entered into some form of disgruntled conversation. One day the normally sullen assistant was replaced by a cheery happy welcoming soul who said good morning and went about her business treating us with a little kindness and human dignity. My reaction was to ask her if first of all she was new or alternatively on happy pills. It turned out she was new and the usual assistant was on the next counter and lgave a look that should have resulted in my immediate demise. It was an experience that was going to repeat itself every fortnight for the next 11 months.

During this period I refused to simply sit on my backside and watch the world pass by. I volunteered to anything and everything during this period and having in recent years moved into my self-build house I was able to spend time finishing various jobs. I improved my woodworking and brickworking skills and helped to lay block paving. I was even shown how to use a Mig welder and created a lot of wrought iron work along the back of the property. Folks often came asking for little welding jobs to be done and this gave us a few pounds to cover basic needs. A friend of mine ran a record stall on the local market and whenever he needed cover I would help him out. I found that really enjoyable, being able to interact with other stallholders and shoppers. Another friend repaired cars so I would help him out doing a bit of welding for him, and ran various other errands and jobs. It was he who actually showed me how to weld and whilst he was like an artist with a welding gun, being able to weld in what they call "three positional," I was only ever able to achieve "two positional" even with all his patience and guidance. His work was incredible. I have never seen anyone being able to weld two pieces of metal together so quickly smoothly and professionally. It really was a work of art.

The Giant Fire Extinguisher

Another friend needed someone to go with him for a week over to the RAF base at Woodbridge in Suffolk. This was during the time of the first Gulf War when the Americans were using the base for their tank-busting aeroplanes. They would take off from Woodbridge and fly to the gulf. The week would help to break the monotony and I would also see a new part of England. Naturally, I also had the pleasure of helping out a friend. He had a rather peculiar job of replacing the rubber inner tube of a rather large fire extinguisher located on the inside of one of the massive aeroplane hangers and was a task that needed at least a couple of pairs of hands. As this was likely to take three or possibly four days we towed his caravan to Suffolk and found this most picturesque village of Shottisham for our camp base. It is in the heart of Suffolk just south of Woodbridge.

From here we could daily drive the few miles to RAF Woodbridge where we found a hive of activity. First of all we had to get past two very smart armed American guards who, whilst extremely polite, were very through in their checks before letting us in. Even then we were escorted to and from the place we would be working. Our task over the next four days was to empty the contents of what looked like a huge fuel container sitting inside one of the large aeroplane hangers. The large fuel tank in fact turned out to be an enormous Fire Extinguisher that had reached its safety date. It needed to be emptied before the thick rubber liner could be removed. A fresh liner was installed and the container re-filled.

Emptying the tank was quite easy. We turned off the water supply, removed the top of the tank and using a mobile electric pump drained it through a pipe. The rest of the day was a case of watching the tank busters doing circuits and bumps around the airfield along with the remainder of the hustle and bustle of an air base on full alert and ready for war. The next task was to drag the largest inner-tube I had ever seen in my life out of this tank. It took two of us a great deal of huffing and puffing to release it and remove it. Once out, the new liner had to be unrolled and laid into the tank. It then took another day to refill. Once the huge vessel had been filled the fun bit arrived. Once word had got round that this particular task had been completed and all forms of uniforms started arriving with all sorts of braiding and medals sewn to them. Shortly before testing the very senior uniforms arrived and they all stood around for this spectacle. Now one does not imagine how large these fully-equipped aircraft repair hangers can be till you are standing in the middle of one contemplating an escape route, should the hanger fill up with fire fighting foam. This was what was about to happen and some poor soul had to be the volunteer. Luckily we were merely the workers who serviced the tank and were not able to test the actual system itself. This task was given to the base health and safety officer, who looked thrilled at the prospect of making a total fool of himself. We stood back beyond the hanger door and there was a anticipatory silence as our volunteer walked to the middle of the hanger carrying what resembled a square torch. This infra red device fired a beam up to the fire sensor situated in the ceiling high above. At a given moment he lifted the torch, pointed it at the sensor, fired the button and then started to run for all he was worth because all hell let loose. Alarms and sirens started off and this huge cloud of white foam suddenly burst up like some science fiction creature and started its way across the floor to towards the entrance. Our volunteer with all his speed and agility managed to just clear the building as this white wall engulfed the entire hanger and he still came out with his back covered in the resistant foam. It was certainly a spectacle that had been worth all the hard effort over the past four days. Certainly the top brass were all impressed as well.

I have been back to the camp site in Shottisham several times over the years but alas the actual base is now no more than a ghost town full of empty buildings, empty houses and empty sentry boxes. The place has gone to sleep with no soul to use it or protect it. It is a far cry from the days we were working on the base.

The end of our own camp site is a rather sad tale. It was run by a lovely elderly couple who shared their back garden, previously an orchard, to keep up to some 25 caravans. They had a further area amongst the fruit bushes for tents. right next to the pretty church and pub. This helped them raise sufficient funds each year for one of them to go and visit their son in Australia. As the couple got older their ability to travel became more restricted and in the end they both died. Their other son who was middle aged was a bit of a recluse and had no personal skills, or management skills and would rather hide in the bungalow than talk to potential customers. The site was neglected and the Caravan club withdrew its support. The site got poorer and poorer even though the villagers tried to help out with the running and maintenance. They even put a sign on the gate, "Please drop your fees through the door of Number so and so in the close round the corner." In the end it failed and fell into very poor state and repair. I did drive past recently and it seemed that the adjoining field that the old couple had purchased many years ago to stop a developer building on it had now been turned into a camping field; the orchard looks like it had been cleaned up, but I was unable to stop to see how as the pub was full of May day revellers. Perhaps this year will reveal what happened.

Making the Best of It

During this 11 months of being out of work I would have to confess I actually enjoyed my time out. I rediscovered myself found skills I didn't know I had and built up tools and a workshop that I still use today. I did think at one time that I would re-train and get into another profession entirely. Thoroughly enjoying getting my hands dirty and using the welding equipment I did approach the training centre to enquire if I could be sponsored to go on a welding course as I felt sure I could earn a decent living in this field. I was advised that the welding course only lasted 6 weeks that really there were no prospects or careers in this field. The only way that I could properly re-train would be to take an engineering course at either college or university. This would be either a 3-year or 4-year course. This was a non-runner; as I could not stay out of work and support the home and family for that length of time. So it would be a case of going back to what I knew best although I was not sure when this was going to be.

However, there was one emotion that I had not encountered before, and one that would prompt me into getting back to work quicker than I had anticipated. As I have said I was now out of work some eleven months. My very good friend Norman who had followed me to London and had been working for Shell had been an absolute godsend. Because he was back in the work force he was able to feed me up-to-date job vacancies.

I was into a routine of our fortnightly trips to the job centre signing on and retreating for a coffee and bun morning. One thing I had noticed when I was first made redundant was the number of actual men that appeared out of work. Also their very appearance that reflected their "no hope" situation. Their dress, was demeaning their unshaven and un brushed hair also showed their hopeless situation and I promised myself that this would be one thing that I would not allow myself to sink into. I made a point of each day when I got up to adhere to what is basic military training of washing shaving and making sure I dress reasonably tidily unless I was about to launch myself into manual work when the old clothes were put on instead. However, on such a trip to the job centre, and afterwards to the coffee and bun retreat I caught a reflection of myself in the glass of the shops, and instantly recognised myself as now being one of the hopeless brigade. I was dressed the same way, my hair was dishevelled I had not shaved that morning. I had my old clothes on and really looked the part of someone with little pride and no hope. This had to stop and at that instant I remember saying to myself, it was time to re-join the world, get myself a job, whatever type I could get, and fall back in with a routine. I was I suppose very lucky as my good friend Norman Perry from our days working together both in Milton Keynes and Northampton, had found a job for me, working back in Northampton for a large practice involved in repossessions. The strange thing was I had attended an interview with them only several months before in their commercial department by the very same partner who actually told me I was "too qualified" for the job. clearly I had over sold myself which mistake I would not make this time. I dutifully applied for the job attended the interview and to much relief amongst the family found myself re-employed to start right away.

10 Back to Northampton.

After several years travelling to London on the train I had become accustomed to it and had used the time to study Italian. I had not been able to do any studying during my period of unemployment so I was quite looking forward to being able to get back to my routine. The train journey from Milton Keynes to Northampton was not as long but it still gave me half an hour of peace and quiet and it is quite surprising what can be accomplished during that hour travelling to and from work each day. Over the next two years I was to re-write the entire book "Buon Giorno" twice over, and bring myself up to my previous the standard.

In my new job I was part of a small team of lawyers handling sales of repossessed properties for a large national Building Society. We were still very much in the recession and a lot of folks had either failed to meet their mortgage repayments or had simply abandoned the properties. In either case the property was repossessed. Lenders at that time were bombarding the market with a huge number of repossessed properties, trying to obtain whatever amount they could. If there was any shortfall against the original loan they would then pursue the defaulting borrowers. It was a very harrowing time for anyone caught with a mortgage that they could not pay. There was little understanding or tolerance for non-payment. The property was repossessed sold as quickly as possible to recover the amount owing.

At first I worked under the departmental Manager Geoff a very larger than life character who was very knowledgeable, had the entire job worked out to the finest detail. He ran his department very firmly the way he saw it should be run sometimes contrary to the thinking of the partners or even the clients. I was just glad of a job so I simply kept my head down, did not get involved with any of the politics and spent my time doing my job. At that time we were split into two groups. Geoff and part of the team worked with him in a separate part of the building to the colleagues I worked with. It all seemed to be working out very well and I soon settled into the routine.

The Computer Management System

Time never stands still. The first change was the introduction of a new computer file management system. Geoff had little to no experience of computers, and because of my own experience with the file management system I had been using in my previous job in Northampton, he felt I was the ideal person to give a considered view on what was being offered. I must confess the system we looked at was so completely different to that which I had been used to. The designer and programmer had created a system that was so easy to use, that it must have been extremely complicated from the programme writers point of view. I was very impressed, especially as the system designers offered to meet us once a month to see if there were any ideas we might have, any improvements we could suggest. They made every effort to work with us towards a successful adoption of this system. Needless to say, Geoff and I were both singing the system's praises and the practice adopted the new programme to be used in the repossessions department for the time being.

City Buildings in Fish Street, with the old "Fish" pub next door. My office was on the top floor, behind the circular window.

At about this time it was recognised that repossessions were increasing. The practice had to keep up with the increasing flow and needed to bring on board more fee-earners and support staff. It made better sense now to bring the entire department together under one roof, rather than have them spread out in different offices. An old office block in the middle of town had just been refurbished and modernised and so the practice decided to take it over in its three floors in its entirety. The conveyancing department was established on the first floor while the litigation department that actually took possession of the properties and pursued the defaulting borrowers occupied the second and third floor.

The ground level was the entrance and housed a retail unit that was not part of the practice lease. We moved in to the building, and had the new computers installed. Now Lawyers as a general rule do not like change. and so the new computer system had to be adapted to their ways rather than the other way round. It was not going to be easy to convince those who were rather committed to the old ways. I was summoned to the partners office where Geoff announced that I would be the "departmental champion" for the new system. When I asked what exactly that meant I was told that I would go live on the new system. Starting right away I was given a month to get my entire work load onto the system and at the end of that time report on the operation of the system. I was to identify any pitfalls and suggest improvements before the rest of the department went live. I preferred to describe myself as "office guinea pig" rather than "office champion."

I had seven filing cabinets full of files, all at different stages, which had to be put onto this computerised management system. At first a month seemed a long time, but it soon became apparent that the manual input of all the data from seven cabinets was going to be a race against time. There was no point worrying about it so I decided upon a two-pronged attack. First, with the help of my secretary, the most recent active files were entered into the system. Once that had been achieved, the second stage was to bring anything that was coming up for completion into the new system, followed by anything that really was left. Under this approach the whole workload was accomplished in less than three weeks and by the time the month was up I had become totally reliant on the new system. It worked incredibly well. We designed a bank of standard letters for a complete transaction. These included opening letters, contract letters, exchange letters, post-exchange letters, completion letters and post completion letters. The computer could also compile bills and completion statements. The system was so simple that all that was required was for the file number to be entered as a new computer "file". Then five separate sheets of information appeared for required fields to be completed such as address of the property, the estate agents, the buyer, the buyer's solicitors, sale price details of the title and whether it was registered or unregistered. Once I got used to it I was able to feed the information required for a file in less than five minutes. Here my typing skills and previous computer skills came in handy. Now the magic could be worked. When the post arrived each day the unique file number was entered onto the screen which brought up all the details. It was then a matter of choosing one of the categories that the file had reached: opening, contract, exchange, post exchange completion. Then one of the standard letters was selected, instructed to "print" and the system took the standard letter and introduced the pertinent information. The printer then produced this completed document, ready for signing.

I never got over the novelty of this piece of technological magic. It was not so many years previous to this when I had employed two secretaries, to take away dictation and churn out on electric typewriters the letters and documents that I was now producing in seconds by hitting a button. I was now producing a high volume of post each day and my secretary was having difficulty getting it all folded and put into envelopes. One evening I asked if I could have some help and the partner agreed that one of the juniors could take on the task. A little while later the partner rang me and said that the junior were complaining that he was having to fold the entire department's post and was fast running out of time. I met him at the junior's desk and pointed out that in fact what he had in front of him was my own post that I had created during the day. There were one hundred and ninety two separate letters that required folding. These letters also included contracts, and all sorts of documents that this magic system had been able to work its miracle for me. Needless to say, both myself and the partnership were sold on this new piece of technology and so the entire department were instructed that they too would have to convert their own files and they too had a month to get their entire case load onto the system and running live. Not everyone was thrilled by the prospect.

"Christine"

At this time it was my second wife's 40th Birthday fast approaching. She had confessed on her 39th that she had never actually had a real birthday party given there were quite a few children and her parents were unable to afford a full and proper party as we would expect. I therefore set out to give her a 40th Birthday to remember and incorporate a "This is your life" theme, where friends and family would all get involved in contributing something hilarious to the book. Through the year all sorts of information and stories started pouring in we had enough material to half fill a book of its own. I had travelled round various counties to take photos and information but there was one person that was evading me. My second wife had spent time living in London and one of her best friends at that time was called Tina. Now I had written to Tina, called at her home several times, dropped notes through the door but had no reply whatsoever. This was disappointing, as she really was quite a lynch pin in the story and it was a pity that she would not be at the actual event. I had to come to the conclusion that with every party or function there is always the natural "wastage" that involved people who were invited said they would come and would not turn up, and I just put it down that Tina was going to be one of these. To my surprise, a lady about the same age as my second wife that I did not recognise, turned up on the night. It was Tina.

She apologised about not replying but dare not phone the house because the name "Ainsworth" was not known to her and she thought it might be a hoax. In the end she decided that she would take a chance and simply turn up. As some insurance against the possibility that the evening might be wasted she brought her friend Christine with her. Christine was about the same age, in her early 40's, and quite attractive. She was slim, and, as we might politely say, well-endowed. As the evening progressed her assets were noticed by other males at the function. She found that she hardly sat down and was dancing with various men throughout the course of the evening. Eventually my Father, who looked like all his boats had arrived at one time with the silly grin that appeared on his face, took his turn. Now he had been and was still a very good ballroom dancer. Nonetheless Christine was able to partner him through the dance, and through the next dance and through the third and fourth and it got to the point when my Mother was beginning to notice and was beginning to look rather uncomfortable at the growing situation. So much so that I approached my second wife and asked who this Christine was and would it be a good idea to perhaps have a word with her to try to calm her down. I noticed she did not wear a wedding ring. My second wife whispered something into my ear which prompted me to straight to my mother and invite her join me on the Dance Floor. She kept looking over to where my father was, still with that silly grin on his face. At this moment point I leant over and whispered in her ear that there was nothing to worry about. She tried to make out that she did not know what I was on about so I again whispered in her ear. Luckily I had my arms outstretched as my Mother collapsed into my arms. She was laughing so much she had tears pouring down her face. Whatever I did to try to pacify her did not work as every time she looked over at my father so she fell back into her limp state of total laughter. It got so bad I had to literally lift her and lead her backwards to the side of the hall and pitch her down into one of the spare chairs. I have never in most of my life ever seen my mother in such a state of hilarious hysteria. I started to get worried that she was going to blow a fuse or have a heart attack. What I had whispered into her ears before the collapse was "Mum – don't worry – She's a sex change!!"

"Christine" was once a man and during the late 60's early 70's he had undergone numerous operations required to achieve femininity. At that time there was no National Health Service provision and he/she had to pay and had resorted to shop lifting to meet the cost. On one of the shop lifting sprees she/he was caught and assuming she was a female committed to Holloway female prison. The story hit the headlines as she was the first male to have ever been locked up in Holloway. It turned out that Christine was a real character. She had so many glorious stories to tell I just wished I could have got to listen to her more.

Office Politics

Eventually I am afraid, as with all offices, politics took over. Our client, the national lender had sent in a trouble-shooter from their head office to try to speed up operations, stream line and co-ordinate a tougher regime that would suit themselves rather than their lawyers. Unfortunately there was a bit of personality clash between the trouble-shooter and Geoff. We heard on the grapevine that the trouble-shooter gave the practice an ultimatum that if they wished to continue receiving their business then Geoff had to be replaced, as they felt they could not work with him any longer. This was a terrible blow for all the staff as he really was the captain at the wheel and steered a very good ship in our opinion. Morale sank as most of us had come from redundancy situations and were all rather looking over our shoulders in case the same was going to happen again. The casualty was Geoff who was unfortunately removed from his position as departmental manager. I was called to a meeting by the partner, who announced that they would not continue with the old system of departmental manager and deputy manager. So whilst they appreciated that I probably felt that I should be promoted from my position as deputy manager of the department up manager that they would instead be creating three teams. Each team would have a team supervisor of which I would be become one.

Now this was complete news to me as I had no idea that I held the role of deputy to Geoff. He certainly had never mentioned it. Although I did feel at times that certain members of staff were sometimes rather abrupt and to the point of rudeness. At the time I considered their attitude wholly unreasonable as I was no more than one of them and merely a conveyancing assistant, which I learnt later I was not. As part of the two teams, very quickly to become three teams, we continued with our tasks of opening the files, taking in the deeds of the properties, making sure that these had good and marketable titles so that they could go for resale by the agents. If there was a problem we would instruct the litigation department so that they could in turn pursue the defaulting borrower's solicitors. Sometime, if the solicitors had made a mistake, it was possible to recover the amount owing through the lawyers insurance fund. We had so much fun with so many stories that it would take a book in itself to write. However, I will pick out a couple to illustrate the time spent.

One Christmas I recalled my team to the old days back at the County Council and Dear Robert Earle and the illustrious sewing of documents. To test the progress of time I placed some pages of A4 paper, a Needle and a length of china grass (green Tape) alongside together with a bottle of red wine. I invited for any member of either my team or the other two teams, to step forward and show how the old fashioned sewing was undertaken for the prize of the bottle of wine. Nobody actually took up the challenge as nobody actually had a single clue how to do it. As far as I know I have not come across one person who has been able to meet the challenge, and as each year passes and more of us older lawyers either retire or pass on, the secret becomes less and less available.

Repossession Stories

With the majority of Repossessions the forced sale comes about due to the failure of the borrower to meet their payments. Thus they run into arrears and eventually default. At this time the lender must try to sell the property being sold for the best price they can achieve, settling as much of the outstanding debt as possible and going after the defaulting borrower for the remainder. Very occasionally, a situation arose where after the sale and all costs and expenses settled there was a surplus. In this instance the lender always tried wherever possible to locate the defaulting borrower. In one instance it turned out that the property had belonged to a middle-aged couple, not married and the gentlemen had died. The lady had abandoned the property and was now residing in the Bournemouth area. I duly wrote a very polite letter suggesting it was in her interests to telephone me and if possible pass the letter to her solicitors who also might like to ring me. Eventually a rather concerned lady did ring and I explained that whilst there was nothing to worry about it would be in her interests if she could ask a local lawyer to ring me as I suspected I would have good news for her. She explained the background of why she abandoned the property as it turned out that the children of the deceased partner had been very cruel to her, more or less mentally forcing her out of the property, which they considered was theirs as an inheritance from their father. The lady basically abandoned the property to them in the end giving up any fight she might have with them as she considered it just was not worth the continuing hassle, and therefore moved away and as far as she was concerned, whilst very hurt, came to the conclusion that this part of her life was now over and she would have to make the best of a raw deal.

On my advice, I received a telephone call several days later from a local Bournemouth lawyer who was rather mystified as to what his client had tried to explain him and why I would prefer to actually speak to him rather than to the lady herself. I explained that I didn't feel the lady would fully appreciate the technical point that I knew as a conveyancing lawyer he would understand. I pointed out that the couple, whilst not married appeared to have bought the property without any restrictions registered against them on the registered title. Indeed without any notices or restrictions registered it would seem that they had purchased as "Joint Tenants". If I was correct it meant that immediately the gentleman had died his legal interest in the property passed immediately and automatically his co-owner. The only constraint I requested of the Bournemouth Lawyer was that he investigate with the land registry, that prior to the gentleman's death he, or anybody on his behalf had lodged a declaration or served a formal notice severing the joint tenancy. This would have the effect of putting up a legal brick wall between them thus preventing his share passing automatically to her. If after his investigation of the land registry he would then like to write to me in the capacity of the lady's lawyer confirming that the legal relationship between them had not changed I could then release funds to him. I duly received my letter, and by return of post I was so pleased to be able to send him a cheque for nearly £12,000, which back in the early 90's was quite a nice little sum especially to a lady with little resources. I still hope to this day that I made that lady's day and gave her a certain "satisfaction" over the greedy children.

Another transaction that stands out was one where we were acting in the sale of a re-possessed property in Surrey. This property was so grand that the Agent's particulars described the garden by the large number of mature trees contained in it. The house was sold subject to contract and the preliminary conveyancing procedures were being processed when one Wednesday I received a rather agitated phone call from the member of the team in the repossession department to say that they had received another offer from, we believed an elderly lady, of nearly £80,000 on top of the purchase price. This was a colossal increase in the price. The constraint was that completion had to take place by that Friday, in two days time. My advice was that since we were under an obligation to obtain the best price, then we really had no choice but to run with it. We duly broke the news to the old buyer's solicitors requesting that they make available paperwork to be collected by courier that afternoon to be delivered to the new buyer's solicitors. We did not actually complete by the Friday, but we did indeed exchange a few days later, on a full 10% deposit to be held to order pending completion.

After the completion had taken place, funds received and keys released, I rang the new buyer's solicitors to confirm that all was well and at the same time asked them about the story of an elderly lady buying the property at such break neck speed. It turned out that it was not an "Elderly Lady" at all as we had been led to believe. It was a young, high - flying lady working in the city, earning pots of money who wanted the house to complete quickly. She had found out that her ex-partner and his new girlfriend were about to complete the purchase of the property next door and she wanted to ensure that she was in her new property first. This is probably one of the best illustrations I have come across under the heading "Woman Scorned."

During our heyday with repossessions we went through a General Election at the time when repossessions and unemployment were major political issues for the opposition parties. With fears of losing the next election, word was passed to the lending institutions that it would be better to ease back on the number of repossessions and instead adopt a policy whereby every local Branch Manager would take it upon himself to get out of his office, bang on a few doors of defaulting borrowers and try to come to some deal whereby arrears could be somehow cleared. Sometimes this exposed some unusual problems. One I remember, was a property visited by the local manager and found to be abandoned. This in itself was not unusual' with this latest exercise. However, when he returned to his office, checked his records, it seems that the defaulting borrowers had volunteered to hand the keys back to the local building Society manager 13 years previously. Nothing had been done, records were ignored and the property stayed empty for those 13 years. Building societies have a duty of care to their members. How were they going to come clean that they allowed arrears to accumulate for 13 years without doing anything? Very simple, they didn't. A buyer was quickly found, the property was quickly sold and the sale proceeds quickly set against the debt the remainder being wiped off.

Charity Fund Raising

I told you the tale earlier of my charity cycle ride from home to work one Saturday morning and back again. A new challenge arose. The offices were trying to raise money for a very sick child to go to Disney World in

141

the United States. Wanting to do my bit, I volunteered to help on the basis that I gave two thirds of any funds raised to the chosen cause but one third would go to my own charity, the Willen Hospice in Milton Keynes. I drafted some sponsorship sheets and started to collect sponsors for my challenge. When I felt there was sufficient sponsorship I nominated a Sunday morning when, instead of cycling to work and back, I would try to run the 15 miles back from Northampton to Newport Pagnell. I had been doing quite a bit of running at this stage and had indeed managed to get the miles up to over 12 although this was on the flat and around the grid roads of Milton Keynes. This was a slightly more arduous run as it involved the main road back from Northampton with its dips and highs, bends and twists. I arrived on the borders of the town and with independent witnesses set off on my run home. Everything went fine and with light traffic got into my rhythm. An hour passed without any problems and beyond the half way point, I still felt very at ease with my legs and breathing legs. It was not until I had passed the twelve mile level that I hit the famous "wall" that marathon runners often talk about. This was now a battle of mind over body and I did feel that the body was winning fast. I then spotted Newport Pagnell in the distance and with a second wind put my head down, gritted my teeth and made sure I was going to finish. After the last spurt I arrived after exactly 2 hours non-stop. However, I had a slight shock when I reached the edge of Newport Pagnell. My support vehicle that was there to greet me and my daughter thoughtfully announced that as I had told everyone I was running fifteen miles, and that this was only fourteen, I would have to carry on. With much giggling the car drove off. The punishment continued for another very long mile. I climbed into the back of the car, only two mile from home, having achieved my goal. I seem to remember I was able to raise £1,200 for the fund to America with a further £500 to go to Willen Hospice.

Tales of Colleagues

In my early days at the Corporation I used to visit various law firms on a Friday afternoon for general chats about problems or issues that I might be able to help with. One of the offices I visited had a well-dressed young solicitor charge. Not long after I joined the legal practice next door and saw him more often, but these offices closed and he moved to new offices. Later they closed and he disappeared. I did not see or hear of him again for some years.

One day I was walking into the lift in our main offices at Northampton and there already ahead of me was a gentleman who

142

seemed to be cowering in the corner, with hardly any sense of confidence or ability to hold a conversation with anyone. I looked closer and it was the same man that I had admired so many years before for his confident manor and charisma. When I spoke to him he went red in the face with embarrassment and as son as the lift door opened quickly disappeared to avoid further contact with anyone. What on earth had happened to him? Shortly after I left the practice I learnt that he too had seen it necessary to leave. He set up his own practice and the last time I spoke to him, shortly before his retirement, I recognised the same old character with a bit more life in his voice. I hope that his move away from this large practice had given him back his spark his dignity and his enjoyment of his old profession.

As the time rolled we became a more tightly knit team. So much so that on a Friday lunchtime the team leaders of the various departments would meet next door in the Fish pub. This was a time to have a good old gossip about the weeks events, swap stories and generally wind down ready for the weekend. One of the team leaders, Lynne, had a dry sense of humour but not everyone understood it and often it was funnier to watch their reactions than laugh at the joke itself. One time we were in the pub one of the new team members came in, ordered his food, found a stool, and started to eat his lunch. Our fellow team leader Lynne, looked at me and with a straight face said, "Don't you just find that bad mannered?" at which I looked over and raised an eyebrow, "Somebody eating their lunch while I am trying to have a smoke!" Before I could burst out laughing and share the joke this poor chap, went absolutely red faced with embarrassment, stood up apologised and moved to the back of the pub to another vacant table to eat his lunch on his own. I did feel really sorry for him as he had not quite caught up with the sense of humour that was bandied about at that time.

However, such light humour was replaced by a very serious issue one Friday. As normal we had gathered, had a few beers and were generally enjoyed our Friday gossip before the weekend. Suddenly, one of the girls came and joined us, sat down and without saying a word took a cigarette packet out of her pocket opened it on the table and removed what was clearly a tin foil containing cannabis. She really could not have been more stupid because round the table were three or four of the practice supervisors and team leaders. What on earth was she thinking? That we would turn a blind eye to a criminal offence that could also implicate the law practice? Needless to say this was immediately reported to one of the partners upon our return from lunch. The Personnel Manager was called and the girl asked to report immediately to the partner's office where she was challenged as to whether she was carrying drugs. She had to admit that she was. She was then escorted to her desk for a further thorough search the result of which was very unfortunate. She was dismissed on the spot escorted to the door of the building with her personal possessions and advised not to return. I suppose the only advantage of this very unfortunate situation was that it was Friday afternoon and the staff had the weekend to recover from this upsetting event, especially as the girl in question was well liked.

Travelling by Train

Now in the latter days of working in Central Milton Keynes and having taken over the offices next door, previously occupied by the very firm of solicitors I was now working for, my colleagues and I would introduce a bottle of wine every Friday afternoon to celebrate the approaching weekend. I introduced this tradition in to our Northampton teams and it was quickly adopted by the partnership, and it came to be the civilised way to end the week. I was still catching the trains to and from home. The train left Northampton at 5.35pm, and finishing at 5.15pm a quick stroll could normally get me to Castle station in time to catch the train. On Friday I was always going to be late but it didn't matter as the next train was only half an hour away at 6.05pm. However as the weeks and months rolled by, and the Friday evening drinks became more enjoyable the 6.05 train became an impossibility. There was no 6.35 train so it would have to be the 7.05. Having worked all day and relaxed with several glasses of red wine, I frequently tended to doze off to sleep. I did not always wake up at Milton Keynes Station, and would obliviously snooze my way down the line until I woke up, got off at the next stop and returned on the down line. On one occasion knew I was in trouble when I woke with a jolt going past the flats at Camden. In a few minutes I was at Euston Station. Here I got off, bought a cup of coffee and a warm roll and walked back down the platform where the train was happily waiting to take me back to Milton Keynes. Needless to say I was quite a bit late home that night.

On another occasion I recall waking up in a panic that yet again I had missed the station and had gone on to the next station. Grabbing my case I shot off the train, stood on the station working out whether it was going to be taxi, local bus or swallow my pride and ring up home once again to confess my sins and ask for someone to pop over and pick me up. At that point reason took over from panic and I realised I had darted off the train one stop before Central Milton Keynes. The train doors started to go

144

beep beep beep as they were closing and I was able to shoot back inside to arrive at the correct stop without having to admit my sins.

One other daily traveller was a character who worked in the main offices as part of the commercial team. Howard used to travel down from Watford. Whenever possible I tried to avoid him as I was really trying to study in the mornings and once he caught up with where I was sitting the rest of the journey was taking up in idle gossip where really all I wanted to do was study. Anyway he was a likeable chap although he seemed to live for work rather than work to live. One evening he caught up with me on the way home, and said, "Oh well never mind, it will soon be Monday again!" At this I started chuckling but his face was deadly serious. He actually meant it. He hated weekends and much preferred to be at work. His claim to fame however came in the middle of one working week, when the trains had been having all sorts of problems with delays and cancellations. Usually the trains from Milton Keynes to Northampton were not too badly affected as they were main stops for fast trains so the chances of being delayed was a rarity. Our friend from Watford knew that, so on this day, having problems with the trains coming down from Watford, he worked out that he would jump on an inter-city that from Euston stopped at Watford and then onto Milton Keynes From there he could take the train to Northampton. Once aboard the inter city at Watford, he asked the conductor what time the train pulled into Milton Keynes. "Oh no," said the conductor "this train doesn't stop at Milton Keynes sir, the next stop is Penrith!" Howard had to be given a special dispensation pass by the guard, giving him free uninterrupted passage first of all to Penrith, then to meander his way back down the country, catching various trains, stopping at various stations before finally arriving at work at 3.30pm later that day. I believe he was still being ribbed about his excursion long after I left the practice.

My Friend and the Gulf War

While I was working in Northampton the Gulf War, that I had seen being prepared back in RAF Woodridge, was well under way. Now over the years I had met many friends from my contacts with Estate Agents, Banks and other Firms of Lawyers. One such long time friend was an insurance broker who had ended up working for a national estate agency as a mortgage consultant. In his spare time he used to ardently attend the Territorial Army where he enjoyed the rank of Sergeant. Now the Territorial Army took him off for various weekends away, which he really enjoyed as a release from his daily routine. Unfortunately the British Army itself was being stretched with the numbers of personnel that were

145

being allocated to the Gulf and so in late autumn he was actually given a letter to report to Aldershot with the possibility of being called up. He dutifully attended was given a medical and advised that because of his rank and skill he would most probably be called up but was assured that if he was he would remain in the country at the very worst Northern Ireland because of his experience in stores and supplies. A few weeks later he was indeed called up to report to Aldershot for basic training. After basic training and yomping round the hills of Wales with the Paras he was told to go home and have a great Christmas but he would need to report back before New Year. There had been a change of plan and he was to be sent to the Gulf. he was assured that because of his rank he would remain with the stores and supplies well back from the front line. We all attended a Christmas party with all friends and family and our newly fledged regular soldier disappeared between Christmas and New Year and dutifully caught his plane to Kuwait where his next surprise was waiting for him.

On arrival he was advised that he would be given a platoon of men and it was his job to be prepared to plug the gaps that the expected advancing opponents were expected to break through. Our recruit protested that because of his rank and skill he was supposed to be at the back working in the supply and stores section but unfortunately that fell on stony ground, and so he spent New Year's Eve not back in England watching the fireworks but on the front line watching Skud Missiles being launched over his head. Some months later, we drove his wife down to Aldershot to pick up our hero, fresh in from his flight back from the Gulf, complete in his desert fatigues to get him home as quickly as we could for the huge welcome home party we had all organised for him. I had managed to find a charity with a large sack of bunting and that now stretched down the street from lamp post to lamp post. We had single bed duvet covers in the shapes of union jacks now hanging from the garage and along the sides of the house. It was a great party to bring our friend home safe from his wartime exploits.

Betting

Since I was a youngster I have always avoided betting in any form. I do not understand one-armed bandits, have never been in a betting shop in my life and even the lottery is a foreign word to me as I have never bought a ticket. My aversion stems back to an uncle who would gamble away his wages away to the detriment of his family. A much needed holiday to his Mother's flat near Folkestone turned into a disaster when on the second day he went to the Folkestone Horse Racing meet. He lost all his holiday money and he had to return with his wife and family on borrowed money. I would not enter into card games or any other form of game where money parted hands. I would happily play for matchsticks but that was really the limit of gambling for me. However now that I was a team leader I came under pressure each year that I should support the staff and their annual sweepstake by buying a ticket for the annual grand national. This wholly went against the grain, but the ticket was bought on the strict understanding that it was to support the team and if by any remote chance we won then the prize would be donated to my favourite charity. A ticket was purchased and was selotaped to the diary and the weekend arrived of the race. Now not really being interested in Horse Racing I never watched the Grand National and could not to this day name more than probably two horses that have ever competed in its history. It would a surprise to me on arrival at the office that Monday morning to find out which horse had won, and if we had a winning ticket. I saw the group gathering to discuss the weekends events and my first question was, "Who won?" I received a startled look from the group. Thinking they did not know what I was talking about I repeated, "Who won the Grand National?" I was still met with confused faces and I pressed some volunteer to share the secret with me. I was politely informed that due to a threat of a bomb scare the actual race was for the first time in its history duly cancelled. My morals therefore remained intact as I was handed my £1 sweepstake ticket money, which I promptly put into the charity box.

Offices in Upper 4th Street, Central Milton Keynes

They say that all good things end badly otherwise they wouldn't end at all. I was slowly becoming embroiled into politics again which I really was trying to avoid. The partner in charge had decided that the "Team Leader" idea was not working and that he wanted to revert back to the "manager and under-manager principle. Although I had been appointed, unknown to myself, as Geoff's deputy, that would not mean that I was going to be promoted to Manager now and was offered the post of Under Manager to work under someone else. This situation was not acceptable and certainly would have been embarrassing and intolerable and so with great regret I had no alternative but to leave. I was further saddened to learn that within a year, the number of repossessions had fallen, and through no fault of the staff or partners the client decided that there was insufficient work to continue the relationship. All their work in future was to be handled by their in house legal department at head office. Thus the entire building at Northampton, all those members of staff who had loyally helped to create such an efficient and profitable division of the practice were inevitably reduced to only two, one being part-time the other a secretary to continue what few repossessions were given to the practice.

11 Back to Milton Keynes (Finally)

It had been now nearly twenty years since I left the practice in Central Milton Keynes to travel to Dunstable, to Northampton, to London back to Northampton and with nearly a year of unemployment sandwiched in between. I always felt that my working career was best served in Milton Keynes. I had grown up here and witnessed the old towns and villages grow into this vast new town. Here too I had worked for the Corporation and become familiar with the land titles and the peculiarities of shared ownership. This is where I had matured emotionally and professionally and was where, in my heart, I really belonged. I knew the agents, local lawyers, building society and bank managers; it was familiar territory.

Once the situation in Northampton had become unworkable I felt I should perhaps have put the cart in front of the horse should have found another job first. However, luck was on my side as the local paper advertised a conveyancer position n Milton Keynes. I was even more surprised to learn, having put in my application, that it was with a growing firm that brought together more or less the old gang from my previous days in private practice in Milton Keynes. The firm comprised two partners from the earlier practice Alistair and Roger and several other familiar names and faces. Talk about turning back the clock! It was fantastic to not only get back to Milton Keynes where I felt I belonged but back with people that I knew and worked with before. What a huge stroke of luck!

The first thing I did was to sit down and devise a computer programme containing the entire pack of standard letter forms. These included for sale, purchase, re-mortgage and transfer of equity. I worked well into the early hours past midnight compiling these forms and drafting each section of Opening, Contract, Exchange, Post Exchange, Completion and Post Completion files for each stage of the process. I worked for weeks building up the bank of nearly 300 standard letters. In addition I built up a bank of another 100 macros (chunks of data that could be accessed by a single keystroke) containing all the names and addresses of local solicitors, estate agents, banks, building societies, along with standard letter clauses and certifications. This gave myself and my colleagues a mechanical form of file management. It was not as sophisticated as the systems I had previously used, but it worked extremely efficiently. Most of it I still use today although it has been adapted for today's more advanced operating systems. In those days the keyboard was the main input device. The mouse and visual interfaces would have to wait for more computer processing power. However, we were all able to quickly produce standard letters, which helped with our daily work load and my "clear desk" policy.

Once back, one of my first cases was to act for a young lady buying a property in Milton Keynes. She was moving from one of the outlying villages to be closer to work and facilities. Nothing peculiar happened during the transaction. There were the usual searches, reports, exchange, applications for funding from the lenders until the day of completion arrived. We dutifully sent the funds through to the seller's solicitors who dutifully released the keys and rang me to confirm all had been completed. I in turn then telephoned the client advising her that all had been accomplished and she could go an collect her keys and move in. About half an hour later, I received a call from the young lady in question who sounded very sheepish and announced that she didn't want to complete. I asked her what she meant as clearly we had already completed, parted with funds and really there was little I could do. She apologised as she didn't mean "not complete" but that she didn't want to live in the house. She didn't like the house. I politely pointed out again that it was rather a little too late and there was not a lot I could do. So again she explained that when she viewed the house she was slightly unsure, but now she has seen it empty she really does not like the house, and therefore, if she put it back on the market would I act for her in the sale. I said that obviously I would be more than pleased to so do. The upshot was that the young lady pulled the door shut, locked it, drove back to the agents, gave them the keys and asked if they would like to re-market the property. She then drove back to the village where she had come from. The property did in fact sell quite quickly as it was in a popular location. Not so many weeks later completion took place and she received back her money, less what she lost in further legal and estate agents fees. There were of course questions raised as to why she had re-sold so quickly.

One of the partners of the practice, Alistair, whom I had worked with previously was, I very much regret to say not very technically minded. In fact really he had no sense at all for anything mechanical or technical. One day in my office I was asked if I could pop down to reception. There, Alistair asked me if I could pop outside and have a look at his car. When we got to the vehicle I noticed that his back tyre was completely flat. He asked me if I thought he might have a puncture. When I said that this was more than a thought he confessed that he thought the car was sliding a bit at the back end while he was driving down the motorway the previous evening! On another occasion he asked me if I could jump start his car as the battery had gone flat. I asked him to pop open the bonnet while I went and got my vehicle. When I returned he was in fact sitting in his car reading a book. A little annoyed as I did have rather a lot of work to do I suggested if he could open the bonnet I could get him started and get back to the office. He confessed that he had not the foggiest how to open the bonnet and the "book" was in fact the manual which he was studying to find out the secret. I then pointed to the lever next to his right knee and suggested he pulled it sharpish which he did and found a familiar sound of the bonnet opening. Really, some folks are all brains and no sense I fear!!

A very good friend of mine asked me if I could act for his Mother who was quite aged and felt she should move into a smaller, new property close to where he lived. The property was part of a new-build by a quite well known builder. The property had not been completed and so we would not complete the transaction until a surveyor, who was also a friend, had inspected it and confirmed that the property had been built to a reasonable standard. Unfortunately there were quite a lot of items that had not been finished satisfactorily and, in some instances, not even installed. However, the builder who was very pushy, was only interested in another tick on the wall chart to show yet another successful sale and was not prepared to accept that the house could not be completed before the incomplete items were finished. Incredibly he started a campaign of harassing the client. First of all they rang the elderly lady directly and advised that they required exchange and completion within ten days. This then was followed after three days with a warning that they wanted completion at the end of the seven days. In the meantime the son, my friend and surveyor, got on to the sales office reminding them that his mother was indeed elderly, and asked them to stop hounding her. He suggested that they deal with him and perhaps their energies would be better spent completing the property rather than persistently upsetting an old lady. Clearly they had not intention of doing this and continued a daily count down till the actual day of when they wanted legal completion and then continued a barrage of phone calls giving the old lady literally hours to complete or loose her property. In the end, on the Friday afternoon the old lady collapsed and ended up in hospital having had a suspected heart attack.

Luckily, it was not a heart attack but a collapse from nervous exhaustion. The sale was aborted and after that this well-known firm of builders announced that they would not entertain either the surveyor friend on any of its sites, or indeed allow me to act for any of the

151

prospective purchasers in the future. The old lady did survive and went on to buy an alternative property. without the stress that had been previously caused and of course in a condition that was satisfactory to her.

I was re-building my contacts and trying to re-construct a list of regular clients and agents to recommend my services. One of the agents who was supporting us had arranged for a charity night in a local pub shortly before Christmas. I seem to remember a date in late November, and when asked whether I would like to attend I gladly agreed. On the evening of the event I arrived a little later than expected but to my amusement one of the agents came up to me and told me that they had a fellow lawyer from another practice who had arrived earlier. They had primed various guests to ask him if he was Allan Ainsworth. At first this was very amusing but as the evening wore on the joke became rather grating to him especially as I was a rival lawyer working for a rival practice. I too was asked to maintain the ruse a little longer by going up to this poor unsuspecting chap and ask him if he was in fact myself, and then, to bring it all to a head, I could finally announce to him that I was in fact the notorious Allan Ainsworth. that the poor chap had been played a trick by the rest of the folks attending. Now I had never met this chap before although I did recognise the name and had been trying without very much success to get to speak to him on the telephone on various occasions over the previous weeks. A quick thought entered my mind, so walking up to him, offering my hand to shake, asked him if in fact his name was my own. I say the poor chap winced at the question to which he politely confirmed his own correct name. At this point, rather than put him out of his misery, I continued the joke against him by saying how wonderful it was to meet him because now I could confirm that I had finally won my bet. "Bet?" he asked. "What do you mean?" "Well," I replied, "you see my name is in fact Allan Ainsworth and I had a bet with my work colleagues that I would get to speak to you before Christmas. I have done one better than that and have actually met you, and spoken to you so I can now confirm that I have definitely won my bet. Needless to add, this went down like a lead balloon especially as the rest of the "audience" joined in with a loud roar and cheers.

I had mentioned in my previous employment in Northampton that I had experienced a rather unpleasant ending with a secretary due to her being somewhat disloyal and had to ask her to leave the practice. At the time it did leave rather a bitter taste in my mouth as being unpleasant and getting rid of staff is never really a nice thing to do. The episode had somewhat been put to the back of my mind with all the events that had

152

occurred since. However, in the early days of joining the practice there was a get together one lunchtime at the wine bar opposite the office. I drifted along and came across the other fee-earners and partners in a group, and who should be the centre of attention was this ex-secretary? On seeing me rather glared menacingly in my direction. The remainder of the lunchtime was, shall we say, polite but frosty and eventually I returned to the afternoons chores and work. I discovered that this girl had taken a job with the area manager for another well-known builder, and that quite a lot of the work was being recommended to the practice that I had now joined. I was obviously summoned to one of the partner's offices to go through exactly what had happened, where it now left me, and more importantly the dangers of possibly loosing work from the builder. The compromise was reached that we would in effect stay away from each other, that I would not get involved with this particular builder, or the work recommended, and that I would not jeopardise the good relationship with them or their area manager. This I was more than happy to agree to and in the end it did work out very well as I was not reproached again on the subject.

My Association with Paul

Another strange connection also came about while I was at this practice and which would cement events yet to happen. The practice was growing from strength to strength. Two of the partners came from the practice that I had joined straight after leaving the Corporation and knew them very well. They were great ambassadors for the practice, great motivators and certainly very good at looking after their staff. Their visions were that the practice would, with the team being built, grow to be a major competitor in the new town and be a force to compete with more established and larger firms. One of the weaknesses of the firm was that while it had a strong conveyancing department, a strong litigation and criminal department, it lacked in the commercial field. With the right persons and right connections this field could bring in a good profit. In the September Paul joined us, and he turned out to be a very good, very capable commercial lawyer from a large, well-respected firm in the city of London. There he had achieved successful multi-million pound deals and would admirably suit the vision that was being created. He was wooed by another partner of the practice, Sam, who had worked with him some years previously and could vouch for his good name and experience. He was interviewed, offered an incredible package to leave the London firm and move himself and his family to Milton Keynes. We quickly became good friends.

153

Fate might have brought us together in another way. At the time when I was leaving the Corporation I had applied to a firm in Plymouth for a job, and was accepted subject to my selling the house and moving down there. He too had attended an interview in the same week and had also been offered employment in their commercial department. We both turned the jobs down for other positions and so, many more years elapsed before we ended up working together.

At it turned out, the promise of high profile work and profit never materialised and several partners started to drift away from the practice. Instead of the work and the fee earners growing in volume and status the practice started to decline. Paul was very badly treated and was told that his salary would be cut and various bonuses removed. This made it intolerable and he could not continue with a tangible position within the practice. Sam, the partner who Paul knew very well, was also being given a hard time by the senior partner and he too was being given awful grief and he was fast reaching the realisation that his position too was untenable. In exasperation Sam decided to leave and set up his own practice. He took his assistant and secretary with him. The atmosphere was now becoming very tense and very difficult. Everyone was beginning to look over their shoulder fearing they too would be next in line. Paul asked me if I would meet him for a drink outside work one evening. He then went through the whole sorry scenario of what was being done to him. He advised me that really the only move he could make was to leave but what he was working on was the possibility of opening up a Licensed Conveyancing practice as he was by now a fully qualified Licensed Conveyancer. I listened and confirmed that if he did this that I would want to help him as it is always good to have someone the other side of you on a transaction that you knew and trusted and could work together. By this time the computer package that I had been working on was proving very successful and time-saving and so I offered that if he wanted I could set him up with the same conveyancing package for his own computer that would help him do the daily work should be open in his own name. At that point he asked me how I felt going in with him although I was not qualified like him. I said that, metaphorically speaking, I would sign a blank cheque there and then as I was so fed up and wanted out of this unacceptable situation. So we shook hands and agreed to put together an opportunity for us both to move away from the practice that was now causing us quite a lot of grief. Now the web of circumstance and previous contacts really came into play. When Paul had turned down the position in the Plymouth Office he went to work for an national builder. He met and became a life long friend of another member in the legal team Brian who would eventually leave the

154

builder and set up himself in private practice and then join forces with David to operate a successful firm of Licensed Conveyancers in Hampshire. Paul had stayed friends with Brian ever since and approached him and David after our own meeting to see whether the four of us could possibly put something together as a franchise. We duly met and both Brian and David very kindly agreed that we could open an office here in Milton Keynes in the name of their practice and run a form of satellite office until such time as I got myself fully qualified as a Licensed Conveyancer. Then Paul and I could break away and sail the ship under our own names.

This was all very secret as we were still working for this rather difficult and unbearable practice. We both quietly looked at the possibility of raising capital to finance the move to a new office, and support ourselves for the first six months. Once this was done Paul handed his notice that he would leave the practice after the expiration of the three months required contractual period. Some little time later, Paul myself and another had gone out to lunch to cry on each others shoulders with another partner of the firm who had been made redundant that day. As we returned to our offices to carry for the afternoon we encountered a lot of shouting and yelling. It actually sounded like a fight. I shared ground floor offices and so went to the window looking out the back expecting to see several hooligans having a confrontation. Nothing there. In the reflection of the windows of the offices behind us, that happened to be another firm of lawyers, I saw another work colleague also looking out the window. She also must have thought the same thing as I, that there was a problem in the forecourt behind us. She then raised her eyes and pointed upwards and so we now realised that something was going on above us. Suddenly the screaming and shouting got louder and coming down the stairs to the side of us. It turned out to be Paul, carrying his brief case with the senior partner coming behind him screaming at the top of his voice for Paul to get out of his offices leave. Now Paul being the character he is would not respond to shouting and screaming. He is a very placid calm person and I could see from the expression on his face that he was very upset and even frightened at this turn of events. Nobody would expect this kind of behaviour from your employers, especially a law firm. After he departed the atmosphere was most unnerving. Then, I received a call from the partner asking me to go to his offices. I am not quite as placid as Paul, and will not allow anyone to treat me or speak to me in the same manner. I took my jacket off rolled my sleeves up to stand and face what ever was about to be presented. However, when I arrived in the partners office, he had calmed down sufficiently and I was not threatened. I was asked if I intended to leave.

It appeared that Paul had been accused of mentioning to one of the firm's clients that he was going to be leaving. The partner had taken it upon himself to assume that Paul was trying to "steal his clients" as the partner put it to me. I spent about three hours, till quite late after normal working hours, with the Partner discussing in great depth how I was not a very happy bunny because of the way we were all treated and that I would go away and consider my position and advise him whether I was going to stay or not. Needless to say I had already made up my mind and the events that afternoon left me in no doubt about what I was going to do. The next day I too handed in my notice to leave. Unlike Paul I was not given "gardening leave" and had to work out my three months notice before I was able to escape.

The Last Days of Peter Collier

One personal difficulty adding to my dilemma in leaving was that several weeks prior to my decision, my old mentor and friend Pete Collier, started working for the practice. I had not seen him for quite a few years. This was the man who had given me my job after leaving the Corporation all those years ago and had faith in me and my abilities, I felt so bad that I was not going to be able to work with him again, and share all the experiences of computers systems as well as my subsequent work experiences with him. I thought we may well have made a great team together, now that I had matured and I thought I might possibly have been accepted as an equal by this man who was one of my great work heroes. Tragically by now Pete was a shadow of his former self. The pressures that he had put himself under over the years were beginning to show. His brother, whom he was very close to had died. The jobs he had gone to had not worked out very well for him and even the last job he had was a bit of a rain cloud for him. His eyes had begun to deteriorate and he was not computer literate. I think deep down he still believed he could work and operate in the same manner as the good old days,. These were the days when we all had two secretaries each, worked hard in the mornings, went out for lunches, came back late in the afternoons, entertained in the evenings, and everyone knew each other in the brotherhood of the closed legal profession. Nowadays folks did not take long lunches, most of the work we had to produce ourselves, from the computers in front of us that acted as our secretaries, expenses were kept to, and evening entertainments were rare. Our sources and backups also were too busy and under the cosh to spare time out for lunches or evenings and we rarely got to even meet fellow lawyers. Some events, such as monthly curry clubs, law society dinners, birthdays, local newspaper Christmas events had long since end. It had all ground to a halt. So Peter really was still living the past glories that had long since gone. He tried very hard, and I tried to help him not only to settle into the practice but to come to terms with the requirements of the daily production of volume conveyancing but I could see that it was a struggle. I tried wherever possible to see clients for him as even in that his confidence had gone.

Shortly after I did leave this practice, my own second marriage had split up and being on my own again I was back to shopping and house keeping. One evening I had heard that also Pete and his wife had sadly parted but shortly after they had moved from his beloved village where he had lived for many years knew all the locals to an area of Milton Keynes where he knew nobody. He was unable to drive as his eyesight now was that bad and couldn't get to work so I felt I should try to get down to see him before I disappeared for my own weekly shop. I turned up unannounced and he seemed pleased to see me and invited me in. He asked me whether I wanted a cup of coffee and going into the kitchen he found it difficult to find cups and coffee, so in the end I made the two drinks myself. I noticed that the shelves had very little to nothing on them and the fridge was virtually empty. He was unable to get to the shops, and because he was on his own now, was running out of resources and indeed the incentive to re-stock. He had injured himself by falling off a ladder, which didn't help matters either. After I finished my coffee I drove straight to the supermarket and choosing a huge trolley, went round filling it up with the attitude "one for me – one for him" and then drove back to Pete's house where, when being let in I carried the bags of shopping into his kitchen, loaded what I had bought into his fridge and cupboards on the basis that this would see him through till he got better and could get himself to the shops. I left him knowing at least I had done some small deed for my great friend and mentor. I was never to see Pete again. A few days later I heard that he had fallen down the stairs, and when he was found unfortunately he was no longer alive. I believe that I may have been one of the last people to have seen him alive. I went to his funeral, back in his beloved village, and when I get the opportunity take a private and quiet drive over to spend some time at his grave. Each New Year when the clock strikes midnight I always take myself outside, with a glass of wine, and raise it to my grandparents, who had more or less brought me up, and to Pete and wish the three of them a Happy New Year so that they all know I am thinking of them and still after all these years miss them all terribly.

Another tragedy I was to learn at that time was one of the first characters I had ever worked with at the County Council, Richard, who had left shortly before I had in 1973 to pursue a career in private practice had also met a rather unfortunate fate. I happened to know one of the partners quite well of the local practice; a branch office of the same practice that Richard had gone to work for. Having not spoken to Richard for many years I asked the Partner whether he was still around and if so how he was. The Partner was not pleased to hear his name. It turned out that Richard, was discovered, together with the branch partner, to have embezzeled some client's funds. This led involved a criminal court case and, I understand, a custodial sentence. At the end of the sentence of course Richard would not be allowed to return to the law and apparently had taken himself off to the West Country to end up with a small holding raising livestock. How true the latter was I have never had verified as despite efforts to contact him all avenues never materialised.

Do I really say that?

It seems that we all are guilty of expressions that probably half of us do not know we are actually saying. On day, shortly before I left the practice, I came back into the office to find my computer had been tampered with. The screen saver, instead of being its usual swirl of stars and planets had some writing going across the screen, looking a bit like an advert you see in one of the television shops, advertising the deal of the day. As I stood there, and read what was going across, suddenly I recognised the sentences as what I sometimes say, unwittingly, during the office day. I quickly realised that someone in the office had been playing a practical joke on me. It was not long before the secretaries were found giggling and laughing at my embarrassment and young Morag held her hand up to confess her sins. She was absolutely right. I did come out with those sayings completely unaware that this was beginning to grate on other folks.

Apparently one of my favourite sayings is, and I must confess still is, "Let's get the aeroplane on the ground, then argue with the pilot," Another, "This is not going to get the baby a new hat." and "Let's get the show on the road." Now this was all very embarrassing as you can imagine. It was now quite funny now that I had become aware of what I was saying. As soon as I dropped another clanger I would try to retract it and the office would burst into laughter. "Here he goes again!" Even today I can't get out of the habit, but I suppose at my age now it *would be difficult to teach an old dog new tricks*, or perhaps *change his ways at such a late stage*, as the use of these well-worn phrases illustrates.

12 Days of Johnston Allen

The three months working out my notice made it difficult to find time to set up a new practice. Paul, on the other hand having been "drummed out" and given "garden leave" was able to do his homework and spent his days very wisely and proactively getting the business off the ground. By the time we formally opened our first little office we already had clients ready to use our services. All the furniture and equipment was in place anon our first day we were ready to roll. There were three of us to start the Practice, Paul, myself, and Pat, who was also from the old firm. Between us we managed the day-to-day running of the offices and bringing in the work necessary to make it a success. Paul and I had set a certain sum aside, which would cover our own personal expenses for the first six months of practice. If we had not succeeded by then I suppose we would have been in serious trouble.

After opening on the 1st August it took us only a couple of months to start bringing in our first drawings and my first amount was duly paid into the account just prior to the Christmas holiday and was for the grand sum of £350. My second marriage had broken up by this time and not really wanting to spend Christmas on my own the money was spent on taking myself on a skiing holiday to a resort in Northern Italy. This itself was nothing too exciting but the little village I stayed in was absolutely divine. Local men dressed as Father Christmas and stopped children under the ages of 8 years old to give them free presents. The local choir who looked like the back row of a very successful rugby team, gathered on the steps of the church in the middle of the village to sing Christmas carols while all the village and tourists came together to share this wonderful time. I have travelled to Italy many times and I have always found the Italians to be a warm and welcoming nation, more so at this special time with everyone being so cheery and full of Christmas spirit. During the day we would all ski together stopping for the typically Italian two-hour lunch, and stopping at a local hostelry at the end of the skiing day for a beer or three before returning to our hotels to change for the evening meal. Even though I arrived on my own I had made loads of friends by the time I left - tourists and villagers alike.

Only several weeks after arriving home I was shocked by the tragic news that the cable car, in this pretty little village called Cavalesi in the Italian Dolomites, had been wiped out by cowboy American forces pilots, showing off by trying to fly under the cables. One of the jets caught the cable with its tail and cut the cable. Over 80 people to plunged to their deaths. I can just imagine what the villagers felt at the time and the anger towards pointless stupidity that was repaid by the Americans quickly getting the pilots out of the area and back on to American soil to avoid any repercussions.

The Allan Ainsworth Double

In the New Year it was back to winning over hearts and minds, to prove we were going to be a success story. I was a little disappointed and rather aggrieved, when Paul returning from one of our many lunchtime jaunts round the Estate Agents, reported that he had visited one Estate Agent who, while promising that he would be more than happy to recommend work. had had a rather serious falling out with myself. In consequence he was reluctant to deal with me. I must confess my memory has gone a little haywire over the years but I just could not recall ever meeting the man let alone having a falling out with him. This played on my mind for several days until in the end I decided, without mentioning anything to Paul, to confront this agent. I walked through the door and the only person in the office was, it turned out, the very person that thought I had upset him. He put his hand out and shook mine and welcomed me to the office. I introduced myself as Allan Ainsworth. This chap's face changed and a frown appeared as he wasn't sure that he recognised the face, although he certainly knew the name. I asked him what on earth had happened that I had upset him. It turned out that just before Christmas, the local newspaper held an annual Christmas party which local lawyers and estate agents could attend free. It was always considered a very good afternoon/evening and we all got rather well oiled by the end of it. Paul and I were unable to attend this particular event but the friendly estate agent did. During the evening he had got into a discussion that turned into an argument with a local lawyer. At the end ,as the lawyer was walking off, the agent asked him his name and was told, "Oh I'm Allan Ainsworth." So I was blamed for something I had not said at a function I had not attended. Further examination revealed that the impersonator was tall, with curly hair and a bit of a beaky nose. I immediately recognised him and told the agent that I knew the blighter. It was Andrew Ray, the same partner who driven me for a Curry many years ago and had ripped off the front of my car. I did meet Andrew some years later and relayed this story. By this time I saw the funny side of it so we did have a giggle over the incident.

Let me give some background to my partner Paul. He had come close to working with me years ago in Portsmouth but events determined otherwise. He worked for one of the large building firms where he met Brian Johnston who became a life long friend. Brian eventually left this

160

builder and went into practice with David Allen.. When we were first thinking of setting up practice by ourselves I was not qualified as a Licensed Conveyancer and it would have proved difficult, if not impossible, for Paul to set up on his own. Both Brian and David, agreed with Paul that we could open the offices here in Milton Keynes on a sink or swim basis flying the flag their name. Thus the name Johnston Allen came into being in Milton Keynes.

The First Offices of Johnston Allen

Working with Paul

This was to prove very successful and it was a wonderful relationship for us all for the next ten years. Paul was, and still is, albeit retired, an incredibly talented and capable lawyer. His field was commercial law and I will take my hat off to him and say he has forgotten more than I would ever know. He could put deals together without emotion or hesitation and in our partnership he steered into commercial work and I managed the more mundane day-to-day business of the buying and selling of domestic properties. However, for all his brilliant capabilities Paul had one failing, he was extremely accident-prone. To say he was the "Frank Spencer" of the legal profession was an understatement. Paul and I divided our first little office, which was a open plan area, into a T-shaped office with a glass partition across the middle then one half being divided again so that he worked alongside me while Pat sat in the main office.

The first time I became aware that Paul was accident-prone was when, one day, out the corner of my eye he vanished! He had fallen off his chair! This was the first of many such mishaps. On such occasions Pat would look up astonished and I would turn my head sideways to find him sitting on the floor, or sprawled on his back. Each time he managed to tip off his chair by leaning too far back or unbalancing himself executing some manoeuvre that chairs are not designed for.. Over the next few months he would walk into drawers left open on his desk, and get up to all sorts of scrapes and accidents at which I marvelled he never hut himself. One day he came into the office asking me if I knew what the green flashing light meant on his dashboard. I didn't, and suggested he check the handbook as the green light on a Vauxhall meant indicators. The next day he arrived with a rather sheepish look on his face to admit he had discovered the cause of the flashing green light. It turned out I was half right. The green light was the emergency flasher. I asked him how he had discovered this? He told me while he was driving home the horn was sounding and the lights were flashing. I asked him what he did about it? He then replied that he had carried on driving until he got home. I should explain at this point that Paul lived at the end of a very quiet unmade private lane at the top of a sleepy village lane where people would seldom hear a dog bark. So this vision of a car screaming through the village, up the hill, down this sleepy lane with horn blasting and lights flashing really rather made me wince for the neighbours. When I asked him what he did about it he replied, as if we the great general public do this sort of thing all the time, "I opened the bonnet and my wife and I simply pulled wires till it stopped."

I will continue to share Paul's accidents as we progress. Unfortunately they still continue today, long after he has retired for which my heartfelt pity goes to his long suffering wife who I am sure could write her own book on him and his pranks.

Breaking the "Golden Rule"

About this time my own son decided that he wanted to move house. Now there has always been a bit of a golden rule with me in that if I acted for you then I really was not going to move you as well. Somehow that golden rule got broken by the next turn of events. The conveyancing procedure had gone down the usual route and contracts had been exchanged with completion to take place on a particular Friday.

Thursday evening I had returned home to receive a phone call from my son. Could I "advise" him on the best way of packing the lorry? His friends were all there and they could not agree. This was obviously the excuse for Dad to go over and help out. On arrival I suggested that he put on first what you need at the other end last, and make sure that kitchen and bedroom are a priority. In case of any problem at least that way you can get the kitchen sorted for food and have a bed to sleep on. Having directed operations I then returned home, Shortly afterwards a 7 ton truck loaded with furniture arrived and was parked on the driveway. Friday morning arrived, the completion took place and keys were released just before lunchtime. I therefore was able to toddle off, having booked the afternoon off, to get changed, and drive the lorry over to his new house, to start the process of unloading. I was on! I had the keys and armed with a sack barrow and a self-lifting tail on the lorry was able to make a start. After about an hour heavily pregnant daughter-in-law and her mother turned up and announced that son had gone off to work that morning, and would not be back till after working hours, or that evening. Anyway I was pretty well into the task so by 3.00 pm the lorry was empty, the furniture suitably distributed, apart from the Washing Machine. At this point four lads including a very good friend of mine turned up to lend a hand. I pointed out, politely of course, that the task had been completed. They were expected several hours earlier and while they were shuffling their feet looking at the ground I suggested they clear the last item, namely the washing machine.

I thought I could then return the lorry to the yard and go home. This is where disappointment set in at my end ! Now my very good friend Phil then announced that my son had agreed that he could borrow the lorry for himself. I asked why and he told me he was moving that day as well.

"But," I said, "Only my son and I are insured to drive the lorry."

"That's alright," he said breezily, "your son said you would be happy to lend me a hand."

So at 3.30pm that afternoon we trailed over to the other side of Milton Keynes where we started all over again, loaded a second home into the lorry which we took us till about 6.00 pm that evening. When we got to the new rental property it was immediately obvious that someone was still living there. We knocked at the door and a lady answered. She said could not do anything till her partner arrived home. I dropped the keys of the lorry into Phil's hands and told him to contact me when the job was done. He did. At 11.30pm that night he called to tell me that the lady had finally departed and was there any chance I could go back and help him. We finally finished at 12.30pm that night, and by the time the lorry was returned to the yard I crawled into bed at something like a quarter to 2 in the morning. There was no sign of son at any of the destinations. It turned out that he had finished work, gone home to a house ready for his occupancy, had his fish and chips from the local chip shop, washed, changed and went to bed for an early night. The Golden Rule is now written in stone. I do not help anyone move for whom I have previously done conveyancing.

More Unusual Tales of House Transactions

While I was having my lunch one day in the Central Milton Keynes shopping centre I received a call from June, Paul's secretary advising me that there was a policeman in the office wanting to interview me about one of my files. Now I had been tricked several times previously involving bogus policemen so I was a little reluctant to respond to this potential wind-up. She was quite persistent although I detected a certain humour in her voice so I decided to play along with the latest jest. The office was only less than ten minutes walk and so I was soon back in the office facing a plainclothes detective. When asked what this was all about he asked if I had acted on the sale of a bungalow in one of the outlying villages. I had. It turned out that on the day of completion this bungalow had been raided by the police. This rather large four-bedroom, detached bungalow set in quite a large area of land on the edge of a quiet village had been used over the previous several months as a brothel. Was I aware of this and could I tell him anything about the owner? I handed over my file willingly to see if they could obtain any further information from the file. The only hint that something was not quite right was when the buyer's solicitor queried the "strange" decoration in one of the bedrooms. The response from the client that it was about to be redecorated back to its original state and condition.

I gave it no more thought until the day of the police visit. However more and more emerged as time passed that it had indeed been used for nocturnal activities by folks not so innocent as the neighbours would have liked. Certain ladies would be invited to stay from as far away as our capital city and further afield, and the regular clientele included some in the establishment hierarchy and the police investigation and raid was too late by only a couple of days to erupt into a major scandal. The owner who I had acted for had disappeared, and was later found to have moved abroad and only the purchaser, who was not apparently as white as the virgin snow, was left to answer some very serious questions. I later understand that the lender had foreclosed, taken the property away from the buyer had sold the bungalow under its power of sale. It is now

164

occupied by a nice, genuine owner who has restored calm and tranquillity to the village.

It has always bemused me as a Conveyancer just what sellers are prepared to remove from properties in justification of their sale. Over the years I have had clients walking off with toilet seats, doors, garage doors and even front doors. We have even had a couple move out and had to be telephoned later that day for them to come back to collect their dog which was not going to let the new owners into the house for love nor money. I had an argument with one female client who insisted that she wanted to take the lagging from around hot water cylinder tank in the airing cupboard. She did not consider it part of the fixtures and fittings because she had purchased it herself from the local hardware store. It was only when I pointed out that folks lay fresh loft insulation and would not dream of taking it up, did she begin to see sense and left the lagging for the new owners.

However, there was one particular case which has always stood in my mind. A couple were paying nearly four hundred thousand for a lovely house in a very nice area on the edge of Milton Keynes. It was well established, quiet and quite desirable as a location. The couple had saved their money and were able to raise the purchase price to buy their dream home. I did find it rather peculiar that the lady, who was not particularly old, wanted to move into a hotel over the weekend while she had the property professionally cleaned. Now unless you have loads of time and money to have a house professionally cleaned, this is, in my mind rather taking matters a little bit over the top. How wrong one can be! The day of completion arrived, money fired off, the keys released and the satisfaction of another "job well done" until I received a telephone call from this young lady in an extreme state of distress. She told me her sorry story and immediately I got on to the seller's solicitor, who I happened to know, and asked if she had already accounted to her client, and I was told that she had not. I said I would be putting a fax on her desk pointing out that I required the funds to be held until her client attended the property to clean up the mess that she had left. The solicitor was more than willing to do this. While I was preparing and submitting the fax the solicitor telephoned her client and read her the riot act, pointing out that the contract documentation clearly stated that the seller would leave the property in reasonable and tidy condition and remove all unwanted rubbish. When the owner arrived at the property she was very indignant and quite aggressive about the fact that my client had felt it necessary to make her go back to the property after she had left it to clear up all her animals faeces. This mess I have to say was not simply in the very large garden but also throughout the house, including all the bedrooms, the hall stairs and landing, and throughout the ground floor of the house including kitchen, dining room and lounge. In these circumstances I too agreed that I would book myself and my family, into a very long weekend in a hotel, while I left the professionals to put the property into a hygienic and satisfactory condition.

At about the same time I had a couple moving to a smaller property. We were aware that the property was going to be untidy and so a deal was struck prior to exchange that the seller would agree for the buyer to hire skips to remove whatever debris and rubbish was necessary from the house and garden. One particular item that had to be dismantled was a caravan that had been allowed to go green and mouldy. Over the ensuing weeks the couple carefully and methodically worked their way through the house garden garage etc. and we finally forwarded an account for the hire of the skips to be paid for by the seller. The seller himself naturally complained that he thought that twelve skips was a little high because "after all he had not agreed for the shed to be removed" we had to point out that whilst he had not agreed for the shed to be removed he had likewise failed to mention that he had made the roof of the shed out of asbestos sheeting that had to be professionally removed in bits the remainder removed in the skips. We did get full reimbursement although the buyers had spent weeks of unpaid time removing the seller's rubbish.

I sometimes despair at some client's stupidity, especially on the day of completion. We had one couple who were trying to get the keys long after we had completed and made numerous phone calls to the Estate Agents and to the seller's solicitors who were holding the funds. They finally located their client on his mobile and asked why he had not removed his furniture and effects? He thought, that as he was moving to Portsmouth, it would be a good idea to hire a van from that end, drive it up to Milton Keynes, where he could load the van and drive back to Portsmouth. This way he would not have to return the vehicle to Milton keynes. While in theory this was a good idea it fell down in practice because he left it to the day of completion. The reason why nobody could get hold of him was because he was t stuck on the M25 rush hour at 4.00 o'clock on a Friday afternoon. The poor purchasers did not finally get access to their new home until well after midnight, when they could begin unloading. Needless to say compensation was again paid to the dear purchasers for van hire, but never really makes up for the personal inconvenience and all the emotional problems that it causes.

People often sell up due to emotional breakdown. Two cases come to mind. One involved two girlfriends whose relationship had a rather acrimonious and difficult ending. Neither of them would have anything to do with the other, I had to take separate instructions, take separate addresses and phone numbers. Neither could turn up while the other was in attendance and in no circumstances was I allowed to let the other know the address or telephone number of the other. The worse part came when we had completed. After everyone was paid off, the lenders, the estate agents and even myself there left a surplus that was going to have to be divided between our two young ladies. Unfortunately neither of them could agree as to what the split of proceeds was going to be. I therefore had to hold on to the surplus funds until they did agree. Now each of the two ladies in question went off to instruct their own litigation lawyers. Each lawyer was to communicate with the other, putting forward the proposals for the split of proceeds, to which a counter proposal was then delivered. This went on and on for a further 10 months until finally one of the lawyers wrote to me to tell me that they had come to agreement. Not wishing to doubt him but to cover myself I forwarded a copy of his letter to the other lawyer to get final confirmation. Finally, I was able to send off two cheques, one to each of the two law firms. The whole exercise, excluding interest, which had accrued over the course of the ten months, let to a settlement over the grand sum of £36 and a few pennies. I often wonder what the lawyers charged for their part in settling the split for such a pointless sum.

Lark and Night Owl

Now at this point I feel we should go back to Paul and his continuing efforts to keep us all entertained and amused. Paul and I seemed to end up working different hours to each other. I am very much an early bird, preferring to get into the office early, but 5.30pm the brain is tired and insists that I retire and go home. Paul on the other hand was never really very good in the mornings but seemed to come alive in the late afternoon. This may have resulted from his commercial law days when transactions took place at all hours. As a result I would sometimes get phone calls asking if I could do a huge favour and return to the office because he had forgotten his office key or for some other mishap. This particular evening was not exception The phone rang and this rather sheepish voice declared that one of the girls must have gone off with his coat, by mistake, and that his car keys were with it. Any chance of me popping up to the office to lock up while his long suffering wife was on the way over with the car keys? I obliged arrived at the office to find Paul confessing that he couldn't now remember where he had left his car. Since this was a normal event I was not too concerned, so I turned off the lights, locked the office and left Paul and his wife to try to fathom out where he had left the car. The following morning none of the staff knew what we were talking about. Nobody had taken his coat and he never found his car either. The police were called and the insurance company contacted to provide a new car. The Police eventually worked out that somehow the bottom door, that is on a security alert lock somehow did not lock itself. Having access, someone came up the stairs into the virtually empty office, hearing Paul at the far end office, probably on the phone, swiftly half-inched the coat on the hanger. They found the car by pressing the door-opener on the fob and drove it happily away.

The Police did find the car a year later, parked in one of the backstreets where it had remained since being stolen. It was reclaimed by the insurance company.

Home Movies

Now I suppose I should tell a story a gaffe that has led me to have my leg pulled ever since. At about this time I was trying to perfect a computer programme to edit my home movies. After up grading various computers and after years of waiting I finally found a package called *Pinnacle* that would enable me to transpose film from the video camera onto the computer, and then, after editing, burn to DVD for the entertainment of friends and family. Richard, who had become our computer guru, had been racking his brains trying to help me out with my home project. Over a couple of years he had upgraded the computers and tried all sorts of ideas. Finally we managed to get the package loaded, but after downloading the film from camera to Computer via the USB cable, we ended up with a terrible pixelated image that was of no use to man or beast. Back to the drawing board. Eventually Richard, called me to say that he had found the solution. What I needed to do was to take the camera into the Sony shop in the Milton Keynes Shopping centre and ask for a Fire Wire. "No Problem," I thought. So on Friday lunchtime, armed with a Sony video camera I walked into the Sony shop, trying to look as knowledgeable as I could, and explained to the young man that I had this Sony Camera, was trying to edit my video films, but what I needed – was a Fire Wire. Brilliant he knew what I was talking about, but then added, "Certainly sir, would that be a 4 pin or a 6 pin fire wire?" Now I was in trouble so I admitted that I really didn't know what I was talking about and needed to "phone a friend." Richard was often out on his large motor bike, which meant that he did not always answer his mobile straight away.

168

It did take a little while but eventually the phone answered and a voice at the other end simply said "Hello?" I launched myself into my predicament at having two choices of Firewire and which one should I buy the four pin or the six pin? There was a silence – eventually a voice came back, "Allan – I think you have the wrong Richard! – this is Richard – in Hong Kong!" I looked at my watch and it must have been the early hours in the morning. This Richard, another very good friend of mine had gone to Hong Kong for a holiday and I had just woke him up. Oh dear! The lads in the shop were now in fits of laughter. I then phoned the correct Richard who hearing the laughter in the background asked what was going on. I had to admit my mistake, and so had him rolling with fits of laughter – the shop rolling with fits of laughter and customers thinking I had cracked the funniest joke ever. The two Richards have never let me forget. in fact Richard who went off to Japan earlier this year said, "Please don't ring me too early in the morning will you?"

Distant Communications

Technology has always impressed me and I have always tried to embrace it wherever opportunity rose. It hardly seems possible now that we ever functioned without computers and email technology, yet when I started work we were still sewing legal documents together. Telephone were not a common feature in homes and if you wanted mobile communication you needed a radio transmitter or a walkie-talkie, What a distance we gave come!

I received a phone call from a chap that had come back into the country from Thailand and asked if I could act for a friend of his who had lived in Thailand for over 18 years and was now desirous of selling his house in Norfolk. The first task was to obtain formal instructions and this was accomplished by email. Once we checked the title we discovered that he owned the property jointly with an ex-girlfriend, which he had completely forgotten about. After further emails between myself and my client, the ex-girlfriend was located, still living in Norfolk, and now to be paid off her part of the equity of some £25,000. This was slowly watered down to £4,000 and exchange of contracts was imminent. The problem of course was to get the contract and transfer to the client in Thailand and back in time. A normal courier service would take too long. I decided for the first time in my career to try to attach the documentation to an email and send it to Thailand for signing and return. It was very exciting to receive a phone call from the client within an hour of sending the document to be advised that he was now driving to the airport to hand the completed and signed documents to his friend who was returning to the United Kingdom and I would have the documentation in my hands within a few days. Sure enough the documentation arrived, we could exchange and complete and thanks to this new technology weeks were reduced to a couple of days. Email had arrived and suddenly the world became a lot smaller.

A similar tale evolved shortly afterwards. A young chap wanted me to act for his sale of a small property which we did with the hope that we could exchange on the Thursday or Friday on one particular week and possibly complete the next. The young man arrived at the office I explained the contract to him. The transfer obtained his signature and I asked how he proposed getting his Father to sign the documentation as he was a joint owner. The young lad looked a bit sheepish as he announced that his father had in fact just emigrated to New Zealand. Without panic the youngster phoned his father which was Thursday morning here and very late Thursday night in New Zealand.. He woke his father up, sent him to the computer to receive yet another email from across the world, and while we were sleeping the Father was in town delivering the contract. It was then transferred to a courier to arrange passage back to the United Kingdom. It reached us Monday morning. We completed the next day.

The Battling Grannies

To assist in the sales of properties in insalubrious areas, he government decided to designate such areas as *Disadvantaged Areas*. This meant that any property in this area that was being sold for less than £150,000 would not be liable for stamp duty. The problem was that to effect this successfully it would have to be designated to certain voting wards. Of course a lot of these wards did not just include run down properties and included some areas that had quite nice properties and were able to cash in on this loophole. In Bletchley an estate built at the beginning of the 1970's that has always been considered as being such an area requiring some assistance to enable sales of these properties to be promoted. The Water Eaton ward was so designated and sales began to trickle through. Now the ward followed the northern line of Water Eaton Road so anything on one side of this road, or to the north was designated, but anything to the south was not. At this time that an old derelict warehouse was converted into residential care homes for elderly who could buy flats but still have a warden run a protected environment. They sold like hot cakes and were very quickly bought up by elderly folks wanting to live in such a lovely environment. I acted for one of these properties, assisted by the daughter of the client. Nothing peculiar happened. We duly completed, the lady moved in, and the title was stamped and registered at the Land Registry.

However, some months later I received a telephone call from the client's daughter asking why I had charged her mother stamp duty and land tax when she lived in one of the disadvantaged areas that was exempt from stamp duty. Despite my protests that the mother had in fact purchased the property which was to the south of the Water Eaton Road whatever I said did not carry weight and I was directed to "Mrs. Battling Sergeant Major" a lady who nobody wanted to take on as his enemy. It was she who instigated this mutiny and it became known as the "Battling Granny Mutiny." She wrote to the Stamp Office and demanded a refund. After the Stamp Office capitulated and paid up the news spread like wild fire and so each lawyer, including myself, wrote to the stamp office, citing the cases that had succeeded. Sure enough, despite providing the clients with clear documentary evidence that they were not entitled, this was contradicted by the Stamp Office, and full reimbursements were granted. Given the size of the development, this was a massive payout. I forwarded the cheque to my client and was a little disappointed that I did not get a thank you, but assumed I was blamed like the remainder of the lawyers for not doing the job properly.

Having unleashed their wrath on the Stamp Office and getting full reimbursement the "Battling Grannies" then turned their attention to the Local Council. If they were living in a disadvantaged area recognised by the Stamp Office then they should be entitled to a rates rebate. giving such consideration to their limited status. So started a second front with them attacking the Council. The Local Council were under government regulation to administer the Disadvantaged Area program and they knew what they were doing. They were fully aware, unlike the Stamp Office, of the geographical boundary of the Water Eaton Road with the northern and southern divides. They took it upon themselves to advise the Battling Grannies that they were wrong, that the lawyers had acted properly by paying stamp duty and land tax. They pursued the matter further by writing to the Stamp Office to correct the error. Unfortunately the Battling Grannies never rang back to say that they had to repay the duty that they had been reimbursed.

I had been away for the weekend visiting relatives in the north. When I arrived home, late Sunday evening there was a strange message on the answer phone, from Paul with a stuttering request to telephone him when I got home. The next message was the cleaner but not quite so hesitant asking me to ring him urgently. I decided to call the cleaner first to find out what on earth had happened while I was away. It turned out that that we had had a fire in the office and could I perhaps go right away and meet him at the office as soon as I could. I then rang Paul. I drove to the office, met the cleaner and entered the offices where there was a very strong smell of left over bonfire. At the far end, where Paul occupied his office, I noticed that the carpet was looking a little charred, the computer above was black and smoke had left its mark across his desk and up the units and windows. What on earth had happened? The cleaner said that they arrived shortly after Paul left and immediately noticed smoke and flames coming from his room. They discovered the litter bin below his desk in flames. It seemed that he had finished off his last cigarette, put the stub out into the ashtray and emptied the ash tray into the bin. Unfortunately the cigarette was not quite extinguished. In a minute the waste paper bin ignited and flames started to spread to the desk and computer above. Luckily the fire had not reached the point where fire brigade was necessary and the cleaners were able to contain it, There was quite a mess that would need to be cleaned up. What surprised me was how they had put out this fire. Instead of using the fire extinguisher to put out the fire, they used it to jam open the door while they ran upstairs to fill the kettle with water and thus dowse the fire with water. You couldn't make it up!

The Second Offices of Johnston Allen

New Offices

By now we had changed offices, and taken over a larger area with three purpose-built offices for myself Paul and another. The staff had increased to include secretaries for Paul and myself, two office assistants. one being Sue, my Gulf War hero friend Chris's wife. Sue did an excellent job organising stationery day to day running of the office and even being the initial contact for all clients and contacts ringing and calling into the office. They both lived close enough to be able get into the office easily and yet still be located in one of the 11 villages that made up Milton Keynes, This gave them a community life away from work. Chris would be able to walk his dog either round the village or into the linear park or lakes close to his home. It was therefore rather sad that they felt it necessary to instruct me to act for them in their move to their current property. Chris had been designated a special task with his employment over seeing a certain factory unit that they had become aware was the target of a potential raid by thieves. It was in the winter and the weather had taken a turn for the worst and was indeed bitterly cold with night frost and extremely low temperatures. Chris and others had to take it in turns to sit covertly waiting for the tip off to materialise. Unfortunately virtually a week went by and still nothing and rather rejected the operation was called off and he was not required that particular evening. However, on returning home he discovered to his horror that their family car, a mini had been stolen off his driveway which in itself must have been a feat due to the fact that the car was locked, the forecourt was a steep slope and to try to push the vehicle off the driveway with neighbours close by must have been difficult. However, the car had been stolen and all while he was trying to protect other properties from being broken into. What made matters even worse was that he then received a call to say that the very premises that he had been guarding all week was at that very moment being broken into. He clearly did not have a vehicle so had to wait to be picked up before the team could attend and try to apprehend the perpetrators. Unfortunately by the time they arrived the perpetrators had more or less completed their task and made off away from the scene. Now one of the problems of the area, to the criminals advantage was that it was surrounded by Red Ways, purpose built red tarmaced foot paths designed for pedestrians and cyclists alike. However, with a small enough car these Redways could be used as convenient get away routes escaping from the larger vehicles that could not navigate through the narrow areas and bollards that were strewn along the route. What made matters even worse was that the perpetrators did indeed make their getaway using these narrow routes. Their escape from their pursuers was in the smallest car they could find in the area. That happened to be the stolen mini that had been sitting on Chris's driveway only a few hours before. The chances of that coincidence taking effect must have been millions to one but never the less happened. Certainly I fully understood the need to move on and away from the area.

A Journey to Jordan

One of my closest friends Jenny, and her husband John, now lived in Durham where he was a professor at Durham University. Once he retired they stayed in the area as they had by now accumulated a good number of friends. They felt they would enjoy life better there than somewhere else. John is an expert Egyptologist, very intelligent but a somewhat reserved character, whereas Jenny is very open and extraverted. They complement each other well, and when they decided to take specialist tours to the Middle East they formed an excellent team. Jenny makes friends very quickly and has the ability to organise people. John, of course, brings a wonderful fund of specialist knowledge to each tour. The had a particular love of Jordan and visiting the many sites of historical interest covering pre-Christian periods, the Roman occupation and the crusader periods. Unfortunately John discovered that he was seriously ill which meant a long and arduous battle against the disease. They concluded that they should make one last trip to Jordan, while strength and health allowed, and they organise a tour with a group of paying friends to accompany them.

I certainly jumped at this opportunity and duly booked my place on what was to prove a remarkable trip. We went in late March. The climate at this time of year is very temperate and enjoyable, whereas the summer heat can be oppressive. We arrived in Amman and eight of us travelled the country by mini bus during the course of the next ten days. We travelled to the Northern Border overlooking the sea of Galilee and saw the Golan Heights in the distance. We journeyed down the Jordan Valley past the Dead Sea and up to Mount Nebo, where Moses first saw the promised land. We visited the remarkable and extensive ruins of the ancient city of Jerash, still being excavated, and full of temples, theatres, colonnades, fora, a hippodrome and triumphal arches. We stopped at Madeba with its ancient church and mosaic and eventually arrived in Petra where Jenny had organised a splendid hotel right on the edge of the main entrance to Petra, where we would stay for three days.

By now the weather was quite warm but each day we would rise and launch ourselves down the three-quarter mile track, through the famous gorge coming out at the even more famous treasury. Each day we were able to explore parts of the fifty square miles or so that made up the Petra Area. Inside this vast area there are various routes leading up to what the locals affectionately call the "high places". The first one which we took on the first day was a slow morning climb up what John humorously called the trade route because apparently the ancients would drag all the merchandise and other wares up this route to the top where there was a huge plateau which was used for animal sacrifices. After several hours of climbing we gained a magnificent view of the whole Petra area and the other four high places including the mount where Moses brother is buried. Jenny then whispered to me quietly that this is where she wanted her ashes to be scattered. The cloud began to clear from my fuzzy memory because only a few months earlier she had called me to say that she had made her will, that she had elected me as one of her executors and had made provision for a few thousand pounds to cover expenses. At the time I thought it odd as there normally are no expenses amounting to that sort of sum. So standing in this high place it dawned on me, that as her executor, I would not only have to over see her cremation, in Durham several hundred miles away, I was then to arrange to collect her ashes, book a flight to a closed country where entry visas and exit visas still apply today. I then had to obtain transport to take me to this remote area, where I would have to conceal an urn containing the ashes of my dead friend in a rucksack, to then yomp the three-quarters of a mile into an area still considered sacred by the local inhabitants. The journey involved climbing for hours on a trail that even donkeys suffered to conquer, and once there, with nobody looking I then had to scatter human remains over a desert and rock terrain without letting others know. I came home hoping that this would not take place after the end of March and not before the end of September when temperatures reach in excess of 40 degrees. I am so glad that Jenny is my friend, but I am rather hoping that perhaps she outlives us all. As for John I am glad to say that he fully recovered from his ordeal. He has gone on to lead other friends and tours including a later one that I joined back to Jordan. He has gone further afield to the Egyptian desert, Syria and even Iran, as one of the first westerners to enter the country for many years.

Tales of Friends

Now it would seem obvious that a mechanic working on his own car would be aware of the basic requirements that he is exposed to on a day-to-day basis. The same I suppose could be said about most trades and most folks in those trades. It transpired that one of the secretaries working for us decided that she and her partner would finally tie the knot and get married and we were all invited to the wedding. On the day we all gathered and went into the registry office together, waiting for the hour to arrive.

The blushing bride arrived on time and in she came with her bridesmaids. They all looked lovely and the groom and his best man looked very smart. As the ceremony was about to start the inevitable happened, when the child that every wedding seems to have, decided to start playing up. The ceremony took on a rather a different flavour with a youngster performing in the background and after a few moments of this the parents took the child from the room and dignity returned to the ceremony. After the couple had gone through the motions and vows, it was time for then to retire to the corner for the signing of the register. It was at this point the evicted couple, reappeared with child to rejoin the congregation. The couple were then invited down to where the happy couple to formally witness the afternoon's events. Most people would not give this a thought, but as a lawyer it did occur to me that a witness who had not been a witness was committing perjury by setting down written confirmation that he had witnessed something that clearly he hadn't. I voiced this concern and people did accept that if this couple did sign the register it would make nonsense of the entire ceremony. A substitute couple was invited to come forward and enter their names into the register. I did think that as the room contained quite a few lawyers, this should have occurred to them I drew their attention to the fact.

A very good friend of mine, Phil, had suffered all sorts of traumas both emotional and medical for years. So much so that in the end after his marriage broke down and he was left on his own. I helped him sell his house and what few belongings he had and suggested he came to live with me, given that my second marriage had failed and I was living on my own. For several months his mental and spiritual state improved but he was still suffering medically from stomach upsets and indigestion. He was regularly referred to the hospital and in the course of quite a few months had been to visit numerous hospitals in the area for various scans and medical check ups. They could still find nothing wrong. He was diagnosed with possible ulcers and was prescribed medication to try to help his condition. Everything he tried failed and his health was becoming worse. I really felt as a friend I should step in and try to do something. At that time his brother, living in Manchester, was also suffering from similar problems. He had been admitted to a Manchester Hospital where they had carried out a pioneering operation, which reduced the size of the oesophagus so that food travelled more slowly to the stomach. This limited the build-up of bile and acids in the pipe. It appeared to work. Phil, in desperation had made several enquiries as to whether this was possibly his own problem and whether the illness was family related. His own father had died mysteriously in his early 30's and I knew Phil was very fearful he was going to go the same way. Watching him deteriorate more or less daily was not very pleasant so much so that I decided that I must try to do something. At that time the Labour Government under Blair was suffering adverse publicity for all sorts of National Health Service scandals, so I felt this might be the time to complain. I found out the fax numbers of the local MP's constituency offices and office in Westminster and drafted a letter describing the case. Within days Phil was summoned to appear at Reading hospital quite some miles away and after his medical check was more or less booked in straight away. Within ten days he went through the identical operation that his brother had undergone earlier in the year. Now this was quite a major operation, which involved deep anaesthesia. I was totally taken aback when early in the afternoon I got a call from the hospital to say that Phil had had his operation and was ready to be picked up. I left and with all speed drove to Reading, arriving just over an hour later. My friend, still pasty-looking from his operation, and still under the influence of drugs and anaesthetic. To any layman he should be laying in a bed somewhere in the hospital receiving care support and medical assistance rather than being discharged like this. However, discharged he was. The drive home was horrendous. I took the smoothest route to minimise too much movement that would cause him pain and finally we reached home. Phil stayed in his bed for quite a few days being too sore and too ill to move. Eventually he regained his spirit and his strength and very quickly it was clear that the operation had worked and he gained weight and colour and was quickly on the mend.

In the meantime he received an appointment to attend Reading hospital for a post-operation check up. The surgeon that had performed the operation examined Phil and was extremely curt and rude. When he finished the examination he advised Phil that he did not need to come back to the hospital again. As a parting remark, he said, "And tell your friend, Mr. Blair's friend I believe, that he won't need to write any more letters to him complaining about the medical profession!"

These last words were rather haunting but did rather put into context a few questions that didn't seem to make sense. How Phil had suddenly been given an immediate date for his operation, how he had been basically ejected the day of his operation, and how he was roughly treated with extreme rudeness and arrogance. It turned out that my letter that had been forwarded to the local constituency office rather lay there for some time gathering dust as our duly elected Member of Parliament was spending more time in London than here in his constituency due to pressure and adverse publicity effecting the current government. He received my other copy though in his Parliamentary office and he was walking down the corridor reading it when he passed "Tony" coming the other way. He showed the letter to the Prime Minister who apparently frowned turned to the health minister who happened to be there with him, and told him that he wanted this sorted out urgently to avoid any further adverse publicity. So Phil had his operation. It proved successful and he has now gone on to re-establish his life, has subsequently married and I speak to him from time to time. He is very happy level and enjoys good health and prosperity.

Tales of Clients

I have always been fascinated by the sheer eccentricity of some clients who never cease to amaze me. This eccentricity manifests itself at the first meeting, or in some cases a rather belated first meeting. Taking instructions can be arduous in itself and in just these next examples rather memorable. One client I had previously acted for was, frankly, a total pain in the backside. He wanted everything to be done urgently, had no patience, wanted everything done as cheaply as possible and never bothered making appointments. He would turn up when and how it suited him. I decided that I would not want to act for him again. The day came when the phone rang and yes this awful client was on the phone deciding that he wanted to buy another property and wanted me to act and had to see me straight away. I really didn't want to act so I advised him that I was busy and couldn't see him that day, especially as it was drawing late afternoon and knew this was going to be another painful experience that would take us beyond normal closing hours. He then announced that he knew I was not busy as he was standing in the car park outside and was looking at me through the window He insisted he saw me immediately. I did act again and it was just as painful as the previous experience but we did get the job done finally.

Another couple rang early afternoon to say they were driving down from London to see me and estimated that, given traffic conditions they should be with me by about four thirty. By Five o'clock I was beginning to feel that this could be a late one. By Five thirty I decided that I wold wait another fifteen minutes before giving up as clearly they had changed their minds. At just before quarter to six, the phone rang. It was the client to say that he was going to be a little bit late. Thinking there was a major holdup on the motorway I asked where he was. He said, Buckingham some 12 miles away from the office, but entirely the wrong side of the motorway. Curious, I asked why he was in Buckingham? He said that they came off the motorway from London at the time expected and at the correct junction. They followed the signs and the correct roads to the centre where the office was, and just kept going. Clearly they did not notice that the New Town's lights were fast disappearing, that they drove through the countryside for another 9 miles before they realised they were running late. They arrived three quarters of an hour later, at gone six thirty to attend our belated appointment.

In another matter I was expecting a client to call and again being late the phone rang and a voice announced that she was lost. Again this potential client had travelled from the Motorway exit in the east, passed right through the centre and was now somewhere in the west. She was unable to understand the difference between an H road or a V road so I asked her, "Where is the sun?" She though I was making fun of her making fun or being extremely cynical, which was in fact just the opposite. I had absolutely no idea where this lady had ended up even though she had counted the number of roundabouts she had passed. So I finally calmed her down and established that the sun was roughly on her left. Result! She was driving in afternoon therefore she must be heading north. Therefore she was on a "V" road. I should add at this point that Milton Keynes is made up of "V" Roads standing for vertical of "H" roads standing for Horizontal. Vertical roads run from North to South and H Roads East to West so the grid square system could prove very effective very efficient and rather quick to get from one side to the other as long as the basic concept was grasped. It was therefore a case of asking her to travel the next half a mile to the next roundabout, which would also prove to be a junction with an H road and tell me the name of the two at that roundabout. We established that she was in fact on the V3 and had reached the H7, which meant if she turned right, kept going over roundabouts finally turning left she could be directed in. I am sure by the time she reached our office the lady thought I was some form of magician reeling her in by some sorcery or magic invisible line to the office. The logic was completely lost on her.

I had finally succumbed to continued nagging by Paul my work partner and had been attending college now for several years. It was not easy in my late 40's. There was a marriage split, a teenage daughter, trying to maintain the house, daily issues at work and keeping up some form of social life. The need to study to gain my final practicing certificate was now becoming urgent. The partners had announced years before that we would be tied by the waist until such time as I could qualify then we would be expected to launch ourselves off and run the practice on our own. I had managed over several years to pass the three required passes in Domestic Conveyancing, Commercial Conveyancing (which I found particularly difficult to understand although I eventually achieved the requisite pass at the end of the college year), and finally my dread and fear, the Accounts examination. It would have been far easier for me to take an exam in Chinese or Mongolian as I had no comprehension for at least the first year what on earth this subject was all about. I had always had others work out double accounts, costs profits, losses. However, the fog of ignorance cleared, I took the examination and surprised myself by passing with a merit, which astonished me. I then was able to apply to the Council for Licensed Conveyancers for my Limited Licence. Limited, as I was for all intents and purposes in the employ of the practice. I attended my interview and was confirmed. Not long after this achievement the partners decided that they really should now start to shake the tree and persuade Paul and I that it really was time, after 9 years to grasp the oars and start rowing our own boat. They, the partners of Johnston Allen, were planning to retire within the course of the next year. Paul and I then decided that I would go it alone and take over the practice; he would take a part time job closer to where he lived in preparation for his own pending retirement. I was to reapply rather ahead of schedule, to the Council for a full licence to enable me to run the practice. It was a rather difficult year, driving over to Chelmsford for a further interview in front of a table full of Council members, all questioning me why after only just a few months I was back again. I did get the initial nod but had to put in a business plan, which involved references from lenders, submission of bank accounts, and demonstration of sufficient funding.. I finally heard the following January and it was decided that come 1st April the old name would be replaced by my own and I would be rowing the boat alone. Paul took his job and his files and existing clients to the practice close to his home, which meant he was basically out of the Central Office rat race and could enjoy a more comfortable working week. As for me it was a harrowing first few months.

13 Allan Ainsworth & Co.

I remember my Mother telephoning the offices shortly after we opened under the new name and asking how I felt. The only description I could give her that she might understand was that of being an experienced sailor who all his life had successfully sailed all the lakes of his country and others, in all sorts of conditions. However, the day arrived when the lock gates finally opened and he would be sailing off into the open sea. He had all the theory had all the practice but finally this was the big deal and he was terrified of going off into what he considered to be un chartered waters. And so Allan Ainsworth & Co. was born and the old name became another chapter of this book. The partners of Johnston Allen did in fact keep to their schedule and in fact one year to the day that Allan Ainsworth & Co. started they in fact disbanded their own practice and retired.

As for us it was business as usual. I remember one of the early clients that we had was a lady buying an ex-Council property where the seller had, years previously, replaced the old windows with new double-glazed units upstairs. Now whilst the conversion was prior to the new Building Regulations that demanded that full consent needed to be obtained or at the very least a F.E.N.S.A certificate issued by the installation company, I still brought my clients attention to this. The logic behind the changes in building regulations was all to stop the cowboys from interfering with structural alterations. Luckily practices had kept up, so that we were now preparing full reports in writing for clients to explain the processes of the transaction, the documents to be signed and the reasons behind it all. This kept up with the litigious minds who were prone to sue anyone if anything went wrong. The client was now under extreme pressure by the agent and the seller to proceed to an early exchange. Despite having to put right all sorts of problems with her own house in respect of regulation requirements the penny did not drop that she should protect herself with regards to her own purchase. My advice to consult a surveyor was shouted down by the seller and the agent and despite my best effort she wanted to go ahead with her purchase. As she was paying cash I highlighted my concerns and at the end of the report where the client signs to say she had read the report, I added the words in bold letters, "despite my advice . . . and so forth." The file was duly completed and closed and life moved on. In the following February I took a call from this screaming banshee of a woman demanding that all had gone wrong, she had got one of the local double-glazing firms in to quote for downstairs windows, and having inspected the property, refused to do the work due to structural movements caused by the windows replaced by the previous owners. What was I going to do about it? I dragged out the old file and quickly realised who she was, and what advice I had given. I read out the report section and she replied, "So you're not going to do anything about it for me!" I never heard another word from her after that.

Thank goodness for full reports that David and Bryan introduced us to years before and which we adopted as a good idea. It certainly saved my bacon that day.

Lawyers have to be on their toes most of the time and not always believe that what their clients say is the gospel truth. We hear various stories and events that maybe could be true or at least warn against certain actions. One such story has been reported several times in the law society disciplinary reports, and can have dire consequences for the not so cautious lawyers, nearly happened to myself. I was acting for an elderly lady who was selling her flat to move into her daughter and son in law's property. She was rather frail, and as often happens in these circumstances you tend to deal more with the son or daughter than the elderly parent. The instructions arrived, and we went through the procedures required for the sale of the Mother's property. This dragged on a little longer than expected but the day finally arrived when exchange of contracts was due to take place. I had by this time obtained a signed contract by the Mother, my client some weeks earlier. On the day of exchange and having taken a phone call from the buyers solicitors advising he was ready, I then telephoned the daughter's house and spoke to her husband. I explained that I really needed to speak to my client, the Mother to take her actual instructions to authorise me to exchange, agree the completion date, and of course discuss with her details of when where and how to send her the balance funds on completion. The husband seemed a little hesitant and simply suggested that he would get his wife to ring me, from Prague! Curious, I waited for the phone call from the Daughter in Prague, which duly arrived within the hour. I explained that whilst I had dealt with her all these weeks, I now needed to speak to her mother. There was a silence, then she said, "Oh did we not tell you? Mother died several weeks ago!"

As all conveyancing lawyers know, to exchange contracts without client's authority is in fact breach of instructions and leaves the lawyer personally liable for negligence. The fact that the client had died several weeks ago certainly would have reflected serious negligence, and there have been several cases where lawyers have done just that. I advised the daughter that this placed a serious problem on the transaction. I explained to the buyer's solicitors what had happened while I sent the daughter off to a local probate lawyer to gain Grant of Probate for the dearly departed Mother. The buyer was very sympathetic and patient and in fact exchange was delayed for several months but finally went through with the daughter now acting as Attorney for her deceased Mother.

Another example of never entirely taking what the client or purchaser says as gospel, came when I was acting for a client, who now working more in Canada that this country. He found it necessary to sell his house for just under one million pounds. It was a beautiful house but purchasers at that price were rather rare, at that time, given the poor housing market. However, the Estate Agent, who was actually a very reputable local agent, introduced a purchaser who did not have a related sale and could move very quickly. Draft papers were issued to the buyer's solicitor, Alistair, being the very same lawyer who showed how to jump-start his car and how to open his own bonnet when I finally returned.

As the weeks rolled by and we seemed to have little response from the buyer's solicitors by way of approved contract, or for that matter, any additional enquiries. I did start to question the validity of the buyer with, the Estate Agents but was assured this purchaser was really keen to get the transaction sewn up. The buyer had taken quite a few trips to the property with relatives and friends, was in constant touch with my client and even assured him that he had ordered play equipment for the garden and for the children's bedrooms. My own doubts and warnings were all taken with a pinch of salt. We were put under extreme pressure by the Estate Agents and the clients, to ensure contracts were signed. The week before the allocated completed date I contacted Alistair to ask him to confirm these dates, only to be advised, yet again, that he was still waiting for the client's formal instructions. This was denied by the client, who said that he had dropped them off "that very morning" with a bankers draft to the Solicitors office. He then tried to make out that these had been "lost " by the solicitor and now he was arranging for funds to be telegraphically transferred. All this time my fears were growing and certainly reinforced by Alistair's confirmation that the guy had not been anywhere near him. The day before completion, and on the day of completion, the buyer was still giving his assurances. As for my client, he had arranged for all furniture to be taken out and stored, for his wife and family to move out of the family home and was now quite excited that the surplus funds were going to be transferred to him and that he could then arrange for family and possessions to move to Canada to join him. Unfortunately, my misgivings were proved right. The day of completion came and went and so the days stretched on with no sign of exchange, no sign of completion and slowly the client and the agents had to come to the conclusion that they had a very serious time waster on their hands. After retracting draft papers from Alistair we did get another instruction from the agents for another buyer and re-submitted papers but this time on a much reduced sale to ensure a quick turn around. As for our bogus first purchaser, it turned out that he was making a habit of this, with other agents, promising transactions that never materialised and putting sellers to a great waste of time and money.

One of the fears we always have is involving properties out of the area that we are not totally familiar them. Today, with the aid of internet searches clients can at least get a better insight into what the area is like. One such transaction that comes to mind was a client who wanted to purchase in the midlands. Not being familiar we waited for draft papers to arrive and whilst waiting, conducted the usual local search, a water search, a mining search and an environmental search. When the results came back, rather than wait for the replies to enquiries I prepared an interim report off to the client and waited to see how many days would pass before he telephoned to discuss the transaction. I seem to remember that it took about the length of time for the letter to arrive on his mat before telephoning me to say that he had got the report, and the searches and with a rather shocked voice announced that he had decided not to go ahead with his purchase. We were not at all surprised at our end given that the mining report came back that there were old mining shafts in the area that affected his property. On top of that the property was in a potential flood area. To make his decision easier we discovered that the property was close to an infill site, which carried its own health risks as the site also contained toxic waste. These serious issues would not have been revealed 30 odd years ago when environmental searches did not exist.

Environmental issues now play a major role in buying and selling property. In Northamptonshire and Cornwall there the risk of Radon Gas. a natural substance that builds up under ground and needs to be released into the atmosphere. It can pervade houses in strong concentrations. Modern houses that are built in these areas must have some form of membrane as a barrier against such build ups. I am therefore very much aware of new builds and always ask the question so as to reassure lenders and clients that they are not lending/buying into such a health risk and potentially unmarketable property. It therefore astonished me on one development where the developer had gone to great lengths to publicise the fact that they had carried out soil checks. These revealed a high level of Radon Gas and a high level of Arsenic deposits that were rising naturally to the surface. The report then went on to congratulate themselves that they had added a whole 1 foot of topsoil to eradicate the problem. I am not an engineer but with a certain degree of common sense, I tried to explain both to the client and to the lender that if there was arsenic coming to the surface that rather than eradicate the problem by simply adding twelve inches of top soil in my opinion was surely like adding a sponge above liquid that would simply soak up the problem and retain it for some considerable time. However both the client, and the lender gave me written confirmations that they were both happy with the situation and wanted to proceed with completion and so despite my advice the sale went ahead and the client moved into what must be considered a very high risk.

As I have discussed above some of the worse clients I have found are either friends or family. The "shop" is expected to be open from as early as 7.00 am and is expected to close as late as 10.30 at night. This is most of the time free advice as one is not expected to be reimbursed for time and advice given to members of family. One of the worst clients in this respect was my own Father. Despite my advice, which I went at great and lengthy pains to give, he went against it and sold his wonderful, modernised bungalow that stood in some lovely grounds to purchase one of the retirement village properties being developed not far from my own home. He attended meetings, went on coach trips to other villages and was convinced that this was the best future for himself and his second wife. At this time he was suffering very severe heart problems with an aneurism that was forecast to kill him. He had been given at that time probably six months to live, if he was lucky. In the New Year the doctors decided to give him various tests to see if he could physically withstand an operation, which in itself would only give him a 50/50 chance of survival. During the course of January and February the tests were undertaken and they decided that an open heart operation should take place in mid March. By this time the aneurism had reached critical stage. My father then refused the date saying that this was wholly inconvenient given the meetings he was attended for the retirement village and he was hoping to move there in June. Asked by the Surgeon when would be "convenient" he advised he could make a date sometime round mid April, despite warnings by the surgeon that he could be long dead by that time. However mid-April came, the operation was successful and he was soon convalescing to continue his quest for completion of his purchase to his new property. Unfortunately, as all building programmes seem to do, the date of June was put back to September. By this time, again despite my advice, he had exchanged his sale with a fixed completion date, which meant he was going to be homeless. His next scheme was to allow the completion date on the sale to take place, and he and his second wife would take a holiday on a flight to Australia. Flights were booked and off they toddled to Heathrow, but he was taken ill at the check-in, and hurried to Uxbridge Hospital where he underwent tests. When he returned to the check-in the next day the airline refused him passage for fear that something would happen on his flight to Australia.

So now he was homeless, and with suitcases stuck at the airport. He and his second wife returned to Milton Keynes where he rented till the new property was ready. Indeed they finally moved in the end of September early October. No sooner had they moved in, after under going all the traumas of being homeless and experiencing medical problems, they decided that this environment was not for them. They didn't like the complex, the way the social network was set up and wanted to sell up. They had lost quite a bit of money on having the Village Owners sell them their fitted kitchen, fitted appliances and fitted carpets. When they came to sell, the Village owners valuation did not take into account all the extras.

So they decided to move off to North Norfolk less than a year after completing their purchase. Once more, against advice, they decided they knew best and bought a bungalow not far from Sheringham on the north North Norfolk Coast facing the North Sea. At its best in the summer it can be described as bracing, but it can be a rather miserable and inhospitable place in bad weather, and winter is always cold. Again they moved off only to discover just how remote this area was. He was still being treated by the hospital for ongoing medical problems and facilities in that area were poor. He found it very difficult to get out and about, first of all with the summer visitors clogging roads and towns and then in winter being so bitterly cold. In the following February I received a phone call from a complete stranger asking that if it was right that my father was looking to move back to the area. I had no idea of this latest venture and suggested he speak to him direct. Nothing was heard for a couple of months till eventually in June I did receive a call to say that yes he was considering buying back in the area, and in fact the property was quite familiar to me. It was the original bungalow, that he had sold despite my original advice several years earlier! He did complete a couple of months later and moved back now being a lot wiser, but shorter of quite a few pounds for the experience. I had suggested originally that he would have been better off not moving in the first place, but to employ a gardener as he got older and frailer and if necessary even a house keeper and a cleaner.

The story does not end there as the purchaser of the retirement village bungalow contacted me recently to act for him in his sale. I agreed so he popped over to take instructions forms and pay his funds. It seems that when he purchased his property from my Father he was not too happy with the state and condition of the hallway and required remedial work to be carried out to the carpeting. Having contacted a local sub contractor a young man turned up and whilst carrying out the task noticed a photograph on the wall of the hall of a narrow boat. He said to my client that his grandfather would love to have a narrow boat, which was his dream. My client remarked that if he wanted one he could always buy that one and left the conversation at that. Several evenings later a knock at the door and it was the young contractor accompanied by an elderly gentleman, his grandfather. They asked my client if he was serious about selling the narrow boat and my client confirmed this. They agreed to meet up at the mooring. The elderly gentleman inspected the Narrow Boat, fell in love with it and certainly gave all the positive signs that he would love to buy it at the agreed price. The only issue was to find a suitable mooring. My client rather flippantly suggested that he buy the house where the Narrow Boat was moored as well. Somewhat surprisingly the elderly gentleman agreed and the property, together with the boat, were quickly sold.

I suppose one of the biggest nightmares of any transaction is the day of, or certainly the day before, the completion day when both sellers and buyers seem to lose perspective and come up with all sorts of strange decisions and circumstances. One I have in mind was the sale of a flat in London that was close to complete. The client, who was selling, travelled between Milton Keynes and London, and not knowing where she was going to be rang her for her address so that I could send her the actual transfer deed in plenty of time for her to sign and have witnessed. My letter clearly stated how <u>important it was to get the document back by the day of completion.</u> As nothing had arrived on the day before completion I felt I had better ring her. Various calls and no answers but at least I was able to leave a message on her mobile to enquire where the transfer was? Finally, she rang back later that day to announce that she had collected her post from London but instead of actually reading it she simply bundled it into her bag to read later. I tried to impress upon her the importance of receiving the transfer otherwise I could not complete. She would then be liable for all sorts of penalties and costs. She then offered to fax over a copy of the transfer the following morning, but again I pointed out that I must hold the transfer containing an original signature properly witnessed otherwise we were back to square one. She then offered to try to courier it to me the following day but that would not be good enough.

It then became apparent that she was at the airport! While I was talking to her she walked over to the Checking Desk where she had just deposited her luggage to cancel her flight to Spain. She was planning leave the country for a week and was offering to courier the transfer once she reached her destination later that evening/next morning. Having cancelled her flight she then had the problem of disrupting the airport luggage system to try to retrieve her luggage, which was in transit to the aeroplane. Then she had to arrange a taxi from the airport to my office to bring the form of transfer which she had still not signed, and let me have her bank details. After this she had to return to London to go to the Estate Agents in order to hand them the keys to the flat. It then turned out that she was also carrying in her hand luggage out of the country! All these considerations and warnings I clearly put in my reports my exchange letters and my guidance for sale notes. I sometimes wonder why I do this job!

Another completion was due to take place on the last day before the August Bank Holiday, when I was due to catch the late afternoon boat for a weekend on the Isle of Wight. In this instance again I was acting for the sellers. The transaction had been pretty straight forward, exchanged agreed and a completion date. That day finally arrived. As seems to be the normal these days I had to keep ringing the other side's solicitors to find out whether they had sent the money. Again I was told, as I had been several times before, that it was about to be sent. However, by 3.10pm that afternoon I had to read the riot act to the assistant who could not speak very good English as this was a Nigerian law firm, acting on behalf of a Nigerian client. I insisted that I must speak to the partner and failing which I was to carry out all sorts of threats. Finally, a gentleman with a very broad Nigerian accent telephoned me, from his car, halfway to Devon. He at last got involved and authorised his office to send the money to me. The money did finally arrive although I did charge him for 3 days interest on notice and fees. It was interesting to receive a phone call two years later by a firm of solicitors acting for the purchaser who asked if we could assist in having another transfer signed as the original firm had not bothered to have it stamped, or registered. In fact the practice had been closed down.

At one point I was able to boast that I had clients in all five continents. I was obviously acting for folks here in England, at the same time I had several clients in Hong Kong selling their properties here in

England to return to China as concerns about mainland China dwindled. I was acting for a foreign office chap living in South Africa as well as a couple who had emigrated to Australia selling their property. One day my wife was chatting to this person obviously asking about our services prices etc. and my wife Angie found herself talking to a prospective client "up a mountain in Canada." One young man who I acted for was selling his property that was due to complete on the Monday. He came to see me on the Thursday to sign his contract and transfer at which point I asked him where his father was who was a co owner. He confirmed his father had in fact moved to New Zealand several weeks before which caused what I would lightly call a bit of a problem He then rang his father from my office which meant his father was already tucked up in bed. to tell him to switch his computer on as we were about to e.mail him a contract and a transfer. Dad dutifully got the e.mail down loaded printed signed drove into town the next morning couriered it back to the UK so we could complete on the Monday. The buyers solicitors never knew how close we were to being in breach of contract.

Sometimes clients naively believe that they can bypass using a law firm which is understandable given some of the rather excessive fees that are sometimes charged. One particularly lady came to me asking if I could act for her on the sale of her Mother's house in London. Her Mother had sadly passed away several months before and electing to try to sort out the grant of probate herself rather than take the expensive road through a law firm. She had been through a long and arduous process trying to cope with the numerous forms and procedures before finally being granted that elusive Probate. That would finally enable her to legally dispose of her Mothers house. During this time she had already been approached by her Mother's neighbours who wanted to purchase the property. They had agreed a price between them and even instructed their lawyers to start the legal process. I had already opened the file having been given instructions and confirmed with the buyer's lawyers that I would be forwarding a contract shortly once my client could attend with her Mother's title deeds and the Grant of Probate. The client called in with the Title deeds and various other documents and of course the Grant of Probate. As I read through the documents I realised that we had yet another problem for my poor disgruntled client to rectify. I asked her as to what had happened to her Father? She said that he had in fact died nearly twenty years earlier. Unfortunately what she failed to realise was that the property was in her Father's name. I asked her if she could produce any Grant of Probate from her Father to her Mother? She couldn't. Was there any deed from Father to Mother or from Father to himself and her Mother? Again no.

The problem we now faced was that the property was still in the Father's name. The Mother had lived in the property all those years following his death without realising, always assuming as did the rest of the family that the house became hers and nobody had checked the title deeds. The exercise of getting Probate for the Mother was therefore a complete waste of time as she did not in fact have anything to leave, it was all her husband's. So my client then had to go back to the Probate Registry and start all over again reapplying but this time for Grant of probate to herself from her long-deceased Father. Luckily the Purchasers were very patient and were happy to wait till such grant of probate was issued. In the meantime the purchaser's solicitors dealt with the contract all the pre-exchange searches and enquiries so that as soon as the Grant came through we could then exchange and complete.

In modern times I suppose we all get hassled by telephone sales people trying to sell us insurance, accident claims, computer software and in business we get all sorts bothering us. One of the roads I have been down but with much larger practices is that involving file management systems. In the past such sophisticated systems have involved main frame computers and indeed many thousands of pounds for not only the hardware but the software as well. I am a huge advocate for such systems which, in a busy office, can help cut through the day-to-day mountain of procedures and paperwork. In the right skilled hands this can work to the business's advantage. A small practice has less room to manoeuvre because the cost benefits can sometimes be small. This fact, as you can imagine, does not stop the telephone salesmen persistently trying to sell you a system. One particular salesman has been on my case now for several years and each time the costs have been reduced and the "benefits" magnified. The last time he called which was some time ago. I stopped him in his tracks by simply referring to the old cartoon character Andy Capp who used to appear in the Daily Mirror Newspaper. He clearly did not understand what I meant so I relayed a cartoon that was in the newspaper one day where Andy Capp was sitting on a wall with his mate doing very little as usual when his wife, Flo appeared and announced that the local shop had one of the new "all singing, all dancing" washing machines. Andy asked why she wanted one of these machines? "Because it would save so much more time," came the answer. "What would you do with the time you have saved?" he asked, to which a deflated Flo replied "I'll carry on washing by hand then." Still the mist had not cleared so I explained that as a small practice we did not get a huge volume of work each day. in fact most of the dross paperwork was completed really within an hour of receiving post. If I had one of these wonderful file management systems, and it was as efficient and time saving as was being portrayed, then what exactly was I going to do the rest of the day? The deflated voice at the end of the phone simply replied, "Shall I ring you in a couple of years when the market picks up?" I have not heard from him since.

These days we have to be very careful with money laundering and various criminal elements at work. What is not realised by many is that the conveyancing lawyer is a far greater target than most professionals for the criminal. If as an individual one turns up at the bank with large sums of Money then the Bank will ask a lot of searching questions and if not satisfied will refuse to accept such funds. The lawyer's practice on the other hand often receives and deposits huge sums through its client account without the bank ever querying such sums. This is because the lawyer is personally liable and it is a criminal offence if it is discovered that he has accepted laundered monies. However the easiest target for forward-thinking criminals is to ensure that ill gotten gains can some how be quickly converted. Sometimes the ploy would be to give the lawyer large deposit monies, then "abort the transaction" after a short period getting the lawyer to transfer monies back to the client which then becomes clean money. or sometimes purchase properties, sit on them for a limited period of time and at the point of sale the funds become clean money.

The best method of detection is experience and instinct. A woman was trying to do a transfer of equity of a house that she purported to own. I gave her a quote but when she turned up to instruct it seems that she did not own the house but was owned by her "Brother" who was to transfer the house to her as it had been paid for by herself some years before. The client and her brother were both African. The brother who would tentatively be the client turned up with his identification and usual checks but had a completely different name to his "sister" and was very uneasy in the price he was going to receive. The sister was refused one mortgage so another was going to then take the transaction on. The lender telephoned me to ask if I was previously aware of the seller or the buyer with whom I had no previous contact. They were very uneasy and on my instinct and advice withdrew the offer. In the meantime the sister referred to her brother's wife s her sister in law who seemed to be doing a lot of the running around and delivering. When a third party became involved I decided that this was probably the point that I should put in my report to the money laundering authorities. However, the original female client confirmed that her "brother" was not her blood brother but this was a

191

term of endearment enjoyed by her nationality. It was strange that she called his wife her sister-in-law if this was to believed. Needless to say the transaction collapsed and I withdrew from any further dealings and left if to the Money laundering authority to investigate any further dealings.

I have mentioned earlier in this book my friend who ended up a serving police officer. Thanks to him as indeed often with regular client friends, they recommend other friends and working colleagues and so it has transpired that I have over the years acted for numerous police officers in various departments of the force. Several have become and remain personal friends. In fact, for one of these I have recently completed yet another sale and purchase on his behalf. Between the previous time I acted for him and recent transaction I would speak to him from time to time both on and off duty and often he "threatened" that if he was in the area he would try to find time to pop in for a cup of coffee and a chat. One working morning the telephone rang and a familiar voice was at the other end. After the usual pleasantries he said that often threatened to pop in, and he was actually sitting on my driveway. Without further ado I went to the front door opened it rather surprised that he had telephoned to announce his arrival rather than just ring the door bell and then the mystery was revealed. Both he and his colleague were indeed on my driveway. However, their "vehicles" were two police horses. I suppose this was the strangest method of transport any clients have ever chosen to come to the offices and it was rather surreal standing there talking up to them both while they remained in the saddle. It was even funnier seeing folks faces as they drove and walked passed the private home from where I now work looking at these two mounted police officers talking to me. The moment was priceless and certainly required mentioning as part of "it should never happen to a lawyer"

With all the checks, backups and money laundering requirements it does keep most lawyers on their toes. However, sometimes events happen by themselves which are quite honest and above board but can lead to inevitable questions. During the very bad winter a couple of years ago a client wanted to buy a property in a particularly affluent area. She didn't particularly love the house but more the area. The actual transaction was not eventful apart from the fact that the client lived in Scotland and after completion the weather drew in so bad that she was physically locked in and unable to get out of the area to move into her new home. This meant that there was going to be at least a couple months gap from the actual completion date in late January to mid March. By the time the client had moved down the weather was still not wonderful which really didn't help matters as she just did not form a bond with the new house. She called an Architect to enquire what improvements could be made but the costings were far excessive so the client she eventually rang me to say she was not happy was going to resell the property and go back to Scotland. She happened to mention this to a neighbour and soon the jungle drums started to beat and within hours she was approached buying the property from my client. Now my client had paid £500,000 and as such had been landed with 3% interest of some £15,000 plus legal fees and removal fees and other costs, and wishing to recover her costs the price was agreed at £530,000. The transaction went through smoothly and my client duly received her balance funds and moved back to Scotland. It was shortly after completion that I received a request from the Customs & Excise to explain the sale at £500,000 and the immediate turnover at £530,000. I explained the circumstances but this did not satisfy the Customs & Excise who required more detailed information. What they had noticed was that a property had been purchased right on the threshold of stamp duty at £500,000 and then sold a very short time later for £530,000 This attracted stamp duty of 4% being £21,200 a difference of over £6,000. They wondered if some form of double-dealing going on with extra monies being paid to the original seller to avoid my client paying 4% stamp duty.

After a degree of correspondence the Customs Excise then required sight of not only the agents particulars, but also the copy contract, the copy transfer, my client account entries and so on. They then demanded full details from the Estate agents and copies of their accounts to see if they had been paid any extra funds. Then the seller's solicitors had to submit their own records and accounts and it took months before the Customs & Excise finally came to the conclusion that the transactions were both legitimate and above board.   However, it was a good warning to be very much aware that at all times all transactions have to be completely lily white and above board otherwise once the investigations start every record will be turned upside down to reveal the truth.

Another transaction that could prove extremely acrimonious was a one which involved a remortgage, a purchase and a sale. The sale was by an elderly father selling his home some few miles away from his daughter. The daughter and her partner were re mortgaging their property in order to purchase the property next door. It looked as if it was their intention that the father could then move into that house so that the daughter could keep an eye on him in his declining years. At this point nothing seemed amiss and the transactions went through normally.

The re-mortgage funds were made available and the neighbouring property purchased. The buyer of the old gentleman's house was a developer who was simply buying it to upgrade it and re-sell the property. This too went through without a problem and the proceeds would be payable to the old man. Completion took place on the Friday. On the Monday I had a very polite call from the purchaser's solicitors who claimed that the gentleman had changed his mind and had broken back into his old home on the Friday night and was refusing to leave. I contacted the daughter and it transpired that the elderly gentleman was content to leave his home and all went well till he got to his daughters where he was going to live. The neighbour's house was never purchased for his use but to let out to earn extra income. The elderly gentleman decided he didn't like it at his daughter's had an almighty row and stormed out. He then walked the four miles back to his old home, broke in, barricaded himself in and refused to leave. It took the Police and a certification order under the Mental Health Act to have him removed to a secure medical unit. I then had a visit from the daughter and her partner who wanted funds from the sale of his house made payable to the elderly gentleman for the balance of proceeds of sale to be altered payable to the her. I advised that without the elderly gentleman's consent this was not possible and any cheque could only be sent to him and cashed by him. The Police quite rightly took the files to see if some form of conspiracy had taken place by the daughter and her partner against the elderly gentleman to defraud him from his home but were unable to secure any sufficient evidence. I have learnt since that the remaining family members have undertaken their own campaign to right what on the surface appears to be a very poor dealing against an elderly gentleman.

I have acted for a Sri Lankan client now for some 12 to 13 years and over the time I have got know him and his rather eccentric ways. One thing I will say about him is that he adores his family and now his grandchildren. His made a career of trolling estate agents looking for cheap properties and re-possessions, He would make the purchase , take on tenants, make improvements and then sell them on for profit. Whilst not giving him a fortune this has allowed him to enjoy a reasonable standard of living. The problem is that, at times. he can get excitable and to some he appears aggressive, although is not in fact the case. He has fallen out with various estate agents who consider his manner too aggressive even though I explain to them that this is his way and that he really is harmless. However, he tends to get himself into very emotional state and several times came to my offices in tears as to why he was being treated so badly.

He sticks to his trade and between us he has kept me in work and I have helped maintain his life style. His daughter asked me recently how on earth I put up with him? I simply say that I have got to know him. I can control his emotions and talk to him rationally about day-to-day procedures and legal problems and probably in the end he has turned out to be as good a client and loyal client as any. Not so many years ago he suffered a heart attack and was admitted into the emergency ward at the local hospital where he was wired up to all the usual monitoring and life saving machines. I only found this out because he called me from his hospital bed on his mobile. My first question was how on earth was he able to speak to me at all even though it was on his mobile. It turned out that he was on his way to me to get my advice on another of his transactions when he was taken ill. He was not going to take the advice of the hospital lightly as he had to come and see me and tried to "negotiate" that they allow him to come out of the hospital for an hour so he could come to my offices on the promise that he would return. They insisted quite rightly that he would have to remain, wired up, if he wanted to live and under no circumstances were they going to agree to his request. In the end as a compromise they allowed him to telephone me. My reaction was to tell him off for not listening to the doctors and no way was I going to talk shop while he was in such a state. He should get himself right before we would then talk again. He did needless to say survive and we have had many a transaction and fun and games since.

The Land Rover Discovery

A couple of years ago it was time to replace the working vehicle, a Land Rover Discovery which had reached over 100,000 miles, It was beginning to look a little tired and needed work and money spending on it. As I was approaching 60, I decided that now was the time to fulfil my ten-year plan and replace various items that would see me through into my 70s. I decided to purchase a used Land Rover Defender 110 that, from the photographs, looked like it had been well looked after and had been adapted for off-road driving and travel. The mileage was low so, having secured a price, Angie and I took the train to Liverpool to meet the owner. After a test drive we parted with the bankers draft and drove our new acquisition home. Now there were a couple of jobs that needed doing, and having checked the log book, I noticed that the had been previously owned by a chap in Bedford. only 9 miles away from my home. It had been serviced regularly by a reputable Land Rover garage close by. I booked the vehicle in for a service and it was like taking someone's best friend to visit them for the day. I was quietly dismissed while the mechanic walked round the vehicle talking to it like it was human which I found most bizarre. Land Rover Defenders and the series models seem to attract a fraternity of well wishers and enthusiasts, and indeed I had been waved and flashed at more times in the drive back from the Wirral than in all the 13 years I had driven the previous Discovery. We had purchased a very unique and rather special vehicle. Shortly after the purchase, we attended the annual "pilgrimage" for Land Rover owners and enthusiasts at Billing Aquadrome. Angie and I went along and found various stalls advertising off-road adventure holidays through various countries and terrains. We chatted to one chap who ran tours through the Middle East, the Alps, Spain, Portugal and even up to the Arctic Circle. Having both camped most of our lives we had a pretty good idea of what life would be like on one of these adventure holidays but had never actually taken an off-road experience. We settled on a trip to Morocco as part of my 60th Birthday Celebrations the following year.

We paid our deposit and picked up various bits of literature to help us plan for our trip and over the course of the next 9 months purchased a roof tent, side awning, fuel tanks, heavier duty tyres and other accessories, to try to make our trip more enjoyable and comfortable. For a practice run we decided to re visit a little resort high in the Monta Rosa Mountains of Italy for Christmas and New Year and duly packed the Land Rover with enough bags and equipment to take a party of school children to Katmandu. Angie and I were both surprised that the journey down was uneventful and reasonably quick. The only mistake I made was deciding to drive down through France and cut into Switzerland via Geneva, which put another 100 miles on the journey. It also meant we were driving round Lake Geneva in the dark and finally reached the little train station at Brig late in the evening. A quick telephone call to the hotel put their minds at rest as well as ours that we were on our way and that we would not be sleeping outside in the deep snow. The train arrived at Brig, took us through the mountains to Italy and another hour saw us arrive at the pretty resort where we would enjoy a weeks stay in the mountain hotel. The Land Rover performed brilliantly and saw off any snow, ice and other obstacles as expected.

One little story that is worth sharing was the day that the proprietor's daughter went to retrieve her car from the underground car park opposite the hotel. It has been snowing and the entrance was like a skating rink. As the Daughter was driving out, the vehicle lost its grip, slid backwards, mounted the small kerb hit the wall and parked itself half on the road and half on the little access path. Its rear end was supported by the concrete pillar and refused to budge. Despite the numbers of willing Italian men with their shovels and strength the little car could not be moved. So I volunteered the Land Rover. I backed the vehicle into the slope as close as I could, tied the tow rope to the front of the vehicle and gently pulled it out of the spot like a cork out of the bottle. Unfortunately Land Rovers do not repair other folk's car bodies and it did look a bit of a mess in the daylight. However the good deed had been done.

The return journey was equally as uneventful although we had a wonderful night's stopover at Morge on the shores of Lake Geneva on the way home. The shops still twinkled with all the Christmas decorations and people enjoying the warmth and good cheer of cosy restaurants and pubs. We did get quite a few passers-by stand and stare at our vehicle as if it had returned from an overland trip to India rather than just over the mountains from Italy.

Adventure to Morrocco

When the time came for us to depart on our mammoth road trip to Morocco I would say that any fears we had in pre-planning had already been set aside by Peter from Adventure Overland who did an excellent job answering any questions or worries. All this planning reached a climax when we got the vehicle loaded with the array of plastic boxes. Peter discouraged us from spending unnecessary amounts of money on pointless storage systems in case we really did not take to this type of adventure and did not wish to repeat the experience. He suggested plastic storage boxes for the various items we would take. This was excellent advice.

On the evening before departure I made phone calls to friends, family and business colleagues to make final arrangements. The last task was to deliver the house keys to my daughter. On my way back home I received a text message which read, "Sailings from Portsmouth cancelled, please make your way to Dover where P&O ferries will take you to Calais where you can complete your journey from there." Now this was to say more than a bit of a shock. The intended plan was to leave on Friday lunchtime for a relaxed drive down to Portsmouth. There we would catch the overnight ferry to Santander, enjoy a nice evening meal on board and sleep in a cabin. We would arrive in Spain on the Saturday afternoon, relaxed and refreshed, and. drive the 50 miles to our first camp site followed by another days drive to the final camp site before arriving in in southern Spain to meet up with the rest of the group we were travelling into Morocco with.

Assuming that someone was playing a practical joke I immediately texted a reply that I was far from amused. I consider the joke at such a late stage very bad-taste, ill-played and wrongly-timed. I didn't get an answer. I did however check the web site when I arrived home and sure enough due to the French unions causing problems. Brittany Ferries simply closed up shop and sent everyone home until they were ready to start work again. Whilst I empathise with management's efforts stop all the silliness, it really was far from helpful for the rest of us planning to travel with them. So what should have been a relaxed start to a holiday of a lifetime went into manic overdrive. Phone calls to the family suggesting that they should not pop over the next day to wave us off on our merry way. Plastic boxes previously standing in the hallway were hastily loaded into the vehicle. Angie and I then tried to get our heads down for a few hours sleep. The alarm kicked in at 3.00 am and we were up and out the door by 4.00 am with a hectic drive via M1 and M25 to try to get past the expected Friday morning rush hour. We were able to keep ahead of it all and duly arrived at Dover just before 7.00 am.

We had no tickets, only pieces of paper issued by Brittany Ferries so we were not sure what the reception was going to be. To our amazement P&O were brilliant. They directed us straight through onto the quayside, where the ferry was waiting to take us over to Calais, all without any fuss or further payment. Once in Calais we were faced with a daunting 4 day drive to try to catch up our original schedule. To say this was pressure was an understatement. I set myself a goal at Calais to try to to be in Bordeaux by Friday evening. However, with two tons of Land Rover, loaded with survival and camping gear this was not realistic. We limped into our old favourite Camp Site, that we had visited several times previously in the Loire, in the pouring rain just after 5.00pm. We were greeted by the owner who recognised us from our previous visits and offered us a chalet for the night. This meant a warm shower, a comfortable made up bed and a hearty meal at their restaurant. We slept like logs. The next day we were up early and on to Spain. That night we stayed at the scheduled camp site 50 miles from the Spanish port, and the following night at the scheduled camp site three-quarters of the way down the middle spine of Spain. We finally arrived again on schedule at the little camp site in southern Spain on the Monday evening, four days after leaving home. Here we met up with the other 7 vehicles and swapped stories about our adventures in reaching this destination.

After a well deserved evening meal and another well-deserved night's sleep we were all firing on all cylinders for the start of our epic journey the next day. The convoy left at 8.00am, drove to the port, and were loaded onto the ship that would carry us over to Africa. At Tangiers we were introduced to a whole different system than what we had been used to at the English Ports. The Moroccans work at their own speed and entry to the country could take 2-3 hours if we were lucky or 5 -6 hours if we were not. However, we got through managed to keep on the tarmac for about 30 miles before we were introduced to what would become the norm for the next two weeks and that was driving off road.

We first travelled up and over the Atlas mountains on tracks no wider than the vehicle and so steep you allowed the vehicle in front to reach some distance before setting off for fear of stalling. On the way down you had to sit forward to study the bonnet of the vehicle to make sure it was lined up with the narrow tracks. It was not a sheer drop but if the vehicle lost its grip it would have rolled over and over and down quite a long way before stopping, so full concentration was essential. The views for the next several hundred miles were spectacular. Eventually we reached beyond the mountains and into the northern borders of the Sahara desert. where temperatures exceeded 35 degrees. The colours were vivid yellows and oranges and were very photogenic.

The various towns we passed, whilst extremely poor, were nonetheless very friendly and the people just lovely. The final town before hitting the desert proper was like a little oasis and the hotel had its palm trees and looked like something out of Lawrence of Arabia would have expected back in the 1920s. Finally we drove into the desert and remained off-roading for 4 days and nights sleeping out under the stars. I positioned the vehicle at each comfort stop and each evening facing east. This meant that the sun was always on the other side of the vehicle while we ate and and on waking each morning we faced the sunrise. The desert sunrise is indescribable! It is a magic moment. So too is the night time, standing on the roof of the Land Rover, about to climb into the roof tent, with a myriad of stars above shining down with the huge beam of light behind being the full moon.

We then started our retreat back to the coast staying in various locations till we finally reached the port and back into Spain. We drove back up the country, this time along the coastal road stopping in some rather splendid hotels on the way. On our second night we were driving after dark and exhaustion was beginning to take over when we saw this magnificent tall hotel close to the motorway. We pulled up outside the building, which was very elegantly designed in marble and stainless steel. I went in to the reception looking more like Indiana Jones leaving a very dust Land Rover outside to ask if they had any rooms. The receptionist was immaculate and without batting an eyelid confirmed that would be fine and did we have luggage. I confessed we did have some rather dusty and dirty plastic boxes which myself and Angie carried through and up to our room. The Room turned out to be a very expensive looking suite with huge balcony, wet room the size of our lounge at home and a bedroom to die in. By this point we didn't care about the cost as tiredness had taken over. So we showered, fed, watered and had a good night's sleep. The bill the next day was incredibly cheap. It cost less than an overnight stay in a village pub in the Cotswolds in England. It turned out in the light that the hotel was part of a very elaborate golfing complex with its own greens, houses and gardens that were all very immaculately groomed. We had the same experience at our next destination stop half way between the Mediterranean coast and the Atlantic. Finally we reached Santander. The boats were running again and so we finally enjoyed our relaxed cruise back to England where we stayed over night in Devon before finally getting home. Our journey was a life changing experience. The Land Rover has since undergone numerous additions and alterations mostly to replace the 8 plastic boxes with permanent and secure storage along with better communications, ready for my return trip to Morocco booked and reserved for 2015.

One Last Tale

My final story involves a recent purchase by a client of a property where a Ms. So-and-so was selling. I opened the file, wrote off for the paperwork and proceeded with the purchase and conducted searches and enquiries. I then received a phone call from the seller's solicitors. The gentleman at the other end of the line was rather hesitant about what he really wanted to discuss with me but it emerged that the person selling the property, had, at the time of the purchase, been a man. However, during the course of ownership he had undergone various sex changes, which had resulted in the person now taking on the form of a female. Unfortunately the operations had mostly taken place abroad and therefore there was no evidence that "he" was now a "she" although the solicitor had acted for this person for a number of years and could vouch for the facts that he now explained to me and asked what difficulties did I have in dealing with the transaction? I pointed out that the title showed that a man owned the property and as long as that name appeared on the contract and the transfer and the solicitor could vouch that this person did exist, in whichever guise, then as far as I was concerned my client purchased bona fide and really could not question the domesticity of the seller. I did explain this to my client, in case she had any problems living in a property where certain events had taken place. She was not concerned and so I telephoned the solicitor to say that everyone was completely relaxed at this end. I then explained the story some years ago of my ex-wife and her friend from London whose companion had turned out to be the first sex-change man to end up in Holloway. This story seemed to break the ice and so the remainder of the transaction went through smoothly and without further discussion. Sadly, after completion the solicitor telephoned me to say that within a few days of the completion of the sale, his client had purchased a brand new car with part of the proceeds and had ended up having a very serious car accident. He/she was in hospital with serious injuries and it had been touch and go whether that person was actually going to live. Very tragic.

14 The Future

As I progress towards the final stages of my long and varied career, I note that many of the working colleagues I have known for many years, are also in the same predicament. Many are similarly approaching the end of their working lives, and in some cases have already retired. A few have passed on.

The working life that we all have enjoyed has changed drastically over the many years and many of those that have gone I confess I will miss terribly. Their skills, experiences knowledge, wit and character, will never be repeated or matched and I fear that a lot of their charisma and memories have gone with them. There are a few that remain and we speak often about what has happened in the world of conveyancing and what will become of the law and its procedures in the years to come. One of those that I have known for over thirty five years, Michael, who still to this day insists on calling me Mr. Ainsworth, despite my protests that we have known each other for all these years and should be on first name terms. I suppose old habits die hard even though it turns out he is older than me. My last "ambition" before I retire or he retires that he will finally call me by my first name. When I advised him that I would be "naming and shaming" him in these chapters he did break into giggles and the last time we spoke he did actually call me "Mr. Allan" so some progress has been made. With the crew that do remain we still try to make the effort of meeting once a month over a beer or glass of wine. This enables us to chew over days gone by have a grumble at "how the profession has turned out." The consensus is that once the old skills have gone then the world of conveyancing will indeed be a sadder place. They say that when you pass your driving test you then start to learn to drive. It is the same in the law. Your certificates, passes and all the glory of letters after your name, really only heralds the start. It is the ensuing years the experiences and the knowledge gleaned from those far better qualified that leads to become a better lawyer. Hopefully this book will give some an insight into my own personal world, and those who have shaped, moulded and polished me to the man I am today. I have also tried to describe some of the laughs and antics that have accompanied us and maybe some reading this it will rekindle their own memories. Most of all I would like to thank those that have taken the time to read and hope that you have enjoyed reading these pages about my working life as much as I have enjoyed living it. It has been most interesting how various characters and circumstances have weaved their way in and out of my life throughout the years. Each disappointment or opportunity has been there for a reason and the thread running through my career has brought me safely to where I am today. Whether that is fate or some other controlling circumstance I don't know, but looking back now it all seems to fit, and has proved that I have been very lucky to be in the right place at the right time.

As for myself, about 3 years ago, on my birthday, Angie presented me with what I thought was a car trolley jack (be rest assured this would have been very useful) but when I opened up the box it was in fact an acoustic guitar. I should explain that all my life I have accepted two facts about myself: one is that I am absolutely hopeless when it comes to art, being unable to either draw or paint, the other that I was never going to be able to play any form of musical instrument. There is absolutely nobody in my entire family history that has had the remotest connection to music or any form of musical instrument. In fact I escaped from my dreaded music lessons at school when I was only eleven years old after being able to achieve some form of recognisable tune to *Three Blind Mice* and *Twinkle Twinkle Little Star* out of a mouth organ. However the sound I produced did prompt the teacher to conclude that perhaps I should quit while I was ahead. However as a teenage student I attended the commercial course at school, which included learning to type on the old manual typewriter. This gave me in the end the dexterity of being able to send individual signals to my hands and fingers thus producing letters and documents later needed for the career I was to follow. This skill even enabled me to master the early computer packages, which depended entirely on keyboard skills.

I was always curious if the dexterity of touch-typing would help in any way with being able to play a guitar. I did admire those people who did have the gift of singing and playing. In my early days working in Aylesbury, I would spend many happy hours at various musical gigs and gatherings, and after moving to Amersham would go along to the folk evenings and had many friends over the years able to play various instruments. For me. the opportunity never really arose, and I never bothered to try to play nor understand or read music. In recent years someone who belonged to a family of skilled guitar players, even "advised" me that my hands were too stubby and my fingers too short to play the guitar. Now that I had a guitar, my curiosity would be put to the test.

Initially I was very nervous. Nobody likes to volunteer themselves to look silly and I didn't want to let Angie down for the faith she had invested in me. So I persevered and went to my first lesson. Despite jokingly asking the tutor which end I held the guitar and where should I blow I was indeed pleasantly surprised. I was able to pick up playing the basic 6 chords needed for many songs and over the ensuing months mastered a total of 10 chords. I was also fumbling through a few basic songs. Playing every day for as long as my fingers could stand the pressure and pain, (fellow guitar students will understand my predicament here) I had the best of good fortune at being introduced to my current guitar tutor Ian. Ian Entwhistle is an incredible acoustic guitar player and a wonderful tutor who has the patience of a saint. I have always admired anyone in whatever capacity who is able to tutor their students and always remain just that slightly more proficient than their students. As the student improves so does the Tutor. It is not until you see the tutor in his or her own field away from the teaching that you then get a true prospective of that person's capability. Ian is one of those extremely rare breed of Tutor. He has been able to gently persuade, coax and demonstrate various styles, methods and chords to me and now, after two years, he has taken me from my initial fumblings to being able to finger-pick my way through some 45 to 50 songs using 8 or 9 different styles. He has even been able to show me some songs that require two of the finger-picking styles to those songs. I am just overwhelmed with the achievement I have been able to reach. I now am a member of an acoustic group that meets once a month. I also attend other groups to play the various songs that I have learnt and so really I feel I have come a long distance. The level I have reached has enabled me to have the confidence to join acoustic groups that meet regularly in pubs and other public venues. I have joined groups from afar as afield as Boscastle in Cornwall to Scotland. I am hoping to use my new skills to bring some form of pleasure to others in the foreseeable future. I have therefore actively volunteered myself to play at various old folk's homes and indeed am currently awaiting confirmation of my first evening playing for a group for the blind.

In August 2014 my greatest and proudest achievement was when I was able to play four songs that Ian and I have meticulously worked on week after week for the previous nine months at my own daughter's wedding in front of some 140 guests. There was another duty I had to perform at my daughter's wedding that completed a promise made some 38 years previous.

Back in August 1976 I travelled to Cyprus with my first wife and son for a holiday we were both desperately needing to have. I had been keeping down two jobs one full time one taxi driving of an evening trying to make ends meet and was admittedly at the end of my physical mental and spiritual tether. It would appear that Cyprus in those days had a reputation of being good watch repairers. As a result my grandmother who I was very close to gave me her dress watch asking if I could have it serviced and repaired. Taking great care of this precious package I dutifully took it to a watch repairer in Limassol, collecting it several weeks later all working and looking clean and serviced. When we returned back to England after staying with my first wife's parents for a month I cannot describe the sick feeling that I had at learning that my grandmother was not at home but was in hospital being diagnosed with advanced stages of terminal stomach cancer. She had known for some time and was due to hospital but kept the task secret until after we had departed for our break so as not to worry us unduly.

I visited her in the famous Stoke Mandeville Hospital with her watch which she asked me to keep for her till she came home. The months rolled and her health deteriorated and just before she slipped into her final unconsciousness I again asked her what she wanted me to do with her watch given she had a daughter and a son who were more entitled in the ranks than I. She simply replied that she wanted me to keep it as a memory of her. I then promised her that if ever we had a daughter, only my son had been born at that time, that I would give her the watch on her wedding day. There is a slight twist to the tale. Having sat in my "keep sake" case for 37 years I was a little worried that maybe damp or age had got to it. When I tried to wind the watch up as suspected nothing happened. Now being the wife of a railway man and having been in service herself as a house maid I realised that these two did not have a great deal of money. Had I in fact been hanging on to a pup all these years. I researched and found a good quality watch repairer in Tring and took the watch to them with fingers crossed. A quick inspection by them assured me that they could do something with the watch. I collected the watch three weeks later and sure enough the watch is not only serviced but working. To fuel my curiosity I asked them if they could tell me anything about the watch. The gentleman inspected the watch and advised that all he could tell me was that it was Swiss made, good sign, that it had a red 9 carat gold face, another good sign, and that it was made early 1920's . So we hold a watch that is nearly a 100 years old delicately made in Switzerland, a nation that has always been held as the masters of watch making that I could give working to my daughter on her wedding day. That day has now passed and I feel a promise well kept and cherished. Maybe one day my daughter can relay the story to her granddaughter on her wedding day when she passes the treasure on to the next generation.

As I near the end of this book it would be impossible for me to try to even start to list all the characters that have made up this chronology of my working life and to whom I have such a duty of gratitude. I will name but a few with the remaining unnamed still held with fondness and gratitude. I would mention the following: Robert Earl, the old "Dickensian" lawyer who pointed me in the direction that I would take for the remainder of my career; Leslie Weatherall, for his wonderful skills as a lawyer, as a teacher and as someone who has given me such ever lasting memories of his stories and of his own life; Pete Collier, for his charismatic character and for being "the original good old boy" as someone described him at his funeral, who I still greatly miss; Roger Fennemore for taking the gamble to employ me from my local authority background and having the faith and trust in me, and also for being such an incredible leader and manager and being able to get the most out of his staff; Stuart Beeson, who once passed one of the nicest compliments I could have asked for when he remarked that if he was ever stuck at the end of the motorway at 3.00 am in the morning out of all the folks he knew there were only two he could call upon and I was one of them; Peter Harrison, who everyone who knows him will agree, has been the eccentric corner pin for us all over the years here in Milton Keynes, and who has kept us all on the straight and narrow, and who I often boast I wanted to emulate by being as dogmatic and eccentric as hew was by the time I retired; and finally, but not least, all the Clients (many who have become personal friends) who over the years have supported me and given me such pleasure to act for.

When I am able shortly to finally hang up my hat, turn the light off for the last time and drift into retirement, my ambition will be, to continue my guitar playing and to travel. I have spent the past two years since returning from Morocco upgrading the vehicle to replace the plastic boxes. It is now self-sufficient, having an on-board cooker, shelves and drawers holding all the comforts necessary for a touring holiday. It has been tested in various soft camping breaks. Europe will be the first destination, re-visiting many of the wonderful places I have already passed through and venturing into new territory. We are already planning an over land trip via Austria, Croatia and Albania down to Greece. I plan to travel again to Morocco in 2015. I also want to find out more about my own country having never visited many counties. So the future beyond retirement, given the blessing of good health, still looks inviting and exciting. Who knows, maybe a new book will be possible: *Shouldn't Happen to a Retired Lawyer.*

Lightning Source UK Ltd.
Milton Keynes UK
UKOW07f0731061214

242751UK00001B/53/P